CONTROVERSIAL
ISSUES
IN SOCIAL
POLICY

CONTROVERSIAL ISSUES

IN SOCIAL POLICY

Edited by

Howard Jacob Karger
James Midgley

Louisiana State University

Series Editors

Robert Pruger
Eileen Gambrill

University of California, Berkeley

ALLYN AND BACON
Boston   London   Toronto   Sydney   Tokyo   Singapore

Series Editor: Karen Hanson
Editor-in-Chief, Social Sciences: Susan Badger
Editorial Assistant: Sarah Dunbar
Production Administrator: Susan McIntyre
Editorial-Production Service: Kathy Smith
Cover Administrator: Suzanne Harbison
Composition Buyer: Linda Cox
Manufacturing Buyer: Louise Richardson

Copyright © 1994 by Allyn and Bacon
A Division of Simon & Schuster, Inc.
160 Gould Street
Needham Heights, MA 02194

Library of Congress Cataloging-in-Publication Data

Controversial issues in social policy/Howard Jacob Karger, James
    Midgley, editors.
        p. cm.
    Includes bibliographical references.
    ISBN 0–205–13790–3
    1. United States—Social policy. 2. Public welfare—United
States. 3. Welfare state. I. Karger, Howard Jacob
II. Midgley, James.
HN59.2.C66 1994
361.6'1'0973--dc20   93–15267
                                                              CIP

Printed in the United States of America

10 9 8 7 6 5   98 97 96

Contents

II. Issues in the Delivery of Social Services

III. Poverty, Deprivation, and Social Policy

Preface

When Robert Pruger invited us to edit this book, we had some misgivings. The task of editing a large volume of debates on current controversies in social policy is formidable. The time and effort involved in identifying viable topics, coordinating the contributions of more than forty authors, and standardizing the material, as well as the need to make the book lively and interesting, presented an enormous challenge to two already overcommitted people. However, we were excited about the idea of inviting acknowledged social policy experts to examine critically important issues in the field from radically different perspectives. We had both contributed to Eileen Gambrill and Robert Pruger's pioneering volume *Controversial Issues in Social Work* (the first in this series), and enjoyed participating in the debates. We realized then that the debate format is an effective means of analyzing controversial issues in social policy, a useful teaching device, and an important requirement for the development of knowledge in our field. Despite our initial misgivings, we agreed to edit this book because we believe that both social policy and social work will be enriched by the stimulation of intellectual controversy and the articulation of different viewpoints.

Controversy is the essence of intellectual discourse. Although it may produce sharp disagreements between persons of differing viewpoints, the role of critical disputation in furthering knowledge is universally recognized. While scholars may strenuously promote particular positions, these positions must stand the test of analytical scrutiny before they can be accepted as valid. Critical debate facilitates the twin tasks of validation and refutation. Critical debate also heightens an understanding of the issues, permits contradictions to be resolved, and ultimately promotes correct rather than false knowledge.

Critical debate can also be an effective teaching device. Rote learning has an obvious role in the educational process, but the task of helping students to gain an understanding of the most important issues in the field requires more than the memorization of key facts. In subjects such as social work and social policy, where judgment is as important as knowing facts, students need to think critically, to be able to grasp complex nuances, and to analyze issues and defend their positions. We believe that the lecture format, in which students are passive, is not an effective means for inculcating critical thinking. We hope that the debates offered in this book will assist instructors in promoting more frequent discussions among students and facilitating the critical thinking we need to enhance our field.

Critical debate also has an important role to play in strengthening our profession. Unlike other disciplines, social work has not always encouraged critical debate. Although controversial articles do appear in many social work journals, they rarely result in ongoing debates or rejoinders. Much to the chagrin of many social work authors, controversial articles, regardless of their content, soon disappear from the journals. This has led many authors to believe that either social workers do not always read their own journals, or that they simply do not care enough about the issues. It is likely that neither of these suppositions is correct. Many social workers fail to respond simply because there is no culture of critical debate from which to draw reactions and critiques. This problem is especially acute in the area of social policy, which is by nature open to multiple interpretations.

Another problem is the profession's propensity to adopt a single authoritative position on complex issues. For example, one is struck by the consistency of the position statements emanating from various professional associations. Often, particular views are espoused as if they were universally accepted. It is assumed, almost *a priori,* that everyone in the profession has the same opinion on key issues. This is clearly not the case, and the diversity of viewpoints among social workers on these issues needs to be recognized. While it is appropriate for professional associations to take positions on political and social questions that affect their members, these positions are sometimes adopted with dogmatic insistence when, in fact, there are widely differing opinions among social workers on these questions.

There is a tendency within the profession to avoid controversial discussions. For example, there are few articles in social work journals that question whether the welfare state is in fact a failed social experiment, or whether social welfare programs really do increase dependency. Although most social workers, including ourselves, are strongly committed to the values and principles underlying the welfare state, the absence of disagreements on these issues within the profession isolates the membership from much needed critical thinking about welfare policy. Many social workers are consequently both ill-informed about alternative viewpoints and ill-prepared to respond to them.

This situation is unhealthy for the growth and vitality of social work as an academic subject. Social work must not only endorse but also meet accepted standards of intellectual discourse within academic settings, and a failure to do so will undoubtedly harm its growth as a respected academic field.

Not only is the vitality of the discipline compromised by a lack of critical debate, but its own strength and maturity is weakened as its dearly held tenets are isolated from critique. Whatever positions social workers adopt must be strengthened by the clarification that comes from counter-argument. Indeed, the profession's beliefs and values may become calcified if it fails to exercise its intellectual muscles.

We have included debates in this book which will encourage social workers to think critically and develop their analytical skills. For this reason, many of the debates address very difficult issues. Indeed, some of the positions argued by our contributors may be unpopular, but, as was argued previously, it is important that social workers understand them. Of course, we do believe in the ability of our readers to enter into the book's spirit of intellectual discourse and to determine for themselves which arguments are the most valid and relevant.

We hope that instructors who use this book will do so in the spirit in which is was written—namely, to expose students to the various opinions that populate social policy's wide and rich terrain. As suggested earlier, one of the strengths of social policy is the fact that it is open to various interpretations, and this makes it intellectually challenging and exciting. Indeed, we hope this book will transmit the subject's inherent excitement and challenge.

Controversial Issues in Social Policy is divided into three parts. In Part I, we offer debates that revolve around general issues in social welfare policy. Paul Adams and Gary Freeman examine whether the New Deal welfare state has outlived its usefulness; Martin Tracy and Tom Walz debate whether social security should be made voluntary; Terri Combs-Orme and Robert Moffit argue about whether the federal government should provide health insurance for all Americans; Dorinda Noble and Nanneska Magee debate whether the federal government should fund abortions; Edward Canda and Donald Chambers argue with Pat Sullivan about the question of spiritual principles guiding social policy; Norman Wyers and John Longres argue whether legislation is needed to protect the rights of gays and lesbians; and John Pardeck and Roland Meinert explore whether social workers actually have a major impact on social policy.

Part II looks at specific issues in the delivery of human services. In particular, David Stoesz and Howard Jacob Karger argue about whether privatization is a positive trend in social services; Lawrence Martin and Michael Parker debate about whether there should be a voucher system for social services; Larry Kreuger and Jack Stretch argue about whether shelters for the homeless are really doing the job; Mimi Abramovitz and Howard Jacob Karger examine whether the social welfare system is inherently racist and sexist; Michael Robin and Peter Pecora ask if false allegations in child abuse are a major problem; Kia Bentley and John Belcher debate whether community-based services actually help the mentally ill; and Burton Cohen and Brenda McGowan explore whether changing the workplace can dramatically change child welfare services.

Part III examines key issues in poverty, deprivation, and social policy. In particular, Karen Haynes and Robert Fisher look at whether single-issue advocacy organizations are a positive development for the American welfare state; Mary Ann Reitmeir and Kit Christensen explore whether there is a feminization of poverty; Mark Lusk and Diana DiNitto examine whether we should expect clients to change their behavior in exchange for governmental aid; Ralph Segalman and Joel Blau debate the issue of whether workfare programs can bring large numbers of people out of poverty; Murray Spencer Sumner and Michael Reisch examine whether AFDC fosters dependency; Joseph Heffernan and Kathleen Heffernan Vickland debate whether an underclass exists; and Michael Sherraden and James Midgley argue whether an asset development program can really help the poor.

This book could not have been produced without the help and commitment of the contributors. Apart from delivering their debates in a timely manner, many were willing to contribute debates on unpopular subjects. This illustrates their academic ability, their self-confidence, and their intellectual integrity. We extend our heartfelt thanks to all who contributed debates to this book. Their professionalism made the book possible and manageable.

A special thanks to Robert Pruger for thinking about us when looking for editors for this volume. Also, thanks to Karen Hanson for expediting the contract and for believing in the project.

Howard Jacob Karger
James Midgley
Louisiana State University

Has the New Deal Welfare State Outlived Its Usefulness?

EDITOR'S NOTE: Although the concept of the welfare state is an imprecise one, the term is widely used to connote a variety of government social programs designed to meet social needs and solve social problems. Most of these programs emerged at the time of the New Deal in the 1930s. Despite the popularity of these programs, critics argue that government involvement in social affairs is harmful to the economy, contrary to the American values of hard work and individual responsibility, and detrimental to freedom of choice. Some supporters of the welfare state have attempted to refute these arguments, but others believe that the welfare state needs an overhaul. They argue that the basic principles of the welfare state should be modified to fit the needs and circumstances of the time in which we live. In effect, the New Deal's outmoded collection of social programs are no longer relevant to current conditions, and need to be replaced.

Paul Adams, Ph.D., argues YES, that the New Deal welfare state has outlived its usefulness. He is a Professor of Social Work at the University of Iowa School of Social Work and has published widely on social policy issues.

Gary P. Freeman, Ph.D., argues NO. He is an Associate Professor at the Department of Government, University of Texas at Austin. His major interests are comparative public policy, international migration, and the welfare state. He has published *Immigrant Labor and Racial Conflict in Industrial Societies* (1979), Princeton University Press, as well as numerous articles in scholarly journals.

YES

PAUL ADAMS

In a much-quoted definition, Wilensky and Lebeaux (1965) described the welfare state as a set of programs through which governments assure their citizens minimum standards of income, nutrition, health, housing, and education as a political right, not as charity. All advanced industrial countries have developed national policies to protect their populations from such contingencies as old age, sickness, disability, and unemployment, and have adopted tax or benefit measures to support the costs of childrearing. Such common features reflect certain structural similarities of modern capitalist states—the failure of the labor market and the wage system to protect those dependent on them against these contingencies, and the organization of workers in unions and political parties to demand protection for their families.

The Historical Development of the Welfare State

The welfare state arose during a period of increasing state intervention in the economy. Governments sought to organize whole national economies for international competition, which took political and military as well as economic forms in the struggle for markets and raw materials. In the process, they came to see their working classes, and especially children (the next generation of workers, soldiers, and mothers), as a national resource to be educated, kept healthy, and adequately maintained if economic and military strength were to be assured (Harman, 1984). Major wars were an especially powerful stimulus to welfare state developments, since both the health and the loyalty of the mass of the population became vital to the successful prosecution of war (Adams, 1982).

Under the pressures of international competition and labor organization, all industrial countries developed some kind of welfare state. However, the welfare state programs were adopted at different times and in different forms. Modern social insurance developed first in the 1880s in Bismarck's Germany, where a militarist state took charge of ensuring the conditions for capitalist development and confronted a large labor movement.

In the United States, which was less threatened by external military or economic pressures and which had a weaker labor movement, it was not until the crisis of the Great Depression of the 1930s that a national system of social insurance emerged. The New Deal welfare state (NDWS) that developed in this period was a more limited and market-oriented system of social protection than existed in many European countries (Esping-Andersen,

1990). The U.S. welfare state has always been based on a limited core of social security, which excludes health care, sick leave coverage, and universal family programs such as family allowances, maternity benefits, or parental leaves. It is a residual welfare state in which many benefits are targeted to those who can demonstrate both that they are poor and that they fit into a deserving category, such as old, disabled, dependent children, or veterans (Titmuss, 1974). The private market, on the other hand, is prominently involved in protecting the incomes of the better paid through health insurance, retirement programs, and so forth.

Why the Welfare State Doesn't Work

In recent decades, the world economy has become more integrated and states have lost control of their economic destinies. Investment, production, and workers cross national boundaries, and even large and relatively self-sufficient states like the United States are decreasingly able to insulate themselves from the pressures of global markets. Governments everywhere have responded to this situation by attempting to restructure the welfare state and by turning to market-oriented solutions to economic and social problems. Enthusiasm for the market flourished, especially among the ruling classes of Eastern Europe and the former Soviet Union, which had gone farthest in attempting to develop state-organized economies in isolation from the world market.

One might think that the NDWS, as the most market-oriented variant of the welfare state, would be the best adapted to current economic trends. Certainly, many American conservatives argue on these grounds for a return to the minimalist welfare state of the 1930s, stripping away the accretions of the 1960s and calling for increased privatization. In Eastern Europe, liberal enthusiasts for the market look to the American model of the welfare state and seek to eliminate social protection for children and families, even in the face of mounting poverty and homelessness.

Although the NDWS is the most market-oriented form of a welfare state, it is also the form that is the least well adapted to competition in a world market. For example, the NDWS fails to prevent poverty in a fifth of American children (and double that proportion for African-American children); to provide health insurance coverage for some 37 million Americans; and to prevent poverty in old age, especially among women. The NDWS also fails to meet the needs of a competitive capitalist economy for a healthy, educated workforce, and for high employment combined with low inflation.

It was precisely the relative self-sufficiency of the United States (i.e., its lack of dependence on world trade), as well as the weakness of its labor movement, that enabled it to do without a fully developed welfare state. In Sweden, by contrast, "The underlying philosophy is that a small, internationally competitive nation must rely on its human resources, and that optimal productivity is best achieved by assuming that individuals and families are guaranteed adequate welfare" (Esping-Andersen and Micklewright, 1991, p. 45).

Paradoxically, it has been large and expensive welfare states of the Swedish type—with their emphasis on solidarity between social groups, universal protection of their populations, and a collective responsibility for the costs of childrearing, sickness, and old age—that have been beneficial for capital accumulation. They elicited wage restraint, higher profits, and more investment (Cameron, 1984) than the American model. They have also produced much less unemployment and lower inflation. On the other hand, the NDWS has left key sectors of industry (which must compete on the world market) with enormous health insurance costs and a poorly educated workforce.

In the new global economy, the advantages of very large countries that are rich in natural resources are shrinking compared with those that maintain adequate and appropriate public investment in human resources (e.g., the education, health, and economic security of the population). According to one estimate, half the decline in productivity growth—from an average of 2.8 percent a year from 1953 to 1969 down to 1.4 percent from 1970 to 1988—can be blamed on a lower rate of public investment ("Industrial Policy," 1992). The failure to invest in the health, education, and security of the working class, especially in women and minorities who will make up the overwhelming majority of those entering the labor force during the 1990s ("Human Capital," 1988), is costing American capital dearly. The 1989 White House Task Force on Infant Mortality calculated that at least a quarter of infant deaths could be prevented by investing more money in health care programs and that the United States would save $7 billion a year if it could match Japan's infant mortality rate. Lack of child care restricts the access of women to the labor market. Moreover, the NDWS's inability to prevent poverty and school failure in the growing number of children in single-parent homes bodes ill for the present and future quality of the workforce available to U.S. employers.

From the point of view of the interests of U.S. capital, the NDWS is extraordinarily ill suited for the global competition of the future. Furthermore, the drive to restrict and privatize it in the face of those pressures is counterproductive. In short, the NDWS has outlived its usefulness for American capitalism.

Of course, it is not necessary to look at the question from that point of view. What is good for General Motors—for example, the socialization of its health costs through a national health insurance program—is not automatically in the best interests of its workers, their families, or those outside the labor force. However, if we examine the NDWS from their point of view, asking about its relative impact on poverty or the position of women or children, the case for the inadequacy of this form of the welfare state is even clearer.

The NDWS ties social insurance benefits to an earnings record, taking the judgment of the market about a person's worth as the basis for determining social benefits in old age. Despite a benefit formula favoring low-income earners, the net effect is still to provide the highest benefits to those in least need. Those with low or intermittent earnings will not be protected from poverty unless they are attached to an earner with a better record.

The NDWS system was built on the need to protect the earnings of a male breadwinner with a dependent spouse and children, a decreasingly common pattern in U.S. society. Social security depends upon the contribution parents make by rearing children, who will work and pay social security taxes to support the next generation of retirees (parents and non-parents alike). However, it penalizes childrearing by taxing workers without regard to family size and by paying benefits on the basis of earnings alone and not childrearing contribution. Mothers suffer most from this policy, bearing most of the costs of parenting in terms of forgone earning opportunities. They also pay again in old age by receiving correspondingly smaller earnings-related benefits (Adams, 1990).

Unlike either the Swedish or the German model, these (and other) problems of basing benefits on earnings are not offset either by specific credits for childrearing contributions within the insurance system or by universal noncontributory benefits such as family allowances or maternity benefits. There is a sharp contrast between the discriminatory impact of the NDWS on women and the systematic efforts of Swedish social policy to equalize the burden of childrearing between parents and nonparents. There is also a sharp contrast between the NDWS and Swedish social policy in terms of protecting maternal and infant health and in improving the short- and long-term economic security and career prospects of women (Adams, 1990; Stoiber, 1989). Policies that increase the capacity of women to have and rear children without falling into poverty or dependence on a male breadwinner are much better adapted to the needs of current families and labor market conditions than the traditionalist policies of the NDWS.

The insurance component of the NDWS is supplemented by a complex array of assistance (or welfare) and social service programs, which are targeted strictly on poor people who fit into various categories. Does this system produce an efficient mechanism for relieving or preventing poverty? No one claims so. Families must demonstrate a high degree of poverty and/ or pathology in order to get the help that could have been provided more economically and effectively at an earlier stage. Moreover, the help they receive is often inadequate and inappropriate. As such, the NDWS does not foster social solidarity and integration, but division and racism.

The NDWS works best for the elderly. If we compare those in poverty (before considering taxes and benefit-transfer payments) with those who remain poor after taxes and transfers, we see that the United States brings about two-thirds of the elderly poor above the poverty line. This compares unfavorably to the 97 percent of the Swedish elderly who are brought above the poverty line. Nevertheless, this poverty-reducing effect derives mainly from social security rather than from programs aimed exclusively at the poor. For children, the NDWS operates even more badly. The U.S. welfare state lifts only one poor family in six from poverty, and less than one in eight single-parent families. (In Sweden the figures are over a half and three-quarters, respectively.) Despite (or because of) its emphasis on means-testing and targeting resources to those in need, the NDWS leaves more people poor, and it leaves those who are poor with a wider gap between their incomes and the poverty line. The rate of child poverty is three or four times that in more generous welfare states (Smeeding, Torrey, & Rein, 1988).

Conclusion

Compared with other models of the welfare state, the minimalist, market-oriented NDWS leaves the U.S. economy ill prepared for the global competition it faces. It also leaves Americans, especially minorities, women, and children, poorly protected against poverty and sickness. A dogmatic insistence on market-oriented solutions has produced the costly scandal of the American health care system, which leaves tens of millions unprotected and tens of millions more without adequate coverage. The NDWS has also produced a welfare system that is bureaucratic, mean-spirited, and stigmatizing. Moreover, it has created a social insurance system which does well for those with good earnings records but fails to recognize the childrearing contributions on which it, and society at large, depends. As such, it fails to protect women and children.

The answer to these deficiencies cannot be even more privatization, market solutions, and coercion of the poor. Moreover, the gains of the NDWS must be defended against those who would put the clock back even further. Instead, we need a different model of the welfare state, one that provides a health care system in which wealth is not an advantage nor poverty a handicap. We need a social and labor market policy that assures full employment, facilitates the harmonizing of work and childrearing, promotes equality between men and women, and prevents poverty in children and families. A fully democratic and egalitarian "welfare society" may require a different kind of economic system than capitalism, but it is clear that the NDWS has outlived its usefulness even to the interests of American capitalists. For the rest of us living in a society of growing poverty and inequality, the "twilight of the American dream" (Smith, 1992) makes the need for a different kind of welfare state a matter of urgency.

Rejoinder to Professor Adams GARY FREEMAN

I was hoping my adversary would not play his Swedish card, not because I feared it, but because it is so easy to dismiss. Why is there no socialism in America? Why is the United States a welfare state laggard? Why can't the United States be more like Sweden? Please. At this late date in the human experiment with socialist utopias, only the most sentimental ideologues still long to impose a top-heavy, intrusive, and leveling social service bureaucracy on an otherwise free people. Beyond that, my colleague's uncritical praise of the Swedish model is unwarranted. Although some have argued that Sweden and other small European welfare states have managed to steer their economies with some skill through the recession of the 1970s (Katzenstein, 1985), the evidence today is highly mixed. Swedish labor relations have become rancorous, the economy is in serious trouble, and the voters have turned the Social Democratic Party out of office. The Swedes have tried to root out every disparity and inequality in their society with an unending stream of new policies. These have, in turn, generated new inequalities and rising resentments. Indeed, Swedish social policymaking has begun to resemble a dog frantically chasing its tail, and with about as much success (Heclo and Madsen, 1987).

Even if we conceded that the Swedish welfare state is a success, what relevance would this have to our own condition? Sweden is a small country of 8 million people. Moreover, its exceptional homogeneity has made social consensus temporarily possible over limited issues. The United States is wholly different. The social divisions that roil our collective life are largely unknown in placid, plain, and pedestrian Scandinavia. That even such questionably blessed societies are themselves experiencing deep tensions over welfare state arrangements and exhibiting strong popular resentment of social bureaucrats should be ample warning to us. Sweden is not a model that the United States can follow, nor should it try. More generally, the European welfare states, though they have much to teach us, are fast learning that growth of social expenditure has its limits and that voters will not abide unceasing increases in taxation forever (Peters, 1985).

We reach common ground when the discussion turns to what kinds of national policies are necessary to make the United States more competitive against its industrial peers. Education, job training, investment, and saving are all required. More generally, to achieve a decent society, as I have argued, we need to reduce unemployment and upgrade the quality and conditions of jobs. Income support programs are secondary to these essential tasks. Furthermore, misdirected social policy can get in the way of economic progress. What we do not need is to put more people on welfare. Let us concede that our public assistance program is in many respects shameful; but let us also concede that it is impossible to guarantee a comfortable living standard for all, regardless of their behavior and regardless of their willingness or ability to work.

NO

GARY FREEMAN

The system of social provision first established in the Social Security Act of 1935, and later amended in important ways, is an essential and irreplaceable component of the American social and political fabric. The basic structure of the New Deal welfare state (NDWS) is sound and should be preserved. For the most part it is a system that works well. While the current set of social programs has serious deficiencies and gaps in coverage, these can be addressed within the existing framework. No fundamental overhaul is necessary, nor would it be wise to undertake one. Any major transformation of the social insurance aspects of the system would impose large uncompensated losses on those persons who have been participating in its programs for many years. Nonincremental changes in the public assistance program are also ill-advised; instead, less ambitious experiments at the state and federal level should be encouraged. Rather than being outmoded, our welfare system—often maligned by liberals as inadequate (Cates, 1983) and by conservatives as detrimental to economic growth (Weaver, 1982)—is just reaching maturity. The system also has characteristics that make it surprisingly well positioned to respond to the challenges of the coming decades.

The System Is Sound and It Works

The American welfare system is based on the assumption that most people work or are dependent on someone who does. It is also premised on the idea that government will ensure full employment at a living wage. Our income support programs are meant to deal with those occasions—childhood, old age, sickness, and unemployment—when individuals are unable to provide for themselves and their families through work. Contributory insurance programs cover those who work or are supported by someone who does (unemployment insurance, old age pensions, disability benefits, and Medicare). Means-tested benefits (public assistance) are paid out of general revenues to those outside the labor force who are without a working responsible party (Berkowitz, 1991).

Contributory insurance with graduated benefits is the kind of program adopted by most industrial democracies. As such, our basic programs are neither odd nor unusual. They are also especially suited to an American political culture that stresses individual responsibility (Lockhart, 1989). Thus the programs enjoying the most popular support are social security and disability insurance (i.e., they involve direct contributions by employed persons), followed by unemployment insurance (i.e., the contributions are paid by employers only). On the other hand, public assistance is viewed the least favorably since no contributions are involved. Contributory insurance rewards work since it organizes society to take care of its own when work is impossible. Risk is shared broadly, and those least able to provide for themselves are supported, albeit at a minimal level.

The NDWS is often derisively referred to as a "residual" welfare state. Although most people would agree that in an ideal world basic benefits would be more generous, and all of us can think of additional benefit programs that might be desirable, the American welfare state was never intended to be more than residual. It was founded on the notion that people are better off if they earn their living in the private market, but that society has a responsibility to deal with those occasions when this is not possible. That is why the NDWS included important provisions to provide work opportunities and to upgrade the quality of work in general. It was never the intention of the American welfare state to equalize living standards regardless of performance in the market, nor to eliminate the necessity to work.

When the French aristocrat Alexis de Tocqueville visited the United States in the early 1830s, he was struck by the fact that "every man works for his living, or has worked, or comes from parents who have worked. Everything therefore prompts the assumption that to work is the necessary, natural, and honest condition of all men" (1969, p. 550). The best welfare reform that could be adopted in America today would be to reestablish the norm that every adult should work or be in a household headed by someone who does. The government should take steps to create an economy that provides jobs that pay decent wages. The NDWS is perfectly suited to supplement the needs of persons otherwise self-sufficiently employed.

Present Problems Can Be Resolved within the Existing System

The NDWS was designed nearly fifty years ago in circumstances quite different from those we face today. It would be remarkable if it were not in some important respects out of sync with present challenges. But what is more remarkable is the extent to which the basic structure is adaptable to new social realities, allowing growth and change in existing programs and the addition of new benefit schemes. The old age pension and disability programs are now fully mature. The system provides income security for millions of elderly Americans and has transformed for the better the experience of old age for most people. Changing demographic pressures and economic circumstances can put the system under financial pressure, but these fluxes can be dealt with by timely legislative interventions, as demonstrated by the bipartisan reforms approved in 1983 to resolve the social security crisis (Light, 1985). The rate at which benefit levels rise can be altered, the retirement age can be gradually extended, and some portion of benefits can be taxed for those with private incomes. There are, in other words, numerous reforms that can make social security more efficient and fairer that do not involve such radical measures as privatization or voluntarism. New programs can also be attached to the original core, as has already occurred with disability insurance in 1956 and Medicare and Medicaid in 1965 (Derthick, 1979). The most obvious piece missing today is health insurance for the actively working population. Medicare covers those who are retired, and Medicaid is available for the poor on public assistance. While neither of these programs is without problems, the most pressing need is to provide basic medical coverage for the majority of citizens who are inadequately covered by private plans or who are without insurance at all. This will not be easy politically, and no comprehensive plan will come cheap. But, the point is that universal health insurance of some kind can be grafted onto the existing NDWS without altering its logic; indeed, it is the logical next step.

Major Changes Will Create Large Transaction Costs

Scrapping the present system in favor of some other model is simply not realistic, nor is it really worth debating. Even large-scale changes, other than the addition of a health insurance program, are not desirable. Once in place, programs based on the insurance model (pensions, disability, and Medicare) cannot be changed without imposing large uncompensated costs on those who have been loyally paying taxes for years and making personal financial decisions in light of anticipated benefits. A fundamental restructuring of our welfare system would violate an intergenerational compact that cannot be taken lightly.

The U.S. welfare state and those abroad have been experiencing increasing financial difficulties in recent years, and there have been calls for radical change. Most of these calls come from the right of the political spectrum and involve privatization and a reversion to free market arrangements. In the present circumstances, any serious changes in the system are more likely to be of this sort than to proceed in a more egalitarian and comprehensive direction. It is clearly better to leave in place programs that have proven themselves and to make them more effective through marginal adjustments. Proposals for fundamental reforms of American social policy have not often passed, as for example the Family Assistance Plan in the 1970s (Moynihan, 1973). Even if they were approved, they normally didn't work, as was the case with many of the Great Society programs of the middle 1960s (Kaplan and Cuciti, 1986).

The Present System Has Distinct Advantages

The NDWS is reasonably well suited to confront the major challenges it faces, arguably more than those vaunted systems in Scandinavia and Western Europe to which the United States is so often compared. Apart from its incompleteness—which I have already discussed and which I see as an argument for the expansion rather than the replacement of the existing structure—we may think of the problems of the present American welfare state as being of two types. The first has to do with the problems of poverty, homelessness, and the pathology associated with the large and predominantly Black underclass. The second has to do with the increasing fiscal strain imposed on individual workers and the economy by the taxes needed to support the welfare state. In neither of these cases does real progress require that we move fundamentally away from the premises and values of the NDWS.

The shocking condition of the underclass is often advanced as an example of the failure of the NDWS. Liberals claim that persistent poverty proves that welfare benefits are too low. As such, they call for guaranteed incomes and for welfare to be provided without means tests. On the other hand, conservatives insist that poverty is worsened, if not created, by the welfare benefits themselves (Murray, 1984). But these arguments miss the point that the welfare state was never organized to sustain large numbers of permanently dependent persons. The problem of dependence is largely the result of the breakdown of both the family and responsible community norms among certain segments of American society. This will have to be addressed through education, social work, law enforcement, and the labor market. Increasing or taking away welfare benefits is not likely to change conditions in the inner cities to any significant degree.

Those criticizing the failure of the American welfare system tend to avoid the fact that, for whatever reason, the social pathology of the underclass prevents it from obtaining familial and labor force stability. It is not clear that social policy should adapt to dysfunctional changes in sexual and marital patterns rather than seek to resist them. The proper objective of social policy should be to encourage marriage and to discourage the birth of illegitimate children. Moreover, social policies should provide incentives to find jobs and to keep them, rather than to create more attractive welfare arrangements. Such policies are consistent with the NDWS.

Certain features of the NDWS that are often criticized may turn out, at least in the present financial crisis, to be distinct advantages. Welfare states need to be adaptive, flexible, and innovative; and to rely more on individual, familial, and community care. Welfare states also need to restrain what appears to be the ineluctable tendency of citizens to demand more and better benefits while resisting the obligation to pay taxes to support them.

In the United States, only the old age, disability, and Medicare programs are completely in the hands of the national government. Unemployment, public assistance, and Medicaid are jointly administered between the federal government and the states. This situation provides a framework for experimenting with programs without requiring a national consensus or risking enormous costs. These are real virtues, given the complexity and intractability inherent in long-term poverty.

The American residual welfare state has another hidden advantage. It has long facilitated a vibrant voluntary sector outside the federal budget, which has been responsive to local needs. While European welfare states often implicitly discourage private charity as retrograde and inferior to public provision, there has been a lot of rethinking of this issue recently. The total welfare provided by a society is the sum of what is provided by the state, the family, and voluntary means (Rose, 1986). This has long been recognized, but social policy pundits have typically denigrated private provision as inherently demeaning and, while nominally lauding the spontaneous provision of welfare within the family, have usually grumbled that such "labor" is not reimbursed out of the public treasury (Alcock, 1987, p. 32–47). It is as if a father and mother are not expected to love and support their children unless they are remunerated for it. Moreover, it is assumed that limitless resources are available to pay people to do what they should be quite happy to do on their own. Rather than being an obstacle to the development of a complete welfare state, private giving may turn out to be highly useful in difficult economic circumstances marked by tight budgets.

Rejoinder to Professor Freeman PAUL ADAMS

Professor Freeman tells us that the NDWS is basically sound. Yet all the problems he acknowledges, including poverty, homelessness, unemployment, and the lack of health care, are expressions of that system. He tells us the model presumes full employment, but it clearly fails to produce it either through management of the economy or through employment policy and supports for labor force participation, such as parental leave and child care.

The contributory system of social insurance is common, as Freeman says. What is distinctive about the NDWS is the lack of universal noncontributory benefits such as family allowances and maternity benefits. The sharp line between social insurance and assistance programs results in an insurance system that perpetuates into old age the inequalities of the labor market, including those structured by racism and sexism. It also perpetuates a stigmatizing welfare system which fosters social divisions and prejudice.

The focus on a Black "underclass" and its sexual and work habits reinforces this prejudice. Insofar as this phenomenon exists, it is a product of the NDWS. Freeman encourages young people in the ghetto to get married. But how will that help when young men face such high levels of unemployment and such sharp declines in real wages that marriage amounts to the wife's taking on an additional dependent rather than a provider or partner? He may exhort poor young women to change their fertility behavior, but what other opportunities for adult status and emotional fulfillment does his NDWS offer them or their partners? All the evidence is that fertility declines as the status and opportunities of women, including African-American women, improve. Surely Freeman does not mean to suggest that substituting marriage bureaus for welfare offices will contribute to solving the problems he attributes to the behavior of the poor?

The residual welfare state that my opponent favors is not one that interferes minimally in people's lives and lifestyles. For him the "proper objective of social policy should be to encourage marriage and to discourage the birth of illegitimate children." Paradoxically, a comprehensive, universalist welfare state would be much less intrusive. As the Swedish case shows, illegitimacy rates similar to those in the United States can coexist with dramatically lower levels of child poverty. There would be no need for the state to be interfering in the domestic arrangements of its citizens in the way Freeman suggests if social and economic policy were seriously directed to ensuring full employment, harmonizing work and childrearing, and furthering the full equality of women.

The real problem with the residual approach to social policy is that it works against itself. It penalizes work, saving, and family caregiving by providing help only when these are absent or break down. A mother may freely love her children, but be unable to feed them or provide for their health care unless she remains poor enough to be eligible for welfare and Medicaid benefits. Freeman's defense of the NDWS depends on blaming the behavior of the poor for its failure to prevent unemployment and poverty. This provides him with a scapegoat, but not an explanation or a solution.

REFERENCES

Adams, P. (1990). Children as contributions in kind: Social Security and family policy. *Social Work* (35)6, 492–498.

Adams, P. (1982). *Health of the state.* New York: Praeger.

Alcock, P. (1987). *Poverty and state support.* London: Longman.

Berkowitz, E. (1991). *America's welfare state: From Roosevelt to Reagan.* Baltimore: The Johns Hopkins University Press.

Cameron, D. (1984). Social democracy, labour quiescence, and the representation of economic interest in advanced capitalist society. In Goldthorpe, J. (Ed.), *Order and conflict in contemporary capitalism.* Oxford: Clarendon Press, 143–178.

Cates, J. (1983). *Insuring inequality: Administrative leadership in social security, 1935–54.* Ann Arbor: University of Michigan Press.

Derthick, M. (1979). *Policymaking for social security.* Washington: D.C.: Brookings.

Esping-Andersen, G. (1990). *The three worlds of welfare capitalism.* Cambridge: Polity Press.

Esping-Andersen, G., & Micklewright, J. (1991). Welfare state models in OECD Countries: An analysis for the debate in Central and Eastern Europe. In Cornia, G., and Sipos, S. (Eds.), *Children and the transition to the market economy: Safety nets and social policies in Central and Eastern Europe.* Aldershot, UK: Avebury, 35–67.

Harman, C. (1984). *Explaining the crisis: A Marxist reappraisal.* London: Bookmarks.

Heclo, H., & Madsen, H. (1987). *Policy and politics in Sweden: Principled pragmatism.* Philadelphia: Temple University Press.

Human capital: Special Report (1988). *Business Week,* (September 19), 100–141.

Industrial policy (1992). *Business Week,* (April 6), 70–76.

Kaplan, M., & Cuciti, P. (Eds.) (1986). *The Great Society and its legacy.* Durham, NC: Duke University Press.

Katzenstein, P. (1985). *Small states in world markets.* Ithaca: Cornell University Press.

Light, P. (1985). *Artful work: The politics of social security reform.* New York: Random House.

Lockhart, C. (1989). *Gaining ground: Tailoring social programs to American values.* Berkeley: University of California Press.

Moynihan, D. (1973). *The politics of a guaranteed income: The Nixon Administration and the Family Assistance Plan.* New York: Vintage Books.

Murray, C. (1984). *Losing ground.* New York: Basic Books.

Peters, B. (1985). The limits of the welfare state. In Vig, N., & Schier, S. (Eds.), *Political economy in western democracies.* New York: Holmes & Meier.

Rose, R. (1986). Common goals but different roles: The state's contribution to the welfare mix. In Rose, R., & Shiratori, R. (Eds.), *The welfare state east and west.* New York: Oxford University Press.

Smeeding, T., Torrey, B., & Rein, M. (1988). Patterns of income and poverty: The economic status of children and the elderly in eight countries. In Palmer, J., Smeeding, T., & Torrey, B. (Eds.), *The vulnerable.* Washington, D.C.: Urban Institute.

Smith, S. (1992). Twilight of the American dream. *International Socialism* 54, 3–43.

Stoiber, S. (1989). *Parental leave and "woman's place": The implications and impact of three European approaches to family leave policy.* Washington, D.C.: Women's Research and Education Institute.

Titmuss, R. (1974). *Social policy: An introduction.* London: Allen and Unwin.

Tocqueville, A. de (1969). *Democracy in America.* New York: Anchor Books.

Weaver, C. (1982). *The crisis in social security.* Durham, NC: Duke University Press.

Wilensky, H., & Lebeaux, C. (1965). *Industrial society and social welfare.* New York: The Free Press.

ANNOTATED BIBLIOGRAPHY

Berkowitz, E. (1991). *America's welfare state: From Roosevelt to Reagan.* Baltimore: The Johns Hopkins University Press.

This book presents a comprehensive and sensible overview of the development and operation of the New Deal welfare state, including incisive observations about current problems.

Derthick, M. (1979). *Policymaking for social security.* Washington: D.C.: Brookings.

One of the most reliable studies of the politics of social policy in the United States, this book makes special reference to old age pension, disability, and medical care.

Light, P. (1985). *Artful work: The politics of social security reform.* New York: Random House.

This highly readable book describes the process by which the social security financial crisis of the early 1980s was "resolved" through a bipartisan compromise.

Lockhart, C. (1989). *Gaining ground: Tailoring social programs to American values.* Berkeley: University of California Press.

This is an imaginative and balanced discussion of the problems of welfare reform in the United States. It takes the popular parts of the New Deal welfare state as a base for asking what sorts of social policies are possible in principle in the United States.

Wilson, W. (1987). *The truly disadvantaged: The inner city, the underclass, and public policy.* Chicago: University of Chicago Press.

One of America's leading sociologists presents an unconventional and influential analysis of the problem of persistent poverty.

Should Social Security Be Made Voluntary?

EDITOR'S NOTE: Social security programs were created in the industrial countries during the early decades of this century to provide for the maintenance of income when normal earnings are interrupted or terminated through illness, disability, injury at work, retirement, or death. Although social security is generally popular, opponents argue that it consumes large amounts of revenues, is administered under complex bureaucratic rules by indifferent government officials, and is not responsive to people's needs. A major complaint is that people are compelled to belong to the social security system. This, critics claim, violates principles of freedom and choice. Individuals should have the right to decide whether they want to pay into the social security system and, if they do not, they should be permitted to use their social security contributions in other ways. Proponents of social security argue that compulsory membership is essential if social security is to be viable and offer adequate protection against poverty.

Tom Walz, Ph.D. argues in favor of social security being made voluntary. Dr. Walz is Professor of Social Work at the University of Iowa. His major research interests are in public policy, aging, and international social development, and he has published several books and numerous journal articles on these issues.

Martin B. Tracy, Ph.D., argues against the proposal that social security should be made voluntary. Dr. Tracy is Associate Professor of Social Work at the University of Iowa. His major research interests are in comparative social welfare, income and retirement programs, aging issues, and international social development. He is the author of *Social Policies for the Elderly in Third World Nations* (1991), Greenwood, and *International Handbook on Old Age Insurance* (1991), Greenwood. He has also published in leading social work and social science journals.

YES

Tom Walz

Despite social security's widespread popularity, the program may have outlived its usefulness. This is not to say that in its time social security did not have a justifiable place and purpose in American social policy. The reality, however, is that social security is more than a half century old and was designed to meet the needs and circumstances of an era that no longer exists.

The Background of Social Security

The basis of the compulsory social security system is a mandated payroll tax on most workers' wages, including the self-employed. This tax is set at 7.65 percent of one's annual income, and is matched by the employer, covering the first $55,500 of a worker's annual wage income. The tax dollars are then placed in a series of trust funds for payments to qualifying beneficiaries. The idea behind this compulsory universal participation was theoretically to "spread the risk" among all workers, including both high and low wage workers and high and low risk workers.

The laudatory purpose of social security, however, does not make it any less vulnerable to being outdated. Until the Social Security Act of 1935 passed, the federal government played a low-key role in the social assistance of its citizens. Whatever financial support that was available in the early years came through local government assistance, often in the form of subsistence living in a poorhouse. For the past half century the federal government has increasingly assumed responsibility for caring for the nation's poor. Poor families are aided through AFDC, while poor individuals are assisted through SSI. Both programs got their starts, at least partially, as part of the Social Security Act.

The financial protection of the American worker no longer needs to depend upon a compulsory governmental insurance scheme. In fact, retirement is no longer a gamble. Retirement is going to happen to virtually every surviving worker. Survivor and disability insurance, perhaps, is still a gamble of sorts. Even so, why have a social insurance program at all? One argument is to avoid the demeaning features of means tested public assistance alternatives.

"Welfare" and Social Security

Public assistance admittedly is not a popular program, and it certainly does not enjoy the same support as social insurance. Yet society has developed much greater awareness about the function of welfare and its necessity than it had twenty years ago. If it were not restricted just to "unwed mothers and children," or those with questionable disabilities, public assistance would shed much of its criticism. Its strength is that it is paid for through general revenues and thus does not involve the kind of regressive taxation on which social insurance is built.

When the federal government entered the social security field in the early 1930s, America was still experiencing an almost hysterical fear of pauperism. Nearly sixty years of cultivating a Social Darwinist view of the world forced the nation to respond to the economic crisis of the Depression in ways that reduced the appearance of government-sponsored social assistance. Today most Americans may feel nostalgia about the old bootstrap philosophy, but their personal experiences display a different sentiment. "Welfare" is no longer a dirty word for many Americans. The issue is really whether a dual welfare structure is still needed, with one system based on social insurance principles and a second based on means-tested criteria. It will be argued here that the former has served its purpose and could be dismantled.

Why the Social Security System Is No Longer Viable

The core of the argument about the lack of viability of compulsory social insurance is based on the datedness of the original assumptions behind the program. First, the financing mechanism for social security (the use of a payroll tax) was based on the assumption that most Americans would remain wage earners for most of their lives. It was envisioned that workers would remain fully employed over their lifetimes, thus improving their wage levels with the gained work experience. Certainly the coming of a labor-nonintensive, high-tech economy was not anticipated. From the start, the work lives of Americans have been uncertain and unstable. Payroll taxes have not flowed steadily into the trust fund. Workers have experienced both economic recessions and occupational obsolescence. Even more serious has been the breakdown of the wage structure. The shift from labor- to capital-intensive production has greatly weakened labor's bargaining power.

Robert Theobold (1962) warned years ago that advanced capitalism could lead to a "workless world." Building a social security system around the assumption of universal work just does not make sense in a "workless world." The levels of employment that exist today can be viewed as somewhat artificial, as many of the jobs are part time and/or in the low wage service sector.

One could also argue that the assumptions behind the equity of principle in social insurance no longer hold. Wages do not rise steadily over a worker's lifetime and labor's bargaining power has not increased in recent years. With benefits in OASDI tied to earnings experience, the shattering of the wage structure for many workers will drive future benefits down, not up. Recent evidence suggests that social security benefits can be manipulated by public policy to suit the needs of the greater economy. This trend seems to be in the direction of a loss of income adequacy rather than a gain in the benefits being offered.

A third assumption behind social security was that each generation would naturally "reproduce" itself. As a "pay as you go program," each generation is expected to produce a significant work force to pay into the program in order to cover annual benefit outlays. A marked reduction in the nation's birth rate was not envisioned at the time the program was designed. While adjustments can be made by increasing taxes on a relatively smaller labor force, this is neither politically popular nor does it improve intergenerational relationships. It is questionable whether it is even necessary to battle to keep social security afloat, especially if there are viable alternatives.

A fourth assumption behind the social insurance scheme is the belief that we would remain a nation of workers and that most income would be derived from gainful employment. In a capital intensive economy more of the gross product comes from infusion of technology than from added labor (Ross and Trachte, 1988). This means that more of the nation's gross product is a function of capital rather than labor. In effect, this means that more of the nation's income derived from production comes through association with capital rather than labor. The exception is "human capital," wherein high-knowledge workers are paid a salary for their knowledge. However, many could sell their services under contract and be paid as "dividend." Thus the "spreading the risk" assumption behind the compulsory payroll tax does not reach out to capture the growing and important segment of income earned outside of wages. These structural developments in earned income patterns challenge the foundations of the system.

Many of the new capitalists whose incomes come from wages and dividends have chosen to build their income protection through a variety of alternatives—private pensions, individual retirement accounts, mutual funds, and other strategic investments. Private pensions have grown steadily, although not all workers are covered, nor are the programs sufficiently portable given the transitory nature of employment today. Nonetheless, the argument favoring compulsory social insurance is weakened by the expansion of the private pension system. In 1935 the sorts of alternatives for assuring a retirement income that exist today were not available.

As we approach the twenty-first century, it is apparent that U.S. society has moved well beyond the industrial capitalism that existed in the 1930s (Bell, 1973). The image of armies of overalled workers passing through factory gates is one of the past. The age and era of global or advanced capitalism has arrived. Robots, computers, and lasers have replaced many workers by enhancing the productivity and efficiency of others. Although we may not yet live in a "workless world," the predictability and stability of an individual's work and occupation will never be what it used to be. This development is not just a "gamble" within our economic system—it is a structural feature.

It is hard to imagine a social security system based on a payroll tax when unemployment rates run at the 7 percent level; when workers are forced to retire earlier and earlier; and when entry into the labor force is delayed by years of education. With all of the stop-outs, drop-outs, and kicked-outs, payment into any insurance scheme will be terribly unstable, and in the long run, it will be difficult to meet outlays even while greatly increasing the social security tax.

In this new age we need to realize that wealth is principally a function of the infusion of capital, not labor. Marx's argument that surplus wealth is derived from the "value added" by labor is less and less true of the workings of a modern economy (Collincos, 1983). The choice of moving in this high-tech direction has been a policy decision of the political economy. Yet it is the American worker who suffers the consequences. It is extremely difficult to understand why the worker should then have to pay the price of this policy decision, especially since it is the corporate industrial sector that benefits most from a capital-intensive society through profits realized by lowering their wage payments and increasing the productivity and efficiency of their operation. It seems logical, therefore, to expect the private sector to bear most, if not all, of the income security protection of the American worker. If there is to be a continuing compulsory social security system, then it should be supported by a 100 percent tax on industry profits rather than the 50-50 arrangement that currently exists.

Benefit structures in social security are believed to be redistributive from rich to poor. At the same time, however, it is acknowledged that the social security tax is regressive. The poor pay a far greater share of their income to social security than do the rich. This is particularly true for the rich whose wealth comes from capital gains and not wage income, since the former escapes all social security taxation. So what does the lower income worker gain from being compelled to pay into the social system? At best a retirement income not much larger than a public assistance payment, without automatic eligibility for a host of important in-kind benefits. Wouldn't a worker actually be better off being able to add social security tax dollars to his or her income while still in active employment, rather than having it put into a trust account for a pension or a disability payment? If the retirement income realized was more adequate and not based on equity principles, a compulsory insurance scheme might make some sense. As it stands now it does not. It is clear that higher income workers do not need social security for their retirement needs. With all the safe investment mechanisms now available, they could easily plan for their income security through noncompulsory, private market alternatives.

Higher income people will not escape the income retribution features of social security if they participate in a private insurance/pension alternative. The basic income tax has fairly well-defined progressive tax features, and, unless they are protected by another policy option, at least a portion of capital gains are taxed. If more of income security were paid from general revenues, those revenues would then come from income taxes and corporate profit taxes, rather than from a tax on the wage worker's income. In short, generational equity is better served through income security provisions that are paid from progressive tax arrangements. We also have a situation arising where fewer workers will enter the labor force at a time when the wage structure has broken down. Still, these workers will be expected to provide support for an extremely large cohort of the elderly (i.e., baby boom group). This could make the compulsory insurance system a source of increasing public controversy.

One must not forget that one of the attractive aspects of social security to FDR was the fact that reserves would build up before any real benefits had to be paid out. This gave FDR borrowed time and access to trust fund money to fight the Depression and later the Germans and Japanese. Postwar affluence fortunately made paying back the trust funds relatively easy. It may not be so easy in the future if the government borrows trust fund dollars to amortize its large international indebtedness, as appears to be the practice.

Conclusion

At the time of the 1935 Social Security Act, Americans were great savers, and many prepared for their old age responsibly. Those that did not were unable to because they lacked the surplus income to save. Under social security there is a small benefit commensurate with a worker's average annual income when he or she retires, but it is not much different than welfare. Those who solidly benefit from social security would probably do even better through investment/interest market mechanisms. The promotion of the IRA, with its tax benefits and improved liquidity, makes voluntary approaches to social security attractive for the non-low-wage worker. Through the proposed alternatives to social security, the federal government would no longer have to administer the massive social security system, however efficiently it may have been run over the years.

It is strange that a society so ready to experiment with its economic "mode of production" is so conservative and restrained in its social experimentation. Social security, like the constitution, is not a program but a concept. Americans need more security protection, but that does not mean it must come through a social insurance mechanism and through a payment that requires a tax on wages. Even though many of us still work, we live on the edge of a workless world. Ours is a capital-intensive economic system. Even the so-called service sector is threatened by advances in computers and robotics. Hence, we must be willing and ready to redesign our income security systems to fit the realities of our political economy and the needs of the citizens, both workers and non-workers. For compulsory social security to make sense it would be necessary to wind back the world to "industrial capitalism." Since this is unlikely, let's move ahead and beyond the "Social Security Act of 1935" (as amended) to a social security system suited to the needs and conditions of a high-tech, global capitalist world.

Rejoinder to Professor Walz   MARTIN B. TRACY

Do we really want to abandon social security in favor of income-tested programs and private initiatives? Professor Walz argues that social security is outdated in a post-industrial society that is less labor intensive. Even if it were true that social security cannot adopt to changing work patterns, which it isn't, it would not be sufficient reason to revert to a system that prevailed in pre-industrial society. Reliance on means-tested government charity and private resources was not suitable when developed under the Elizabethan poor laws of the early seventeenth century. Residual benefits as a last resort of income support in a new work world are certainly not appropriate for the twenty-first century. And Walz suggests that social security is an archaic and outdated approach! One can only conclude that his views reflect a fundamental misunderstanding of the purposes of social security and of its proven ability to adapt to social, economic, demographic, and work-related changes.

A myopic view of the function of social security is not an original one. The debates about social security in the United States have traditionally ignored the role of social insurance as an instrument of social justice, a role that is equally important as a means of ensuring adequate income in old age. It is a dynamic system that could not have possibly continued to exist for over half a century of extreme political and economic turbulence without being adaptable. Are we really expected to accept the charge that social security is incapable of flexibility in the future? Or that the system has been unresponsive to changes in labor conditions since its inception? How, then, does one explain a host of adjustments and modifications that responded to new realities?

In fact, the system has continuously reacted to new social conditions: insufficient income protection of couples led to the inclusion of dependent wives and husbands; the difficulty of protecting nonwage earners was resolved by adding the self-employed; the system shifted from being a strictly "pay-as-you go" system to a trust fund when threatened with a shortage of funds for the baby boomers; the system linked benefits to price and wage indices when benefits were devalued because of inflation; the age of first eligibility was lowered to 62 when it became apparent that some individuals were unemployed before the retirement age of 65; and social security raised benefits for people who delay retirement and increased the amount of wages that "retired" persons can earn without being penalized when the need to retain older workers emerged.

True, the system has not yet responded to all the emerging changes in the work place, especially the increase in women workers. But social insurance systems outside the United States have made great improvements in their programs to compensate women by moving toward parity in wage levels, by giving social security credits for homemaker services, by setting minimum levels of social security credits regardless of actual taxes paid, by permitting voluntary contributions, and by splitting credits equally between married partners in the event of divorce.

The social security systems of other nations have also responded to new work patterns such as early retirement, reduced work time, and changes in careers. This has been done with innovative provisions that include partial retirement (the worker reduces work time and receives a partial pension), pensions for the long-term unemployed, and pensions for partially disabled persons and for the prematurely aged. Social security systems in other countries are very similar to our own, and they face the same shifts in labor and capital. There is absolutely no reason why we cannot make similar, and even better, adjustments in our social security system to meet changing social and labor conditions.

Should we give up a system that is based on earned benefits for one that awards benefits simply on the basis of need? Should the government's role in post-industrial society be to dispense charity only to the deserving poor? It took the world two centuries to get beyond the antiquated notion that government-supported programs of income security in old age should be related solely to need. If the history of social welfare programs has taught us anything, it is that income-tested benefits are demeaning and intimidating and are acceptable only as a last resort. History has also taught us, most of us at any rate, that social rights protect individuals against the risks faced by everyone. Social insurance is a proven and effective way of guaranteeing these social rights to all.

NO

MARTIN B. TRACY

Social security should not be made voluntary. In fact, it is not possible to have a public social security system that is wholly voluntary. Social security is, by definition, intrinsically linked to the principles of social insurance which require compulsory contributions from virtually all of the working population. A true social security system exists only when protection against the risks of the loss of income is shared among all workers. It is certainly possible to have a privatized system of voluntary benefits, but voluntary social security is an oxymoron, a contradiction in terms. Proposals that would substitute a voluntary system of social security for the current program of old age, survivors, and disability pensions (OASDI) reflect a basic misunderstanding of the purpose and structure of social security systems.

The Basis for the Social Security System

The question of why there is mandatory participation in the OASDI program under social security in the United States is usually raised by persons who are convinced that most individuals would be financially better off if they were free to save and invest their surplus income without government involvement. Indeed, it is not difficult to demonstrate that prudent investments in individual retirement accounts, mutual funds, money markets, certificates of deposit and private pension programs would often yield a higher return than the monthly annuities that are paid under social security. In addition to this economic argument there is a concern in a market economy that individuals should have the freedom of choice as to how they prepare for their income security in old age. It is further suggested that decisions about individuals' economic futures should not be forced upon them by a faceless government bureaucracy which knows nothing of their personal circumstances and desires (Blinder, 1988).

In contrast, those who support compulsory participation in OASDI make the case that if individuals were totally responsible for all of their retirement income, poverty rates among the elderly would increase dramatically because many workers do not have the will to set funds aside regularly when they are faced with the choice of spending or saving. Moreover, many spouses and part-time workers (or sporadically employed persons) who do not have a regular income over a forty-year work period cannot realistically be expected to voluntarily save for their old age. Further, there is a greater risk involved when savings are invested in private pension programs or in stocks and bonds.

Proponents of the current OASDI system also justify mandatory participation on the basis that social security is egalitarian and redistributive. It is egalitarian because of special provisions in the calculation of OASDI benefit amounts that pay benefits to lower income workers at a higher rate. It is redistributive because it transfers income from one generation to another by taxing the earnings of the employed and giving the money to the unemployed elderly and their spouses or survivors.

Compulsory Social Security and Social Justice

The question of voluntary versus compulsory OASDI has been the subject of debate in the United States since the 1920s. The central issue since the inauguration of the Social Security Act in 1935, however, is often misunderstood and seldom discussed. The dispute is not over whether families should have a decent level of income following the loss of earnings due to the retirement, disability, or death of a worker. No responsible person contends that society would be better served if more older persons were eligible for income-tested benefits under the Supplementary Security Income (SSI) program. No, the essence of the argument is over whether old age, survivors, and disability pensions should be driven by economic efficiency through individual efforts or by economic adequacy through universally enforced income transfers. The central question is: Does society want a system that emphasizes individual rights or one that stresses social rights?

I will argue that the most important benefit of a compulsory system of social security is not economic security but social justice. Individual rights for the sake of economic efficiency are secondary to social rights for the sake of economic protection against the risks that threaten to reduce the income of everyone.

It is apparently difficult for many Americans to fully appreciate the role that social security plays in social justice, although most other societies place social rights obtained through social security on equal footing with civil rights and political rights as an essential feature of a just society

(Perrin, 1985). The foremost reason that there are social security systems in 135 countries (U.S. Department of Health and Human Services, 1990) is because social security is a vital instrument of social justice. The level of economic security is obviously a major program goal, but the role society plays as a whole in providing economic security is an even more important one.

This is not an original idea; indeed, it is one that is very commonplace in other societies. Outside the United States, the relationship between social security and social justice is not an obscure or esoteric issue that is discussed only by scholars and philosophers; it is part of everyday discussion and media coverage. In Europe there are constant reminders of the interrelationship between systems of income support and social justice and social solidarity.

The theme of social security as an instrument of social justice is clearly stated in the logo of the International Social Security Association (ISSA). The ISSA is an independent affiliate of the United Nations, with 306 member organizations in 121 countries. It is headquartered in Geneva, Switzerland. The logo proclaims: "No Lasting Peace without Social Justice, No Social Justice without Social Security." It is a simple maxim, but one that resounds with complex yet elementary truth.

Although social security is a system designed to assure social justice, the process of funding and awarding benefits that gives social security its unique characteristic is social insurance. Social insurance is the program mechanism that is used to implement a system of social security. There are several fundamental precepts of social insurance which help to explain why the system must be compulsory. One is that benefits are based on work and earnings; thus, benefits are earned. However, contrary to what many people believe, few workers actually contribute as much money as they receive in benefits. In the United States, as in most other countries, benefits under OASDI usually exceed contributions. The only way that this is possible without government subsidies is to tax current workers to pay OASDI to former workers and their families through a system of income transfer from a generation of workers to a generation of nonworkers. Under this system, sufficient funds can be raised only if there is a pool of resources which, in turn, is possible only if contributions are compulsory. Some systems are partially subsidized by general revenues, but, by definition, social insurance systems are funded by compulsory payroll taxes.

The concepts that link social security and social insurance with social justice (by way of mandatory government-administered, work-related national social insurance) began to develop in Western society in the middle of the seventeenth century. It was advanced through the ideas of various leading French and German thinkers of the eighteenth century and through the writings of Thomas Paine, the American political philosopher. One major concept that evolved from these early advocates of state-supported public income programs was the notion of "social solidarity," which suggests that humankind has a natural inclination for social organization in the pursuit of common needs. The idea was that certain social conditions, particularly poverty, are viewed as injustices that are contrary to equal rights. Equally important was the view that these social injustices and inequities are conditions that are the responsibility of the state to resolve.

Paine, for example, called for a comprehensive system of state-financed benefits to guarantee civil rights by fighting poverty with a statutory minimum income for children and the elderly; by providing universal education; and by giving allowances for births, marriages, and deaths (Paine, 1792, cited in Perrin, 1985). While these proposals were not accepted in the economically fledgling United States of the time, they played an important role in the evolution of the doctrine that society should provide income protection to the needy, not as charity but as a state obligation. Similar ideas contributed to laying the foundation for social insurance programs in Europe beginning with old-age pensions and workers' compensation benefits in Germany in the late 1800s.

In the United States, the need for mandatory state protection against the loss of wages or salaries accelerated in the mid-1930s because of the economic devastation of the Great Depression. While it had previously been assumed that wage earners would protect themselves from the risk of losing their income through individual savings, voluntary collectives, or the help of other members of the extended family, the Depression made it clear that the loss of earnings and savings was seldom the fault of individuals.

It was recognized that protection against the loss of earnings through savings was unrealistic for many wage earners because the opportunity for employment was beyond the control of the individual. Even if they were employed, wage levels were often insufficient to enable workers to set aside money for future needs. In addition, extended families had become less and less capable of meeting the needs of unemployed family members, including the elderly, becuse of the shrinking size of families. The nuclearization of families meant that fewer children remained with their elderly parents and many services that had previously been provided by children had to be purchased. This reduced the ability of extended families to meet the income needs of family members who had lost the capacity to earn wages: the old, disabled, or widowed.

Why Social Security?

The federal government's response to the uncertainty of employment and earnings brought on by the Depression was a compulsory social security program. Although the term "social security" was coined by the 1935 Act, similar systems had been introduced in many other countries as much as thirty-five years earlier. By 1940 there were fifty-seven countries with mandatory social security systems.

What exactly did we intend to accomplish in adopting a social security system? Why not adopt one of the numerous alternative proposals that were in vogue at the time? The answer to both of these questions lies within the historical evolution of social security as an internationally accepted instrument of social justice. As such, social security is not merely a way of reducing poverty among elderly, nonworking persons, but it is a comprehensive system of income maintenance and health care programs that are largely financed by payroll compulsory contributions.

Social security in both the United States and in foreign nations has not developed in a haphazard and unplanned way. Particularly since World War II, it has been the result of concerted efforts by representatives from virtually every nation to establish national standards of income, health care, and work conditions through the conventions and resolutions of the International Labour Organization (ILO). Perhaps the best known and most influential ILO Convention is No. 102, which establishes minimum standards for benefits provided under the nine branches of social security: medical care, sickness, unemployment, old age, employment injury, family, maternity, invalidity (disability), and survivors' benefits (International Labour Office, 1989). Under this Convention, which was adopted in 1952, the state bears the responsibility for administering social security, including securing funds, usually through compulsory payroll taxes.

Few Americans are familiar with the standards of Convention 102 or with the ILO for that matter. This is a situation of considerable irony, given that the United States government, as well as U.S. labor and business leaders, has long been influential in establishing minimum standards for social security in other nations through their activities in the ILO. The irony is even more profound in that our Congress has never ratified Convention No. 102, even though our official delegation to the ILO has historically encouraged other nations to follow it.

Why not follow the same standards we help set for others? One clear reason is that employers and the medical profession in the United States have consistently and successfully argued against government imposed minimum standards of income and health care that are based on the recommendations of international bodies (Alcock, 1971). I would also venture that we have not ratified the Conventions because so few Americans are aware of the existence of the standards, the ILO, or of U.S. involvement in that organization. It is little wonder that the American public does not comprehend the underlying principles for mandatory participation in social security, which is so readily understood and supported by the general population of other countries.

Conclusion

Social security through social insurance presumes that every member of society has a fundamental right to economic security and health care. This premise is derived from the principle of social solidarity, which assures that benefits provided to those who are unable to work are not provided as charity but as a social right. Such a right is possible only under conditions of compulsory participation in the system. The conversion of OASDI to a voluntary system would not only destroy social security as a mechanism for income protection in old age, but would also ravage our sense of social justice.

Rejoinder to Professor Tracy   Tom Walz

Professor Tracy makes a fairly predictable defense of the government-administered social insurance program (OASDI). However, he does not address the fact that our social insurance program is only one aspect of the nation's social security system. (Public assistance is its necessary complement.) As the world changes and more people are displaced within a modern economy, the importance of public assistance relative to social insurance grows.

Tracy speaks of the egalitarian and redistributive features of social insurance, but gives no mention of the regressive nature of the payroll tax nor of the gender inequities in the program. He also fails to view social security within the world's changing political economy. No mention is made of a shift to a nonwage-based (capital-intensive) economy where "value added" profits are not reflected in the *wage* payroll; nor does his argument even speak to the new mobility of industry to shift to the world's cheap labor sectors. Regarding the latter, either an international social insurance system should be developed where the risk is shared worldwide or the idea of insuring against income loss in a volatile but changing economy should be forgotten.

To me the central question is neither one of individual rights nor of social rights; instead, it is income security protection. Money is money; it buys the same whatever its source. The ultimate insurance scheme is a government concerned for its people. When tragedies occur and one's link to the job market is severed, it should be government's role to respond. This insurance should be paid for by those who can afford it. Those who own property should be expected to be self-financing, at least to a point. Those who are poor should be given what they need to subsist. To set aside a relatively high percentage of a poor person's lifetime income in order for him or her to receive a modest social insurance benefit at the end makes no sense. Even when the benefit has redistributive features, it does not mean a lot to people whose life expectancies are reduced by the hazards of their class.

If social security is not based on an equitable system of getting back roughly what you pay into it (with some interest), then why have it at all? In truth, what we have today isn't social insurance, but a disguised transfer payment program. One might as well clean up the whole mess and go to a noncategorical up-front means-tested transfer payment system with attached in-kind benefits. This could be paid for by general revenues.

The fact that the social security movement is still going and growing perhaps makes sense in the many industrial and pre-industrial societies. Social insurance in its time made sense. It just doesn't fit the capital-intensive, global, high-tech economic world of the West. Social institutions, like social security, are unfortunately slow to change.

REFERENCES

Alcock, A. (1971). *History of the International Labour Organization.* London: Macmillan.

Bell, D. (1973). *The coming of post-industrial society.* New York: Basic Books.

Blinder, A. S. (1988). "Why is the government in the pension business?" In Wachter, S.M. (Ed.), *Social security and private pensions: Providing for retirement in the twenty-first century.* Lexington, MA: Lexington Books, 17–34.

Collincos, A. (1983). *The revolutionary ideas of Marx.* London: N.B. Books.

International Labour Office (1989). *Introduction to social security.* Geneva: International Labour Office.

Paine, T. (1792). *Rights of man, being an answer to Mr. Burke's attack on the French Revolution, Part II.* London: Hypatia Bradlaugh Bonner.

Perrin, G. (1985). The recognition of the right to social protection as a human right. *Labour and Society* 10(2), 239–258.

Ross, R., & Trachte, K. (1989). *Global capitalism: The new leviathan.* New York: State University of New York Press.

Theobold, R. (1962). *Challenge of abundance.* Chicago: American Library.

U.S. Department of Health and Human Services. (1990). *Social security programs throughout the world, 1989.* Social Security Administration. Office of International Policy. Research Report Number 62. Washington, D.C.: U.S. Government Printing Office.

ANNOTATED BIBLIOGRAPHY

Bell, D. (1973). *The coming of the post-industrial society.* New York: Basic Books.

> The author explains the workings of a post-industrial economy and the dynamics of a service society.

Bernstein, M. C., & Bernstein, J. B. (1988). *Social security: The system that works.* New York: Basic Books, Inc.

> This volume describes what social security does and how and why it has been successful.

Brocas, A. M., Cailloux, A. M., & Oget, V. (1990). *Women and social security: Progress toward equality of treatment.*

> The authors discuss the major issues confronting women and social security coverage in industrial countries.

Collincos, A. (1983). *The revolutionary ideas of Marx.* London: N.B. Books.

> This book provides an excellent overview of Marxian economic theory.

International Labour Office. (1989). *Introduction to social security.* Geneva: International Labour Office.

> This volume provides an overview of the primary principles of social security from the perspective of both industrial and economically developing nations.

Perrin, G. (1985). The recognition of the right to social protection as a human right. *Labour and Society* 10(2), 239–258.

> The author traces the philosophical roots of the development of social security in industrial societies.

Ross, R., & Trachte, K. (1989). *Global capitalism: The new leviathan.* New York: State University of New York Press.

> The authors explore the nature of the current global economy and how it has changed from its industrial smokestack years.

Should the Federal Government Finance Health Care for All Americans?

EDITOR'S NOTE: In recent years, the American health care system has been severely criticized. Many people are unable to afford health insurance, the numbers of families without any insurance coverage has reached alarming proportions, and many ordinary citizens are highly dissatisfied with the cost of medical treatment. Numerous proposals for reforming and even replacing the health care system have been formulated. They include a federal national health insurance program, such as exists in Canada. This bill would introduce employer mandated provisions and greater cost containment through managed care. However, these proposals have been rejected by those who believe that the health care system would function more effectively if it were deregulated, and if greater competition and market-driven provisions were introduced. Obviously, proponents of this approach are vigorously opposed to federal involvement in health care, and to the idea that the federal government should fund health insurance for all Americans.

The health care issue is examined in this debate by two experts who take very different positions on health care policy. Terri Combs-Orme, Ph.D., argues YES, that the federal government should fund health insurance for all Americans. She is an Assistant Professor at the Department of Maternal and Child Health, the Johns Hopkins University School of Hygiene and Public Health. Her primary research interests are in maternal and child health, access to health care for poor people, and barriers to prenatal care. She is the author of *Social Work in Maternal and Child Health* (1990), Springer, and she has published on health care issues in many scholarly journals. She previously served as a member of the Governor's Advisory Council on Infant Mortality for the State of Maryland, and is currently a member of the Arkansas Child Welfare Compliance and Oversight Committee.

Robert Emmett Moffit, Ph.D., argues NO. He is Deputy Director of Domestic Policy Studies at the Heritage Foundation in Washington, D.C. His major research interests are in health care, education, welfare, and urban policy. He has published in several academic journals and in the *Wall Street Journal* and the *Washington Times*.

YES

TERRI COMBS-ORME

It is surely a sign of the times when it is unnecessary for a debate like this to begin with a justification for restructuring America's health care system. In his 1992 State of the Union message, President Bush declared that Americans "have the best health care in this world because it is private," and thus revealed himself to be the last person in this country who thinks so.

By every measure that counts, the American health care system is appallingly poor and backward. Approximately 40 million Americans have no health insurance. This would not constitute a crisis, except for the fact that these 40 million Americans thus do not have access to care when they become ill.

These uninsured Americans *may* be admitted to an Emergency Room if they are in cardiac arrest (due to legal prohibitions against turning them away), but in less life-threatening situations they may not be so lucky. A child with chronic ear infections may not be treated by a private physician in a rural area that has no free clinics, and may thus suffer pain and permanent hearing loss. A pregnant woman may not get prenatal care in a county that lacks a public clinic, and thus may give birth to a low-birthweight infant. A homeless man most probably will be turned away if he seeks a preventive checkup, or treatment for a cough or other "noncritical" illness. Approximately one million Americans seeking health care are turned away every year because they cannot pay, and millions more forgo the preventive services that might save dollars—and human capital—in the long run.

By other measures America also does not lead the health parade. Our infant mortality rate is twenty-first in the world. African-American babies die at twice the rate of their white counterparts. Statistics are hard to come by because of our shyness about collecting data on social class (we prefer to pretend that it does not exist), but we do know that poverty equals more illness, poorer health care, and higher mortality.

To cap it all off, this defective and ineffective system is very costly. The rate of growth in the cost of health care in this country exceeds the growth of the Gross National Product. More important, the cost for individual families who have insurance is high and growing yearly. It is increasing even as these families worry about uncovered catastrophic illness wiping them out, or a job loss rendering them completely unprotected. Much of the coverage of those families is partial, inadequate, and does not extend to dependents. Over one-third of uncovered Americans are children.

But these days just about everyone agrees that the health care system is a mess. As I write this, there are variations on four major proposals before Congress, and another that came recently from President Bush (after four years without a word on the subject). Conservatives and liberals alike agree that something must be done. However, some of these proposals constitute jumping out of the frying pan into the fire.

Guiding Principles

Before I discuss the various alternatives for reforming health care, it is important to affirm the principles that should guide us in our selection. We don't tend to do that in this country; instead we lurch from problem to problem, making minor changes that seem unconnected. Before making changes in the health care system, it is important to think about the broader principles. The arguments that follow are derived from these six explicit principles:

1. Accessible health care is a universal right of all Americans, not a privilege to be purchased or earned.

2. Quantity, quality, and accessibility of health care should be equal for all, not dependent on income or categorical status. Thus any system that results in differential quantity, quality, or accessibility in health care according to income, gender, age, or any other criterion is unacceptable.

3. Health care should not be linked to employment. A majority of Americans with health insurance have it through their place of employment, but the fear of job loss or changes in benefits that are not under their control undermines the security of this arrangement *and* limits their job mobility. Moreover, erosion of employment-related insurance due to rising costs has reduced coverage for most Americans throughout the 1980s. It is therefore reasonable to expect that as long as employers seek to maximize profits, they will look to employee health care benefits when they are seeking to trim costs.

4. Quality, quantity, and accessibility of health care should not vary according to state. Under the Medicaid program's state governance and due to differing state laws regarding health insurance (and the fact that some states are wealthier than others), living in the wrong state can cost heavily. History indicates that some states will always be more interested in the rights and needs of their citizens than others.

5. Any system must balance the needs and rights of children and the elderly in a fair and rational way. Under the current system the great majority of elderly Americans are protected by Medicare, albeit imperfectly, while eight-and-a-half million American children lack any type of coverage. The cost to their health is a direct threat to this nation's future.

6. Any system must include coverage for and accessibility to long-term care for all elderly Americans. The cost of long-term care is beyond the resources of nearly everyone. Families are not capable of paying these costs for their elderly members, and should not be made to feel guilty nor to mortgage their futures and their children's futures for their inadequacies in this area.

You may disagree with my principles. But, before you lend your support to any measure, make up your own list and require that any plan you consider deals explicitly with your principles. There are a number of options on the table for restructuring the health care delivery system. In general, the alternatives fall into two broad categories. One type would reform the present system, and the other would construct an entirely new way of providing health care in this country.

Reforming the Current System

Reform of the present system could occur through several methods. **"Pay or Play,"** one of the methods before Congress, would be employer based, with employers allowed to either provide health care to employees, as many do now, or buy into a public system that would be provided for the unemployed and those not in the job market. Medicaid and Medicare would remain basically intact.

Another option, which was basically President Bush's suggestion, is a system of **tax incentives and vouchers** that would supposedly allow all Americans to purchase their own health insurance and care. The poor would be given vouchers to purchase insurance (and thus presumably care), while those who are better off would receive progressive tax deductions for the price of their insurance.

A third and pitifully inadequate option is simply to make **a few reforms** in the current system of private care for some people. This might involve increasing eligibility for Medicaid to include the currently large group of Americans who are not poor enough to qualify for it, but not rich enough to purchase private care—the "working poor."

Can it be saved? Reform of the current system is the poorest option. The current system is based on profit and exclusion, and none of the reforms addresses these basic problems. The free market system has been shown to be an ineffective manager of hospital costs, and it results in waste, higher administrative costs, and inequities.

A system based on market forces will always result in less care for the poor, who inevitably need more health care. They are often the least attractive patients and live in areas where providers choose not to be. Any variation on the current system will result in choices by providers that result in inadequate availability of services for the poor, regardless of financing arrangements. Witness the mass migration of private physicians from poor inner-city areas. Many poor women and children are covered by Medicaid, but cannot find obstetricians and pediatricians who are willing to negotiate the paperwork nightmare to treat them.

The most important reason to reject "reform" and build an entirely new system is that any "reform" that perpetuates a two-tiered system of care will continue to discriminate against those who need the best health care. The poor receive the leftovers; those leftovers are scavenged and reduced in times of recession. With such a system, we could expect that in times of recession such as now, there would be efforts to remove both individuals from the program and particular services from coverage. Preventive and social services are always the first to go, despite evidence of the long-term costs of sacrificing such services. And when prevention is reduced, it is children *and thus our future* who suffer the most dramatically.

Building a New System

Another approach, rather than reforming the current mix of private and public, is to construct a brand new approach to health care in this country. There are three ways to build a new system. One is to provide a Medicare-like system for all, with basic care financed by taxes and individual co-payments, either out of pocket or through supplementary private coverage. Another is to set up a National Health System such as exists in Great Britain. This method would abolish the private insurance industry and in effect do away with most private health care providers, in favor of centralized government health facilities.

Many of us do not favor a system like Medicare for all people because the administrative machinery necessary to work with multiple payers is expensive and serves as a barrier to participation. Moreover, it affords little protection for the tremendous cost. Medicare itself is the best evidence against this system. Costs rise yearly; providers make up for low reimbursements by scheduling numerous, possibly unnecessary tests; and individual participants must carry supplementary insurance to be protected adequately. Most elderly Americans find that their Medicare protection against major illness is little more than illusory.

The British system is a very effective one for Great Britain, but it probably would not work for Americans. The great size and diversity of this country argue against centralized clinics; Americans will resist "socialized" medicine, if for no other reason than because American physicians will do so. We like our diversity, and we like our independence.

A final measure would construct a single-payer system of universal coverage such as exists in Canada. Under this system, all Americans would be eligible for health care, financed by tax-supported payments from a single federal health care agency paid for by general revenues raised through taxes. As proposed, the program would be administered at the state level by an agency that would compensate health care providers according to a federal schedule of fees.

The Canadian system stands out as the best alternative for several reasons. Its most appealing argument is the success of the program in Canada. Before the program was initiated in 1966, Canada lagged behind the United States in both infant mortality and life expectancy (two conventionally recognized indicators of a nation's health). Impressive gains there now place Canada above the United States on both measures. Moreover, the great majority of Canadians are satisfied with their health care system. In contrast, in a recent Harvard University poll, 89 percent of Americans indicated that they thought the American system needed either fundamental changes or a completely different structure.

The Canadian system provides comprehensive health care to all Canadians through a system of contracts with the private sector, with fees negotiated between provinces and physicians' groups. Hospitals are paid on a prospective basis. Very few Canadians seek services outside the system. Although the different provinces manage the system, individuals may transfer to other provinces and have speedy access to the system. Health care providers may not collect co-payments.

The Canadian experience refutes claims by private system enthusiasts that a federal program is inefficient and expensive. The Canadian health care budget for 1985 was 8.6 percent of their GNP, 20 percent less than that of the United States. Moreover, although health care costs have been rising in Canada, they are rising at a lower rate than in the United States as a proportion of GNP. Most importantly, the system reduces administrative costs; the Canadian system's overhead costs run at about 3 percent compared to American private insurance companies' overhead of 8 percent. In part, this is due to the fact that in the United States a great deal of our health budget goes for advertising and billing; the Canadian system does not need advertising and does far less billing due to its prospective system.

Finally, the Canadian example is again useful to those who fear that the single-payor system would destroy the initiative of individual physicians and remove the motivation for young people to enter medicine. The Canadian health care system assists in underwriting the cost of medical school, and medical school tuition is about one-tenth of what it is in the United States. Moreover, there has been no drop in medical school applications, despite the fact that Canadian physician salaries are about 85 percent of their American counterparts.

This is an important time for Americans. For once, this nation has the opportunity to complete the historic work begun in the 1930s. This work would protect the security of all Americans, even those who lack the political clout to get what they need on their own. It is possible to seize on the broad dissatisfaction with the American health care system to do something bigger than just repair the "tears" in the current system. This is an opportunity to use the tremendous wealth of this country and the determination and authority of the federal government to invest in the future by investing in all our citizens. We as individuals may not live to see the return on our money, but our children will, and their children.

Rejoinder to Professor Combs-Orme

ROBERT EMMETT MOFFIT

Dr. Combs-Orme's call for a Canadian-style national health insurance plan is another example of what Samuel Johnson, the great English essayist, described as a triumph of hope over experience. According to my colleague, a new monopoly will be good for us. A Canadian-style government health care system will make Americans healthier and happier; and health care delivery will be cheaper and more efficient. With a global budget for health care spending, we will get cost control. This time, in other words, Congress, which seems incapable of controlling the federal budget, will get it right.

My colleague claims, for instance, that the Canadian experience proves that a federal system would be neither "inefficient" nor "expensive." But recent experience proves nothing of the sort. While American health care costs have been rising, adoption of a Canadian-style system is no guarantee that cost increases will slow down. Between 1967 and 1987, America's per capita, inflation-adjusted health care costs rose 4.38 percent a year; during that same period, these costs increased 4.58 percent in Canada. While Americans do spend more per capita than Canada, it does not necessarily mean that Canadians get better value for their money. They get what the government gives them. Likewise, while Canada's health care costs as a percentage of GNP are lower than America's tax-favored, employer-based system, the reported Canadian expenditures do not tell the whole story. There are hidden costs, including the costs to patients of waiting for health care services or the costs of forgone or unavailable medical technologies or procedures. Canadian columnist Geoffrey Stevens, writing in the November 22, 1991, edition of *The Vancouver Sun* of British Columbia, notes the supreme irony of the current American health care debate: "The irony is that at the very moment American politicians and health care professionals are asking whether the U.S. can afford not to adopt Canadian-style medicare, Canadians are asking whether we can afford to keep it. There isn't a province that is not desperately worried about health costs. There isn't a province that is not struggling, not to make medicare better, but to cut back."

My colleague also argues that such a government-run system will reduce administrative costs, citing differences between Canadian government overhead and that of American private insurance companies. Officers of the General Accounting Office (GAO) make similar claims. But much depends on exactly what is or is not counted in comparing such costs. Canadians may shuffle less paper. But as analysts from Lewin/ICF and others note, Canadian administrative data do not always include much of the costs of facilities and medical supplies and equipment, or the costs of collecting taxes as opposed to private insurance premiums. In any case, use of common forms or electronic billing processes can be established within the framework of a market system. A government-run system is unnecessary.

Any government provision of a "free good," in this case health care, is pregnant with shortages. The unlimited demand for the government's "free" medical services always outstrips the government's limited supply of such services. The result is that the government inevitably resorts to some form of bureaucratic rationing, making decisions about who gets treated, how they are to be treated, and when they are to be treated. The wait in Canada for a cataract removal takes four months, a coronary bypass over five months, a hernia repair five and a half months. According to a survey sponsored by the Fraser Institute, a Canadian think tank, about 260,000 Canadians are awaiting surgery.

Even if national health insurance worked perfectly well in Canada, that would still not make it a model for the United States. Costs would not be controlled; they would simply be shifted to the American taxpayer. Nor would government health insurance deliver health care services most efficiently for the huge and diverse population of the United States. While Canada has a younger and more homogeneous population of 26 million, the United States has an older, more heterogeneous population of 250 million people. The imposition of a government-run health care system would not ring in an era of "kind and gentle" socialism. It would rather make American medical clinics look like Soviet grocery stores.

NO

Robert Emmett Moffit

While America's $800 billion health care system is clearly in critical condition, the remedy is not to kill the patient. A single-payer health care system, based on the Canadian model, will simply make a bad situation even worse. Indeed, as the Hon. Constance Horner, recently Under Secretary of the United States Department of Health and Human Services (HHS), observes, "National health insurance combines the compassion of the IRS with the efficiency of the Postal Service at Pentagon prices."

There is no "free market" in America's health care system. It is disproportionately financed by government directly, and is one of the most highly regulated sectors of the American economy. And many of the major problems with the system — including skyrocketing costs, gaps in coverage, and the fact that millions of Americans are without even basic health insurance — are directly traceable to the way in which the federal government already supports the financing of health insurance and distorts the operations of the market. Combined federal and state spending already accounts for 43 cents out of every dollar spent on health care. Instead of expanding the control of the federal bureaucracy, a much wiser policy would be to change federal tax policies and introduce market forces, such as consumer choice and competition, into the system.

Tax Laws and Market Distortions

The rapid expansion of government health care financing and cost shifting through huge government programs like Medicare and Medicaid is not the only factor contributing to rising health care costs. The key to understanding the current health care crisis is to grasp the enormous influence of a huge and largely unexamined federal tax subsidy for the private sector: the special and exclusive tax breaks for private, employer-based insurance.

The character and quality of America's private, employer-based health care system is determined by one thing: the federal tax code. Every year Americans get billions of dollars of federal tax relief for health insurance on only one condition: they are enrolled in a health insurance plan provided by their employer. No other form of health insurance enjoys similar support. In 1991, federal tax breaks, in the form of tax exclusions and deductions for employer-provided insurance, totaled $66.6 billion, according to Lewin/ICF, a Washington econometrics firm. Add state tax exclusions on the monetary value of employer plans, plus some miscellaneous tax breaks for private health insurance, and the total comes to nearly $88 billion in 1991 dollars. The result is that employer-based insurance monopolizes the market to the exclusion of all other insurance options or forms of health care delivery.

This is a huge federal tax expenditure. It is also a very inefficient and unfair tax expenditure. The richer the company's health insurance plan — the more frills, the more "first dollar coverage," the more "bells and whistles," including state-mandated health benefits covering everything from payment for chiropractic services to *in vitro* fertilization — the bigger the tax breaks. If one is employed in a large corporation with "Cadillac coverage," the tax benefit is great. It amounts to a large chunk of tax-free compensation. If one is employed in a small firm with no coverage, then there are no tax breaks at all. If a worker and his family want to purchase individual health insurance, they will have to do so with after-tax dollars, which for most middle income families is prohibitively expensive. If a worker loses his job, he and his family get no tax assistance and must either go without health care services or end up on Medicaid, the federal/state health program for the indigent. The raw numbers demonstrate the regressivity of the current tax relief for employer-based health insurance. Again, according to Lewin/ICF, if a family is poor with an income of less than $10,000 per year, they get just $50.00 per year in tax benefits under the current system. If that family makes between $10,000 and $15,000, the tax benefit amounts to just $207 per year. But for a family with an annual income over $75,000, the average tax benefit for employer-based health benefits amounts to $1,427. The higher the income, the more generous the federal tax assistance.

Because the health insurance "market" is tied up in this old IRS straight-jacket, there is no portability with this type of insurance. For American workers and their families this government restriction on the diversity of health insurance options has profound and often severely disruptive personal consequences. If an American worker wants to change jobs, or, worse, if an American worker loses his job, he does not lose his life insurance, his auto insurance, or his homeowners insurance. He only loses his most important insurance: the health insurance that protects him and his family against severe illness or high medical costs. Back in the 1940s, as a matter of compensation policy, tying health insurance tax relief to the job may have made sense. But in the 1990s, with a highly mobile workforce, this restrictive tax treatment is absurd.

Soaring Costs

Such market restrictions are not only absurd, they are also costly. Given the dominant incentives of employer-based insurance, this cannot be surprising. Virtually all of the incentives in the employer-based model are to increase costs. For most employees, health insurance is a kind of "free good" that automatically comes with the job. Employees, after all, do not purchase health insurance; it is purchased for them by someone else, the company or the corporate benefits manager. Thus, on the most basic level, the normal exchange between buyer and seller, a healthy collision of the forces of supply and demand, does not take place at all. Moreover, once the "free good" is purchased for the employee by the company, the employee has no incentive to curtail his demand for these health care services; they are invariably paid for by "somebody else," the firm or the faceless insurance company. So there is no incentive on the part of the employee to control health care costs. To the contrary, given the employees' incentives, it would be financially pointless; the savings would not be realized in the employee's family budget, but would accrue to the coffers of the company. Naturally, the current incentives to demand government-supplied health care as a "free good" would merely intensify under a huge single-payer system of national health insurance.

On the supply side of the equation, the situation is much the same. No serious incentives exist to control costs. For the doctor or the hospital, there is no incentive to curtail either the supply or the cost of medical services, even highly expensive medical procedures that might be of only marginal benefit to the patient. After all, the patient is not going to "pay"; the payment is borne by "somebody else," the company or some other "third party" payer. For the physician or the hospital administrator, the employee is not only a patient, but also the golden gateway to third-party reimbursement, largely financed by employers. Given physicians' fear of medical liability and the consequent incentive for them to practice "defensive medicine," the ordering of unnecessary tests and procedures, the incentives driving up costs in the employer-based health insurance system are further aggravated.

Since health benefits are legally regarded as employees' compensation, they are also subject to collective bargaining. Union representatives, pursuing tough bargaining with management, naturally have an incentive in pressing the companies to provide even richer benefits, including payment for routine medical services, such as office visits, teeth cleaning, and eye glasses. Expansion of benefits is, after all, an expansion of tax-free income for employees. Bigger benefits packages result in larger tax breaks, regardless of whether or not the corporate benefits package meets a family's specific health care needs. As a result, not only are a lot of American families underinsured or bereft of even catastrophic health care coverage, but a lot of American families are also overinsured, with prepaid medical plans for even the most minor and routine medical services. These inefficiencies and their associated costs are enormous. In any case, because neither the consumers nor the health care providers in this unique third party payment system are sensitive to costs — costs which are always borne by "someone else" — it is no surprise that health care costs are rising much faster than other costs in the national economy. Of course, that "someone else" is all of us.

A Market-Based Solution

Because the government's tax policy has created a system that does not work either efficiently or fairly, a government-run, single-payer system is not the answer. In fact, Americans already have a model of a single-payer government health care system, replete with a morass of unintelligible rules, regulations, guidelines, and cumbersome paperwork. Its reimbursement regime is a complex price-fixing scheme that looks like a Rube Goldberg imitation of old fashioned Soviet central planning. It's the Medicare program, now serving 34 million elderly and disabled citizens.

Medicare costs are skyrocketing. Medicare administration requires thousands of central office employees to monitor both the huge quantity and the quality of medical services, programs, and contracts. And controlling Medicare's annual budget has become a politically charged, painful exercise for Congress, the Administration, the elderly, and the taxpayers alike. Indeed, according to Medicare's own analysts, the high rate of spending in Part A, the Medicare Hospital Insurance program, could render the program financially insolvent by the end of this century. It is not clear how, if we cannot even assure fiscal solvency or cost control in the Medicare program, we are going to be successful in doing so with a Canadian-style national health insurance system.

The best way to provide universal access for every American family is to change the federal tax code. Among others, the Heritage Foundation has proposed a revolutionary overhaul of the federal tax laws to provide universal access to health care for American families within the framework of an open market, driven by consumer choice and competition. Free market forces are the most efficient means to control costs ever devised. The radical introduction of market forces into a system where they are largely absent would not only change and diversify the character of our health care delivery, but would also control costs in the same way that costs are controlled in every other sector of the American economy. In its essentials, the Heritage Foundation Consumer Choice Plan would do the following:

1. *Restructure tax benefits.* The plan would keep the billions of dollars in current tax relief for private health insurance, but restructure it and channel that relief — dollar for dollar — back to individuals and families that need it most. Instead of tying federal tax breaks to only one kind of insurance, the plan would open up the federal tax code and make it neutral. It would provide tax relief in the form of vouchers or refundable tax credits to workers and their families, helping them with the purchase of a basic insurance package and medical services, regardless of their place of work or employment status.

2. *Provide for universal access and target financial relief.* At the same time, the plan would require every individual or head of household to purchase at least a government-certified basic package of health insurance, including catastrophic coverage. The legal requirement to purchase at least a basic package of health care coverage would not be unlike current state requirements for citizens to purchase auto insurance. In both instances, the legal requirement protects not only the individual covered, but also the rest of society. While every family would be eligible for a basic tax credit or voucher to help them with their health care costs, the plan would target more generous tax relief to those individuals and families that need it most. Thus, families with lower incomes or higher annual health care costs would get more generous credits or vouchers to help them pay their health care bills. By blending the credits into the withholding system, families would not have to wait until the end of the year to receive tax assistance. By making companies deduct the balance of the premium payments to insurance plans chosen by the employees, the administration of the system would be simplified.

3. *Introduce consumer choice and competition.* Health care insurance decisions for most Americans would no longer be the exclusive province of either corporate benefits managers or government bureaucrats. Instead of being tied to a "one-size-fits-all" company health insurance plan, workers and their families could choose from a wide variety of health care options.

By giving every family tax relief directly, regardless of where the breadwinners work, the competitive playing field for insurance plans would be leveled, and families would have the opportunity to comparison shop among competing health care options. Workers could pick and choose the best combination of price and benefits that satisfies their specific needs.

Any savings would accrue directly to the family budget, not the company account. No longer would workers and their families be faced with the "take it or leave it" option of employer-based health care. Instead, the company plan would have to compete with other plans. These could include plans sponsored by unions, employee organizations, trade, fraternal, or even religious associations. While workers could decide to enroll in a large, traditional fee-for-service plan, for example, they could also decide to choose a qualified HMO or an innovative medical group practice plan, or a plan that emphasizes preventive medicine, health promotion, or wellness programs. The result: American workers and their families would have access to the same kind of consumer choice and market competition that is now enjoyed by the residents of the White House; members of Congress; and nine million federal employees, retirees, and dependents in the exclusive, consumer-driven Federal Employees Health Benefits Program (FEHBP). Interestingly enough, over 35 percent of all enrollees in the federal system are enrolled in private health insurance plans sponsored by unions or employee organizations.

Such a major national reform would be of direct benefit to most American families, but especially those Americans who have no health insurance at all. Under the Heritage Foundation Consumer Choice Health Plan, according to Lewin/ ICF, most family income groups would be better off both in terms of their tax situation and after tax health care spending. Moreover, by radically restructuring the tax code, and hence the insurance market, the consumer choice model would introduce new efficiencies into the health care delivery system. Within a budget-neutral framework, Lewin/ICF has estimated that the total impact of the market changes would yield an annual savings of $10.8 billion in the American health care system.

America does not need to import an exotic version of Medicare from abroad. Rather, we need to preserve what is best in our system, particularly the high quality of American medicine and our tremendous capacity to generate life-saving and cost-saving medical technology, while assuring universal access and establishing an efficient method of financing health care. A strong injection of market forces will restore an ailing system to robust health.

Rejoinder to Dr. Moffit TERRI COMBS-ORME

Dr. Moffit makes some valid points in his discussion of the American health care system. It *is* unfair, and it *is* costly. The solution he proposes, however, does not solve the problem for two reasons.

The first reason is that the Heritage Foundation's proposal (which resembles President Bush's proposal) does not address the problem regarding the maldistribution of providers. My own state of Maryland is a good example of this problem. Certain wealthy counties surrounding the District of Columbia where there are large numbers of wealthy, relatively attractive patients (i.e., healthy and compliant) and a pleasant life-style are flush with obstetricians. In some areas of eastern and far western Maryland, where the population tends to be poor and at higher risk of poor pregnancy outcomes, and where the life-style does not provide nearly so many amenities, obstetricians are scarce. A private market economy cannot address this issue, even if the system is able to provide equivalent remuneration for all patients (and I'm not clear whether Dr. Moffit's plan provides for this). Private health care providers will always gravitate toward settings where the patients are healthier, more compliant, and more like the providers themselves in their middle-class values. This is to be expected, but it means that only government intervention is likely to result in availability of providers in less attractive areas for less attractive patients.

But a more fundamental problem with the Heritage Foundation plan is the assumption that "competition" and free choice can operate in the area of health care as it does with automobiles. Americans are relatively sophisticated about automobiles; apparently they can judge the reliability record of a Honda and choose it over many American models. But can they select the better physician, or exercise discretion regarding whether or not to undergo a test or procedure recommended by a physician? "I'll let you know, Doctor. I have to check into the rates of false positives and false negatives with the CAT scan. I'm not sure this is an efficient way to determine whether I have a brain tumor." I don't think so. Competition can only govern supply and demand when the consumer has discretion; most Americans cannot exercise such discretion with regard to health care, and with regard to either selecting a provider or undergoing specific procedures.

Moreover, the hospital industry provides an example of the effects of competition on health care costs. Since hospitals have been free to expand and advertize, costs have skyrocketed. Much of that increase is directly attributed to the costs of overbuilding and fancy consumer-oriented amenities, expensive advertizing, and consequent overhead. It's fine to extol the theoretical virtues of competition; however, these empirical data suggest that it doesn't always play out as planned. I am all for a more fair tax code, but let's address that on another day. It will not solve the health care crisis.

ANNOTATED BIBLIOGRAPHY

Butler, P. A. (1988). *Too poor to be sick*. Washington, D.C.: American Public Health Association.

   Although somewhat dated, this book provides an excellent overview of the issues surrounding access to health care for the poor.

Butler, S. M. (1990). A tax reform strategy to deal with the uninsured. *Journal of the American Medical Association,* (265)8, 2541–2544.

This article describes the role of tax policy as it relates to the high numbers of uninsured Americans. It also provides an overview of the health care plan advocated by the conservative Heritage Foundation.

Combs-Orme, T., & Guyer, B. (1992). America's health care system: The Reagan legacy. *Journal of Sociology and Social Welfare* (19)1, 63–89.

This article provides an overall picture of the Reagan agenda on health. It also examines the short- and long-term effects of the Reagan administration on the health of Americans.

Himmelstein, D. U., Woolhandler, S., & Wolfe, S. M. (1991). The vanishing health care safety net: New data on uninsured Americans. Cambridge, MA: The Center for National Health Program Studies.

This booklet provides extensive and recent data on the number and characteristics of the growing population of Americans who are either underinsured or without any health insurance coverage.

Navarro, V. (1989). A national health program is necessary. *Challenge,* May–June, 36–40.

This article discusses the Canadian health care system and compares it to its American counterpart. In particular, the author discusses how private insurance companies and competition drive up health care costs and suggests that the Canadian system would be a better choice for Americans.

Should the Federal Government Fund Abortions?

EDITOR'S NOTE: Abortion is one of the most controversial issues of our time, with strong opinions being expressed on both sides. Although efforts have been made to prohibit abortion through judicial and legislative action, the constitutional right to have an abortion remains in force. However, abortion opponents have succeeded in curtailing federal abortion programs. Regulations have been promulgated to prohibit federally supported family planning agencies from providing advice on abortion, and under legislation enacted in 1976, the use of federal funds for abortions has been drastically restricted. Supporters of these measures argue that abortion is an evil which should not be condoned by the state. In addition, they contend that scarce federal resources should be used to meet the critical medical and other social needs of the poor and not to terminate unwanted pregnancies. Supporters of abortion rights claim that federal aid is vital if the poor are to have a choice in the matter. They argue that if the poor are to have equal rights in society, they should have access to abortions through federal support.

These arguments are examined by Dorinda N. Noble, Ph.D., who supports the view that the federal government should fund abortions. Dr. Noble is an Associate Professor at the School of Social Work at Louisiana State University. Her major research interests are children's mental health, corrections, and child welfare. She has published numerous articles on these issues in leading social work journals.

Nanneska N. Magee, J.D., argues against the idea that the federal government should fund abortions. Ms. Magee is an attorney with Conant,

Whittenburg, Whittenburg and Scachter, a litigation firm in Dallas, Texas. She has an interest in legal writing and has published several articles on this topic in legal journals.

YES

DORINDA N. NOBLE

In 1944, an American soldier, part of the military force freeing France from Nazi domination, surveyed the bombed-out ruins of a French village. "We sure liberated the hell out of this place," was his wry comment.

The Supreme Court, aided and abetted by the Reagan and Bush administrations (both of which prided themselves on keeping Big Brother out of everybody's business), is eagerly "liberating the hell" out of the fetus. Women, particularly poor women, are surveying the bombed-out ruins of their rights to make personal decisions about childbearing and to secure safe, legal abortions under their federal medical coverage.

Public Funds and Abortions

In 1992, *Parade Magazine* (Clements, 1992) pointed out that, regardless of sex, age, or income level, nearly three out of four voters polled in their national survey said that abortion should be allowed by law. This response is only one of many surveys which indicate that the majority of Americans believe that abortion should remain a legal — and personal — medical option. The same article, however, also related that 56 percent of respondents opposed the use of federal money to pay for abortions for women who could not afford them.

In reality, this is a moot point: virtually no federal funds are used for abortions, whether the woman in need of it is Medicaid-dependent, a Peace Corps volunteer, or a member of or dependent of the military. In 1990, federal funds paid for a mere *165* abortions, a dramatic drop from the almost 300,000 federally funded abortions in 1977 (Gold & Daley, 1991). Since the federal government is now out of the abortion business, governmental funding of abortions has fallen almost exclusively upon the shoulders of state governments. However, almost all of the 162,418 state-funded abortions performed on medically indigent women in 1990 took place in only thirteen states (Gold & Daley, 1991).

Thus, this debate is an academic rather than practical one. Regulations restricting federal funds for abortion stemmed from the Hyde Amendment debates (in an almost all-male Congress) beginning in 1976, and culminated in the *Harris* v. *McRae* decision of the Supreme Court (again, an overwhelmingly male group) in 1980. First, federal funding was restricted to vaguely defined "medically necessary" abortions; then to pregnancies in which severe and long-term *physical* damage would likely result, or those resulting from duly reported rape or incest; and, finally, to pregnancies that actually endangered the woman's life.

These restrictions on publicly funded abortions have demeaned and trivialized the whole experience of pregnancy and childbirth. They have also denied equal protection to poor women, and contributed to the poverty and degradation of mothers and children. They are unfair and foolish restrictions.

The Moral and Social Implications of Denying Poor Women Publicly Funded Abortions

Pregnancy and childbirth are monumental, life-changing events which carry substantial dangers. Pregnancy, after all, does not occur in isolation from a woman's life, her environment, her circumstances, her mental and emotional state, or her physical health. It is not simply another medical event.

Yet we do not treat procreation as a particularly important event, even though the right to procreate is one of the most jealously guarded rights in American society. Anyone can make a baby, and it is done every day. There are no mandatory controls on childbearing, regardless of the parent's health, financial status, criminal record, mental capabilities, or age. In a society which demands training and licensure for jobs from hairdressing to hypnotherapy, we require no preparation for parenting, our most important job. As a consequence, the citizenry's understanding of contraception is limited and spotty. So it is not surprising that many pregnancies, rather than being planned, timely, and welcome, are instead unwanted, unneeded, and unbearable. This is especially true for poor women who are often ill educated. It is also true for teens, who on the one hand, are frequently denied developmentally appropriate, intelligent education about their own sexuality and reproduction; and on the other hand, are bombarded by advertising and entertainment that revolves around sexuality. It is no wonder that we have one of the highest teen pregnancy rates in the industrialized world. One out of ten females aged 15–19 — most of whom are too young to legally buy alcohol, too young to marry without parental consent, and too young to be legally employed in many jobs — are entering into pregnancy. Three-fourths of these pregnancies occur because of a lack of contraception (Colker, 1991).

The results of unplanned pregnancies, particularly among the impoverished, have profound implications for society. Because poor women often receive little or no prenatal health care, both mother and baby face a disproportionate health risk. For instance, one-fifth of low-birthweight babies are born to teenagers. Teen pregnancy disrupts schooling and frequently insures that the mother will always live on the edge—if not in the middle—of poverty. Since children are dependent on mothers, they, too, are forced to live in poverty. Regardless of the mother's age, pregnancy and childrearing interrupt and may end a woman's ability to earn a living.

From a strictly economic viewpoint, the cost of schooling and providing other public supports for a child in poverty vastly outweighs the costs of an abortion (many of which can cost as little as $300.00). For every government dollar spent on abortion for indigent women, more than four dollars is saved as a result of averting short-term expenditures on medical services, welfare, and nutritional services (Corns, 1991).

The debate over publicly funded abortions is not simply about money—it is about values and prejudices regarding the nature and the boundaries of life. It is also a debate about sexuality and about who controls the decisions that affect sexuality and procreation. The argument heats up when statistics about abortions are trotted out: in 1987, 59 percent of females having abortions were younger than 25; 65 percent of them were white; 58 percent had experienced no previous abortion; and 82 percent were unmarried (Henshaw, Koonin, & Smith, 1991). In the minds of many people, these figures indicate that abortion is being used as a form of birth control by "seductive" (or at the least, silly) women who have given way to "carnal lust" and now want to escape "taking responsibility" for their actions.

Of course, pregnant women are not the only ones who "take responsibility"—their offspring, their families, their communities, and the whole society must shoulder the responsibility when children are born to people not ready to care for them. In reality, making women "take responsibility" for their sexuality is a punishment for women—a punishment for having sex. The anti-abortion movement, especially for teens, is really an anti-sex movement. Men are not similarly punished and made to "take responsibility." For example, even when absent fathers are ordered by courts to pay child support, just 25 percent pay the full amount regularly (Waldman, 1992).

The current denial of abortion services to Medicaid-dependent women is discriminatory on several levels. First, because of poverty, these women have fewer real options and are more dependent on government funds. Consequently, they are more vulnerable to the intrusion of government into their lives. Second, women of color are more likely to be poor than white women. The poverty rate for black mothers is about three times that of white mothers (Roberts, 1990), and the poverty rate for Hispanic mothers is even higher. Given an unwanted pregnancy, abortion may be essential to the financial, emotional, and physical wellbeing of such a woman. Yet, if the government will pay for her childbirth expenses but not for her abortion, she may well feel that she has no real choice.

Further, some women may not even get the opportunity to discuss their choices (particularly if English is not their native tongue), since the federal government has restricted the dissemination of abortion information in facilities receiving federal funding. The process becomes even more traumatic when a woman, having made the wrenching decision to terminate pregnancy, is forced to cross lines of intimidating demonstrators to reach medical providers.

On the other hand, poor women will have little trouble in finding out about and securing sterilization, a procedure that is funded by the government. In its decision of *Harris* v. *McRae,* the Supreme Court reasoned that the state has a compelling interest in and "favors childbirth" for indigent women. Despite this "compelling interest" in childbirth, the state seems to favor sterilization more since Medicaid funds are available to pay for 90 percent of the costs of sterilization (Petchesky, 1990).

Government restrictions on abortion do not stop with lack of funding for the actual medical procedures. In the *Webster* v. *Reproductive Health Services* decision of 1989, the Supreme Court upheld a ban on the use of public employees or facilities for abortions for any purpose other than to save the mother's life. The result is that in the United States, unlike most other industrialized nations, abortion services are concentrated in clinics rather than hospitals, and about two-thirds of procedures are performed in specialized abortion clinics (Henshaw, 1991). The lack of abortion services in hospitals is a special hardship on poor women, who tend to rely on hospital emergency rooms for their medical care.

Thus, many abortion patients have to travel long distances since 82 percent of the 3,116 counties in the United States have no abortion services at all (Roberts, 1990). Native American women living on reservations are among the most restricted, as well as the most poverty-stricken women in the nation. Not only are they denied federal funding for abortions, but Indian Health Services facilities (which may be the only available health care within hundreds of miles) are prohibited from performing abortions *even* if private funds are available (Roberts, 1990).

The Supreme Court has stated in *Harris* v. *McRae* that its decision does not inhibit poor women from obtaining abortion help privately. But, the inaccessibility of services and the high costs are serious barriers, even for women who may be able to obtain private funds. For pregnant and impoverished women who are also drug addicts or HIV-positive, getting help is even more troublesome. Drug treatment centers frequently refuse to treat pregnant women because of potential liability problems, while more than one-fourth of abortion providers acknowledge that they will not serve women who have tested positive for HIV (Roberts, 1990).

Conclusion

It is ironic that the government has, in effect, dictated that the fetus has priority over the health—emotional or otherwise—of the mother, particularly if she is poor. This is the only medical situation in which one person is forced by the government to sacrifice her health and well-being for another organism. The current restrictions on abortion funding for poor women seem to be predicated on the belief that pregnancy is a matter of choice, even though in many cases it is more the result of the lack of effective contraceptives, the result of forced sex, or the result of the lack of meaningful sex education. Furthermore, the present governmental restrictions attack the idea that decent health care is a basic need that society should try to meet, even for those unable to pay.

The process of "liberating the hell" out the unborn by devastating the mothers of those unborn is self-defeating to our society and unfair to women and their families. Abortion is here to stay. It should and it must be available to *all* women.

Rejoinder to Professor Noble   NANNESKA N. MAGEE

My opponent wants to make this a class-and-race argument, but that is not what this discussion is about. It is about money. The question here is not whether I should be able to get an abortion. The question is whether the government should pay for my abortions. Abortions are legal, and I can get one if I can afford it or find someone to help me afford it. Plenty of people do. But if I cannot pay, do I have the right to demand that the government (read this as "all of us") should pay?

Of course it is harder for the poor to get abortions. It is harder for the poor to get most things. This is the definition of being poor. If we can figure out how to get rid of poverty, I am all for it. Until that day, things are going to remain generally tough for the poor.

I am not arguing against government funding for abortions to save the mother's life; we have that duty. I object only to federal funding of those abortions that are matters of choice. I say the government should not pay simply because government cannot fund all our social desires—and because there are more pressing problems we need to pay for first. Besides, there are other ways to help people limit the number of children they produce.

Low-cost or free abortions would not solve all the problems my opponent asserts are barriers that prevent women from getting abortions now. My opponent does not explain how those barriers would be lowered by throwing money at the problems of teen pregnancy, crack babies, and children in poverty. My opponent does not explain how government-funded abortions would solve the problem of men who are irresponsible about supporting the living results of their actions. While it is true that absent fathers pay little or no child support more often than not, will making abortion more widely available help? And will subsidizing abortions help drug addicts make responsible decisions about terminating their pregnancies, when they no longer act responsibly in any other part of life?

It is easy to argue that if rich women can terminate a pregnancy, poor women should also be able to. It is easy to argue that if the rich can afford superior education and cultural enrichment programs for their children, the poor should also have these benefits. And I believe they should. In an ideal world. And I support taxes to educate and care for all Americans as well as we can afford to do those things. But subsidized abortions are not among the top ten on my list of priorities in health care for the poor. Neither are face lifts — for either men or women. The point is, while abortions and face lifts may improve the quality of a person's life immensely, they are not necessities. They are luxuries. When we get the necessities taken care of, then perhaps we can give ourselves a few luxuries. But we don't get the luxuries first.

NO

NANNESKA N. MAGEE

The author Harper Lee once said that the only thing that does not abide by majority rule is a person's conscience. Abortion is an issue that proves her point. It is a very personal concern of the conscience, which is nevertheless being played out on a public societal stage. We have arrived neither at conclusions nor compromises. This disturbing lack of acceptance, a scarcity of resources, the problems resulting from burgeoning medical technology, the expense of abortion and related costs, and governmental invasion of women's privacy are good reasons why the government should not fund abortions.

History of Restrictions

In 1973, Sarah Weddington, a young attorney from Austin, Texas, argued *Roe* v. *Wade* before the Supreme Court. Though her client had long since borne and relinquished a child for adoption, the constitutional point Weddington argued was that a state could not unduly burden a woman's right to choose abortion by making regulations that prohibited her the means of carrying out that decision. Within a decade after *Roe* v. *Wade* was successfully argued, almost 500 bills were introduced in Congress, most of which sought to restrict the availability of abortions by promoting a constitutional amendment outlawing abortion, by transferring the power to make abortion decisions to the state, or by limiting federal funding of abortions.

Proposals of the last kind have been the most successful. The "Hyde Amendments," first passed in 1977, prohibit the use of federal funds for abortions except to preserve the mother's life. The 1980 Supreme Court decision in *Harris* v. *McRae* upheld the constitutionality of the Hyde Amendment. The *Webster* v. *Reproductive Health Services* Supreme Court decision of 1989 further restricted publicly funded abortions by giving state legislatures considerable discretion to pass restrictive abortion legislation. During the 1990–91 term, the Court in *Rust* v. *Sullivan* ruled that the United States can prohibit federally financed family planning programs from giving abortion information. Personally, I do not approve of prohibiting a free flow of information; gag rules seem distinctly unAmerican. However, the fact is that these decisions and laws govern our current restrictions on publicly funded abortions.

Scarcity of Resources

Resources are always scarce. Medical services, especially those provided by the public sector, do not and cannot meet the public demand. The woman who needs bypass surgery, the child with a cleft palate, the diabetic going blind, the Alzheimer's patent without funds for nursing home care—these services are not luxuries for the sufferer or for society.

But choices have to be made, because there is simply not enough money to go around. Funds should be spent first for life-threatening conditions. The birth of a child certainly affects the quality of life of the mother no matter what becomes of the child, but that birth does not usually threaten the mother's life. I do not argue that abortion should be made illegal—certainly not in cases where the birth threatens the life of the mother. But most women seeking abortions are not doing so because of a grave medical threat. Admittedly, there are good reasons, besides the specter of death, why a person would not wish to have a child. The mother may have too many children already and be unable to effectively parent another one. She may not be emotionally equipped to parent a child at this point in her life—or ever. The mother may be too young, or she may be unmarried and unwilling to surrender her child to strangers to raise, or she may suspect or know that the child is not healthy.

All these reasons are very human and understandable. Nevertheless, having a child is not in the same category as having massive kidney failure.

If our choices are between saving a life or improving the quality of someone's life, we must choose to save life — or we must rewrite our moral imperatives. This is not to say that abortions are not important to the people who desire them. They may, indeed, be of the utmost importance. Because women are the primary caregivers for children even in this day of "equal" marriages, the ability to limit the number of children a woman has is fully as important as the ability to receive equal pay for equal work. (I think that if women had written the Declaration of Independence, the right to limit the number of children would have been one of those God-given rights listed in the Preamble.)

But the method by which a woman limits her number of children *is* an option. A woman may, after all, avoid getting pregnant. If she does get pregnant, she has options other than abortion to tolerate the pregnancy and provide for the child's future. I do not say that they are easy options; however, I do say that government should not have to fund all of our options.

Lack of National Consensus

Government does for us what we cannot do for ourselves, but government is our creature and does only what we have allowed it to do. If we are going to fund abortion, we must reach a national agreement that abortion is a procedure our nation will allow. We have not yet reached such a national consensus.

In the past, this nation has allowed the federal government to take actions about which the American people were deeply divided, such as Prohibition and the Vietnam war. In each of these cases, the federal government was acting because of some "moral imperative." The government needed to protect us from our proclivity to strong drink, or the government needed to prevent the spread of communism in Southeast Asia in order to protect the American way of life for our grandchildren. Government acted before we agreed with its actions. The results were chaos.

The same is true for abortion. We have seen public demonstrations and violent acts perpetrated by otherwise law-abiding citizens. We have seen spectacular propaganda on both sides. But we have not yet seen compromise, conciliation, or real attempts to agree. We have not yet had a national referendum on this issue. Though polls say a majority of the people in the United States favor the legalization of abortion, this is not the same thing as agreeing that the government should pay for those operations. The government would be well advised to wait until the citizens have agreed before it steps in, once again, to save us from ourselves.

Because there's no national consensus on the issue of abortion and because government has traditionally looked upon increases in population as desirable, it would be less politically divisive for the federal government to fund other, less controversial methods of birth control. Using public monies to fund widely available sex/health care educational programs and provide birth control pills, birth control implants, and condoms would be far preferable to dealing with the social unrest generated by funding abortions. It would also have the advantage of very likely reducing cases of AIDS and other sexually transmitted diseases.

There is also the issue of individual responsibility. It is always easier to make a decision after the fact rather than before, easier to repent after succumbing to temptation than to resist the temptation in the first place. Abortion is often a post-coital repentance. If this is a country where the individual is free and responsible for his or her own actions, the government should not pay to eradicate the results of an individual's choosing not to be responsible.

Problems of Medical Technology

Roe v. *Wade* said that abortion was permissible in the first two trimesters of pregnancy when, according to the court, the fetus was not yet viable. Modern technology is changing the point at which the fetus becomes viable. Infants born three or four months early are now surviving with increasing frequency, though medical costs may be huge. This poses a fundamental problem with the *Roe* v. *Wade* trimester system. Is the Supreme Court going to be faced with examining developing medical technology, adjusting the point in time at which abortion becomes impermissible? Or is modern technology making the whole viability/inviability distinction moot? If children indeed can be conceived in petri dishes, is it not foreseeable that the whole gestation can be carried out without having to resort to any human womb whatsoever? This destroys the argument in *Roe* v. *Wade* that the fetus is not a child until it can survive outside the body of its mother. Abortions pose difficult moral decisions, and government should not spend the public's money until these bioethical dilemmas are resolved.

Federal funding of abortion also involves the expense of keeping alive those children who unexpectedly survive the process. The government may then find itself in the position of paying to have the fetus destroyed and then paying to have the resulting, possibly damaged, child kept alive—likely at great expense.

Expenses

The abortion procedure itself is much more expensive than other forms of birth control; the later in pregnancy the abortion occurs, the greater the cost. Let's be practical. We can pay for pills or condoms for thousands, for less money than abortions for hundreds.

There are, of course, instances of women who become pregnant through rape or incest when, presumably, the woman would not have been able to resort to birth control. Legislation may need to deal with this particular problem. For the most part, however, abortions are performed on women who have other forms of birth control available. It would be less expensive for the government to make those forms of birth control readily available to society than to face the labor-intensive and technology-intensive medical procedure of abortion.

Privacy

In a world where privacy is a diminishing commodity, government funding of abortion means more government rules and more information gathering. If it funds abortions, the government must regulate the decision-making process and keep procedural and accounting records (which are potentially public, particularly in the volatile case of abortion). The poor are already subjected to intrusive indignities in the public welfare system; government-funded abortions would only increase their invasion of privacy.

Other, more private forms of assistance for the pregnant poor would be preferable. The monies that would be spent on abortion, for instance, could provide counseling for the pregnant poor in deciding on adoption processes, or in parenting training if, as usually happens, the child remains with the biological mother. Use of public funds to teach parents to be better parents would save much money and heartache if child abuse and neglect could be decreased.

Conclusion

The mere fact that the poor have certain options closed to them simply because they are poor does not mean that the government should furnish those options. The poor do not typically have the option of attending Harvard, either. While the federal government would be well advised to provide adequate education to the poor, it is not under the necessity of providing the most expensive education to the poor. While we may all agree that the federal government should improve the access of the poor to medical services, it does not necessarily follow that the federal government should fund all possible medical services.

This is an imperfect world in which we must make do with what we have, even in cases where we would wish it were otherwise. There are no easy answers. Abortion is not an easy answer, either.

Rejoinder to Ms. Magee

DORINDA N. NOBLE

I must extend appreciation to my worthy opponent. At least she did not use the "K" word . . . abortion is killing. It is disconcerting to hear the "K" word used in shocked tones, as if people in this society are not familiar with killing. Our inner cities are killing fields; we bankroll Iraq to slaughter untold numbers of Kuwaitis; we practice legal killing in our prison death chambers. Killing is nothing new to us.

And thanks for not offering adoption as the "final solution." I am a firm supporter of adoption, and I am an adoptive mother myself. But adoption, as wonderful as it can be, is still tough for everybody involved. My opponent says that abortion is not an easy answer; I say that adoption is also not an easy answer.

I agree that resources are scarce. Indeed, the world has finite capacities. With population growth out of control, can we afford to encourage unlimited procreation by the very people who can least afford children? Not only can the poor not afford children, but because of their generally poorer health, they are more at risk to produce children with genetic or congenital abnormalities. And children (healthy or not) who are born into impoverished circumstances, which compromise their chances for productive lives, are being conceived *right now*. We can't wait for the national consensus that my opponent promotes. While we're trying to resolve exquisitely difficult moral dilemmas about the beginning and end of life, people's lives are being destroyed by intolerable pregnancies and the crush of overpopulation.

While my opponent bemoans the quandaries that rapid developments in medical technology create, I argue that technology increases our need for public funding of abortions. Well over 300 genetic conditions, many of them devastating, can now be diagnosed prenatally. Infants who, five years ago, would have been spontaneously aborted or would have died naturally after birth are surviving because of medical technology. While their prognoses may not be good — and their chances for independent living limited — they are nevertheless surviving. The very people who are at the highest risk to produce special needs children are also the people who are least able to meet basic, let alone special, needs.

My opponent argues that publicly funded abortions will compromise women's privacy. What can be more invasive of privacy than pregnancy, childbirth, and childrearing?

Rather than pay for abortions, my opponent suggests that public monies would be better spent in intense education about responsible sexuality, contraception, and parenting. I agree. It would be far better to have an educated population than a desperate one. But we don't do this. Until we do, we need to provide abortions for the poor. Those who can pay will always have access to abortions. All of these funding restrictions will not stop abortions. The bottom line is that *poor* women, who may need those abortions most, are not able to secure them. The long-term costs are staggering — and we will *all* pay.

REFERENCES

Clements, M. (1992). Should abortion remain legal? *Parade,* (May 17), 4–5.

Colker, R. (1991). An equal protection analysis of United States reproductive health policy: Gender, race, age, and class. *Duke Law Journal* (Spring), 324–365.

Corns, C. A. (1991). The impact of public abortion funding decisions on indigent women: A proposal to reform state statutory and constitutional abortion funding provisions. *University of Michigan Journal of Law Reform* 24(Winter), 371–403.

Gold, R. B., & Daley, D. (September/October 1991). Public funding of contraceptive, sterilization and abortion services, fiscal year 1990. *Family Planning Perspectives* 23 (September/October), 204–211.

Henshaw, S. K. (1991). The accessibility of abortion services in the United States. *Family Planning Perspectives* 23 (November/December), 246–253.

Henshaw, S. K., Koonin, L. M., & Smith, J. C. (1991). Characteristics of U.S. women having abortions, 1987. *Family Planning Perspectives* 23(March/April), 75–81.

Petchesky, R. P. (1990). *Abortion and woman's choice.* Boston: Northeastern University Press.

Roberts, D. E. (1990). The future of reproductive choice for poor women and women of color. *Women's Rights Law Reporter* 12(Summer), 59–67.

Waldman, S. (1992). Deadbeat dads. *Newsweek,* (May 14), 18.

ANNOTATED BIBLIOGRAPHY

Colker, R. (1991). An equal protection analysis of United States reproductive health policy: Gender, race, age, and class. *Duke Law Journal* (Spring), 324–365.

This essay examines public policy concerning pregnancy-related regulations, and suggests that equal protection arguments better protect women's reproductive choices than do privacy arguments.

Corns, C. A. (1991). The impact of public abortion funding decisions on indigent women: A proposal to reform state statutory and constitutional abortion funding provisions. *University of Michigan Journal of Law Reform* 24(Winter), 371–403.

The effects of abortion decisions on the poor are well outlined in this illuminating article. The author also proposes policy changes which appear to offer more protection to impoverished women.

Petchesky, R. P. (1990). *Abortion and woman's choice.* Boston: Northeastern University Press.

In this book, one finds a definitive history of abortion practices and policies. The social, economic, cultural, and political battles surrounding abortion are discussed in a clear and interesting manner.

Roberts, D. E. (1990). The future of reproductive choice for poor women and women of color. *Women's Rights Law Reporter* 12 (Summer), 59–67.

Roberts gives an impassioned and thought-provoking view of how abortion policies affect poor and minority women.

Should Spiritual Principles Guide Social Policy?

EDITOR'S NOTE: There has been a renewed interest in the role of religion in promoting progressive social policies. The contribution of pious social workers and the Social Gospel movement to the emergence of the modern welfare state is frequently cited as an example of the positive influence of spiritual principles on social policy. Inspired by this tradition, some have argued that social policy should be guided by spiritual principles. Since religion represents one of the highest human ideals, it is appropriate that social policy be informed by spiritual values. However, this opinion is not universally shared. Opponents argue that religiously inspired beliefs can form the basis for very different social policies. For example, while liberal Christian groups regard state intervention as a positive expression of society's concern for its citizens, the religious right vigorously opposes government welfare programs. These different points of view suggest that the issue is complex and that it requires careful examination.

In this discussion of the issue, Edward R. Canda, Ph.D., and Donald Chambers, DSW, argue YES, that social policy should be guided by spiritual principles. Edward Canda is Associate Professor at the School of Social Welfare, University of Kansas. He is interested in social work and religion and cross-cultural social work, and he has published extensively on these issues in leading social work and sociology journals. Donald Chambers is Professor at the School of Social Welfare, University of Kansas. His books include *Social Policy and Social Problems* (1992), Macmillan; and *Evaluating Social Programs* (1992), Allyn and Bacon.

Patrick Sullivan, Ph.D., disagrees, arguing NO, that social policy should not be guided by spiritual principles. He is an Associate Professor at the School of Social Work at Indiana University. His major research interests are in mental health, and rural social work and substance abuse. He has published numerous articles on these issues in scholarly journals.

YES

EDWARD R. CANDA AND DONALD CHAMBERS

Defining the Role of Spirituality in Social Policy

Social policies must be guided by spiritual principles, first because of necessity and second because of desirability. We accept the following definitions for "spirituality" and "spiritual principles" in a social work context given by Canda (1988). At the broadest level, spirituality is the totality of the human process of development that encompasses and transcends its bio-psycho-social-spiritual aspects. It is not reducible to any part of the person; rather, it is the wholeness of what it is to be human. It is what makes a person a "thou"—a personal being with inherent dignity—rather than an "it"—a mere object or thing, to use Buber's expression (Imre, 1971; Edwards, 1982). In a narrower sense, spirituality refers to the distinctive "spiritual" aspect of the person—the search for a sense of meaning, purpose, and morally fulfilling relationships with other people, the cosmos, and the ground of being, however one conceives it. Thus, spirituality is expressed in rival religious and nonreligious concepts of what is human, what is just, what is "right," and what promotes the development of human potential. *All* human endeavors are driven by just such concepts and so become manifestations of the spirituality of individuals and collectives.

Certainly that includes social policies and the programmatic systems that express them. Social policies are about competition for the allocation of scarce resources in a real world where resources like money, life sustaining or life promoting technology, food, housing, etc., are never infinite (Chambers, 1986). Just on that account decisions *must* be made. The finite resources of our planet are always and everywhere rationed on the basis of some vision of life's purpose and meaning, and that vision is contained in these spiritual concepts. Thus they are used to determine the quality of life a nation provides for its citizens; whether and when death is an acceptable civil outcome; which moral imperatives are to be regarded as serving the interest of both the public and private good; when work is to be demanded; when a parent must provide support for children; or when parental behavior ceases to be good for children. At bottom, social policies and social programs are nothing more than the concrete expression and implementation of these rival spiritual concepts.

The Need to Incorporate Spirituality in Developing Social Policies

To say that spiritual principles should guide social policy is, in a limited sense, no more than saying that social policy is always and everywhere driven by the value perspectives that must inevitably enter the judgments whose meaning is captured in social policies—judgments about where the public interest lies in the allocation of scarce public resources. It cannot be otherwise. Judgments absolutely require a perspective generating decision as to whether one condition is better or worse, more or less desirable than others. Choosing one social policy among many is simply making a decision to work toward one preferred "spiritual" viewpoint rather than another—spiritual in the narrower sense we have defined.

But in the broader sense, the idea of "spirituality" goes beyond the idea of values and value judgments. Sometimes the importance of the idea of values and value judgments has limited impact because the "relativity" of values and value judgments is so persuasive—so much so that it is both tempting and common to dismiss them as, somehow, arbitrary and ultimately incomprehensible. Because no perspective can be shown to be universally "true" by a rational or empirical test, it is easy to consider them intransigent and elusive. However, when one speaks of these fundamental viewpoints as undeniably "spiritual," it brings transcendent meaning, purposes, and a moral framework of life and human relationships into the very core of social policy choices.

The idea of "spirituality" also challenges the common relativistic assumption that one value or spiritual perspective is "just as good as another," which makes it easy to ignore them in designing or implementing social policy. It is foreign to the nature of the concept of spirituality to think that, at least for the adherent, one spirituality is "just as good" as another. In denying that notion, it alerts the social policy debate to the possibility that the spiritual perspective chosen to guide the policy and its programmatic implementation may be in serious conflict with the spiritual perspective of those who will be affected. Thus, the "spiritual fit" of the policy to the spirituality of consumer-beneficiaries must *always* be an issue for social policy and program design and analysis.

Second, it sets to the side the insidious viewpoint that there can be some kind of "value-free" or "value-neutral" objective approach to social policy questions. It sets front and center the idea that the meaning of life is the important issue in social policy choices and cannot be a meaningless or arbitrary question. It explicitly denies the seductive notion that value neutrality can be justified simply because there are so many alternate value positions and none can be inarguably "correct" on logical or empirical grounds. Quite the opposite, this idea of spirituality explicitly reveals value relativity to show how spiritual positions do indeed make all the difference in the world in terms of the impact of social policies on consumers and beneficiaries. It also reveals that spiritual perspectives are an important explanation for human variability. It puts in center place the idea that social policies and programs should treasure that variability and should not cast away or give lower priority to spiritual perspectives because of a sense of urgency to provide for equity, adequacy, and efficiency—those most ubiquitous of standard economic criteria.

Social policy or program designs divorced from spiritual principles are at worst dehumanizing, and at least misguided by naivete. Dehumanization results from ignoring individual or group spirituality in social policy because the human being becomes reduced to a machine-like entity when severed from a context of I-Thou relationships and spiritual matters of meaning, purpose, and world view. Social policy and program design can become a purely rational agent of the state or of narcissistic group interests and goals and, in the worst case, unfettered by compassion and respect for the intrinsic worth of all people. In that case, there is nothing to prevent the powerful from marching the disenfranchised off to execution or holding them in perpetual oppression.

Another danger of divorcing spirituality from policy is allowing powerful interest groups to go unchecked in their attempt to subjugate and manipulate. Even in this country, which mandates separation of church and state, religious ideology and language infuse the political process. Presidents and politicians pray to God in their public addresses to justify war and to imply legitimation for their policy positions. Policy debates on everything from abortion to defining the "worthy poor" are fraught with spoken and unspoken spiritual and religious assumptions. Take, for example, the case of requiring willingness to work as a part of the eligibility rules for public assistance. This view is commonly based on the (ultimately Calvinistic) idea that work is a moral virtue leading to better citizenship in the form of workforce participation. Should religious practices (even if not those of some particular sect) be a requirement for citizens to adopt children in custody of the state? Should a judge be able to sentence a persistent drunken driver to attend Alcoholics Anonymous meetings where recognition of a Higher Power is an essential part of this "treatment" course? Should those who are serving as foster parents (or those charged with physical child abuse) be entitled to use their religious viewpoints (based on biblical references) to justify the harsh physical punishment of a child? Is the state entitled to use religiously sponsored child care for children in its custody?

But if neither value neutrality nor exclusive commitment to a single value or spiritual perspective will do, how should value/spiritual perspectives enter into the debate about social policy choices? Martin Rein is helpful, since he has anticipated the problems we have discussed above (Rein, 1983). Rein presents many of our arguments (and more) against value-free and "value-committed" policy analysis, and advocates a "value-critical" approach. This approach will be helpful in answering this question.

In the context of our question here, our interpretation of the value-critical view would introduce spiritual perspectives into the social policy debate by first making explicit those questions that the policy will encounter from the major stakeholders. Specifically, the questions include spiritual perspectives of decision and opinion makers who frame the social problem to which the policy and program is designed as a solution; those of street-level bureaucrats (social workers and other human service workers) who implement it face to face with clients and consumers; those of client and consumer groups who are the intended beneficiaries; and those of the onlooking citizen groups, either those whose taxes pay the bill or simply the self-appointed citizen-guardians of public morality. Rein expects great dissonance among these perspectives. Spiritual perspectives are brought to and emerge from a dialogue among these key actors — the experience of framing a social problem, designing a solution, implementing a programmatic solution, and learning from the experience of clients and consumers who are subject to that policy or program.

One of the particular merits of cross-frame, critical analysis is that it forces the abstractions of policy into contrast with the everydayness of life experience. It requires policy to be constrained from the bottom up as well as by the top-down imperatives of abstract rationality. Rein's contribution is that, far from defining as problems the expected contradictions, incongruities, and paradoxes, he treasures dissonance. In following Habermas, Rein anticipates that this dialectic between divergent views will produce discontent with the old and motivate the creation of something new and better, a "meta-analysis" that accounts for the existent divergence while developing solutions which resolve apparent conflicts — always in favor of what is more useful for the clients/consumers of public policy. Dialectical analysis pushes its adherents to think better and more clearly about divergence and about using it to achieve higher levels of resolving contradiction. It values paradox and capitalizes upon it. Further, it tolerates difference and conflict, allowing it to simply stand as given.

A value-critical approach does not require policy rationality and consistency to be the supreme tests of its goodness. That is of high value in relation to our commitment to support spiritual variation as a distinctive quality of the human condition. We should want to treasure the value-critical approach as a solution to our problem of how spirituality and diverse spiritual perspectives should enter and serve our social policy and social program enterprise.

A Recommendation for Incorporating Spirituality into Social Policy

The reader should not conclude from the preceding argument that there is no spiritual perspective that is conclusive. There is, and the reader may well find it surprising, for it emphasizes how spirituality frames the process of the policy debate, rather than its concrete outcome. Its intention is to maximize the possibility of creative and constructive dialogue on these matters. Note that it is spiritually sensitive rather than spiritually naive or coercive. If our suggestion below is followed, policy formation cannot be either naive or coercive. And, of course, our suggestion about a proper and specific spiritual perspective should also be subjected to the spirit of the value-critical, cross-frame reflection we have advocated.

Our spiritual perspective is a metaperspective which encompasses diverse spiritual perspectives within a process of creative dialogue. It implies three spiritual principles: First, **people are encouraged to express diverse and contrasting spiritual positions** both because of the inherent worth of each and because of the need for honesty and critical reflection in the policy formation process. Paradoxically, this openness supports the inclusion of diverse views, even exclusivist views, within the policy process. It is ecumenical, thereby encompassing spiritual diversity by encouraging open dialogue. It implies a second spiritual principle, **nonviolence or Ahimsa,** to use a Gandhian expression (Walz, Sharma, Birnbaum, 1990). In the context of this argument, Ahimsa means that a policy debate should occur in an atmosphere of mutual positive regard. Even when conflicts of interest are inevitably intense, the spiritually sensitive approach does not dehumanize or demonize the opponent. It seeks mutual benefit and dignified compromise, and/or win-win solutions whenever possible. It seeks to avoid settling disputes by compromises that maintain an oppressive status quo or exchange one set of oppressors for another.

This commitment to nonviolence is rooted in the third spiritual principle, which Gandhi called **Satyagraha,** the truth force. This principle suggests that all policies reflect claims about "the true, the real and the good." Everyone is engaged in a spiritual process of discerning "what is truth" or even whether there is a transcendent "truth" beyond the relativities of truth expressions. As Gandhi emphasized, social policy must support this search for truth and create conditions of justice in which people are at liberty to search for it. Social policy should also support everyone's right to search and identify this truth in various ways.

Authentic spiritually sensitive policy making must involve a heartfelt reflection upon the consistency of policy ends and means with participants' most profound moral, spiritual, and religious commitments. These spiritual principles pose a formidable challenge, but one that is necessary and desirable for extricating ourselves from the pitfalls of the value neutral, the value naive, and the value coercive in social policy.

Rejoinder to Professors Canda and Chambers

PATRICK SULLIVAN

In arguing that spiritual values should guide social policy initiatives, Canda and Chambers present a tautological argument. All matters of life are presented as a manifestation of spiritual principles; therefore, spiritual matters should be of prime concern in the creation of social policy. We are left again with a lofty set of ideas, but with no sense of how the rubber actually meets the road.

Additionally, the authors trap themselves by suggesting that social policy or program design divorced from spiritual principles is potentially dehumanizing. Certainly, my colleagues admit that if all of life is a manifestation of spirituality, then the manner in which policy decisions are currently made does indeed reflect spiritual principles. Those who struggle with difficult policy decisions, both within and outside our discipline, would be offended if it were suggested that they are not concerned about human suffering, dignity, or desires. Certainly, the very process of policy creation that exists today is an attempt to balance competing perspectives.

To counter the dilemma that they have helped create, Canda and Chambers suggest that a dialectical, "value-critical" approach to policy creation will expose competing spiritual perspectives. Furthermore, this process may help us recognize the right "spiritual fit" of policy and constituents. According to the authors, this dialectic process has several additional positive features.

First, the prevailing assumption that policy questions and decisions are value free will be exposed. Who, may I ask, suggests that policy questions and decisions are value free? The very rules, principles, and processes that we have established to make policy decisions are, in part, a reflection of our understanding that competing values are involved. The rules and principles that guide policy decisions, while imperfect, are designed to protect and honor differing viewpoints and human diversity.

Second, it is suggested that this dialectical process will help check the influence of powerful interest groups who affect policy decisions. Is the behavior of these groups anti-spiritual? My dear colleagues, please remember that there are those who believe that their wealth is a manifestation of God's special blessing and that it is their moral and spiritual duty to accumulate as much wealth as possible. Thus, regardless of Canda and Chambers' protestations and claims, the very process they encourage can result in the creation of spiritual hierarchies and the passing of spiritual judgment — just what they fell victim to in describing it. Obviously, they are now moving onto extremely dangerous turf. For indeed, throughout this discussion there is the hint that a preferred spiritual perspective already exists or can emerge. One can only ponder the precarious international situation and reflect on how many global conflicts are driven by notions of preferred spiritual positions.

In the final analysis, Canda and Chambers have described a process that not only is short on the specifics of implementation but also naively suggests that universally agreeable decisions, or metaprinciples will result. Who, for example, will participate in this spiritual dialectic? How will the discussion occur? Reality also dictates that some policy decisions must be made quickly and efficiently. One need only consider the lack of immediate response to the AIDS epidemic to consider what tragedies can occur while we remain stuck in a process that subjugates action. Finally, this perspective can easily lead to the very dehumanization and lack of tolerance for diversity that the authors rightly deplore.

Spirituality is an inherently personal matter. The manner in which we understand the meaning and purpose of life, and the manner in which we express or affirm our views are also unique. Canda and Chambers are correct in asserting that policy decisions are not simply technical matters. However, until there is an established set of universal spiritual principles and further clarity on how these principles can be operationalized in social policy decisions, any reasonable role for spirituality in public policy decisions remains ambiguous and potentially dangerous.

NO

PATRICK SULLIVAN

The Limits of Incorporating Spirituality into Social Policy

Social work has deep roots in the spiritual and religious traditions of our nation. Furthermore, the code of ethics and the cardinal values of social work reflect a philosophical orientation to life that draws from spiritual principles. Nonetheless, spiritual principles cannot adequately serve as guideposts in the development of social policy. This assertion is based on several points: (a) common definitions of spirituality are broad and vague; (b) when codified as a series of guiding principles, spirituality becomes indistinct from religious doctrine, which often has a built-in status quo bias; (c) social policy decisions require one to make choices—at times tragic choices—that pit equally important value positions against one another.

While a plethora of definitions of spirituality could be offered for review, two are presented below. Canda (1990) has conceptualized spirituality as "the gestalt of the total process of human life and development, encompassing biological, mental, social, and spiritual aspects" (p. 13). Titone (1991), more narrowly focused, has defined spirituality as "one's personalized experience and identity pertaining to a sense of worth, meaning, vitality, and connectedness to others and the universe" (p. 8). These two examples highlight common themes expressed in wide-ranging definitions of spirituality. First, spirituality is regarded as a holistic force that shapes and colors the manner in which life is viewed and ultimately influences behavior. Second, as a search for meaning, spirituality is concerned with the relationship between an individual and God, or a higher power.

As defined above, spirituality is too broadly construed to provide meaningful guidelines to direct the development of social policy or to help make difficult policy decisions. To agree, for example, that life should be infused with meaning and purpose, or even that all people should be accorded respect and dignity, does not help a society decide the relative desirability of expending resources for books or bombs. Recognizing these expansive definitions, Canda (1990) has suggested that "if spirituality is the totality of human life, one must ask why use the term at all?" (p. 13).

Spirituality is an inherently personal experience. While religious participation and rituals may suggest accepted canons, beliefs, and behaviors, in reality each person shapes belief systems in his or her own unique way. Siporin (1982) has noted that the values of social work are more concerned with the relationships between people than with the relationship between people and God or a higher power. Indeed, this distinction is important. By focusing attention on relationships between persons, as well as the relationship between people and society, common ground rules are established that, in practice, protect the rights of persons to believe and exercise faith in the manner they choose. While spiritual principles can and do guide the nature of relationships between people, the diversity of beliefs and practices present in America defies efforts to create a universal code of ethics that can effectively inform social policy.

It has been argued previously that common conceptualizations of spirituality are inherently elusive and often unique to each individual. This suggests that as guides for behavior and, for our purposes, policy, these principles must be distilled into precise canons, laws, or values that provide clear direction for each individual. The effort to refine spiritual principles in such a manner is best reflected in organized religion. Indeed, Canda (1990) admits that "we could, as a profession, adopt the term religion in place of spirituality" (p. 14). Yet, Canda astutely notes that social workers often have negative reactions to religion, given the history of competing sectarian perspectives within our profession. Some have argued, for example, that distinctions between private and public morality should be rejected and that social workers should accept their role as guardians of an agreed upon moral order. Siporin (1986) has remarked that "the dangers of religious absolutism and intolerant moralism of a theistic state are not to be risked" (p. 48). One need only consider the disquieting number of global conflicts that are shaped and fueled by competing religious ideologies.

Historical reflection does provide illustrations where religious leaders and institutions have actively worked to craft social policy in America. Perhaps the most vivid example of this is characterized as the *Social Gospel* movement. The Social Gospel movement reflects a period of history where religious coalitions attempted to move beyond the arena of personal redemption to focus on the extant social conditions of society. However, Niebuhr (1932) detected the fatal flaw in the Social Gospel effort, recognizing that:

> . . . it is religion's sense of the absolute that betrays it into social conservatism at the very moment in which it regards contemporary social structure critically . . . the world of injustice is taken for granted (p. 19).

The Social Gospel movement could reasonably claim partial responsibility for any number of progressive policy initiatives in the period immediately before and after the turn of the century. However, at times this movement also degenerated into a crusade for moral purity that resulted in rampant censorship in nearly every endeavor of the human enterprise, including the arts, sports, personal dress, and behavior (Klein & Kantor, 1976). In the end, Niebuhr (1936) surmised that this "rationalistic effort to deal with the problem of emancipated human life in terms of moral-self-salvation and by means of indirect and melioristic action through education and reason failed" (p. 181).

In the final analysis, spiritual principles, by remaining inherently individualistic, and religious doctrine, by establishing rigid guidelines for moral behavior, tacitly support and maintain the status quo. Social policy, in contrast, must be fluid and must react to and anticipate changing social realities. In addition, policy must be sensitive to protect diversity. Unfortunately, social work has been equally criticized as a professional activity that ultimately buttresses the status quo and undermines significant and needed social change. This important criticism supports the movement toward an empirical/legalist approach to policy development.

Policy decisions are, above all, complex. Chambers (1986) states that:

Social welfare policy is about selection, rationing, and the attempt to correct injustice. Social welfare policy is about a concrete empirical world and the attempt to moderate the occasions of its sometimes cruel and inhumane effects. (p. 57)

Several facets of Chambers's conceptualization of social welfare policy bear discussing. First, as Chambers highlights, social welfare policy is about the concrete empirical world. Many spiritual orientations advocate detachment from social discourse and political process. Indeed, views of life and existence from some Eastern philosophical traditions suggest that all of life is suffering and an illusion. Such perspectives can lead one to discount policy creation as inherently fruitless and insignificant. At the individual practice level, one often confronts similarly nihilistic views — that current situations are all a function of God's will and that God's ultimate plan renders individual action meaningless. The belief that current social conditions reflect the natural order of things has been used to excuse blatant injustices and inequitable human conditions. Social policy rests on a belief that individual rationality and action can be exercised in a manner that can balance the needs of individuals and collectives, and ultimately improve the human condition.

Even when the impetus of all concerned is the elimination of injustices and human suffering, social welfare policy involves choice. It is here that spiritual principles fail us completely. Policy decisions, unfortunately, rarely ask us to choose between good and evil. Often the choice is between two distinct goods and/or it requires weighing the relative merits or evils of a policy decision. Policy decisions involve, among other considerations, mediating the demand between such time-honored principles as equity, effectiveness, and efficiency. For as Chambers (1986) notes, policy also involves the selection of beneficiaries and the rationing of benefits.

Far from involving simple spiritual choice, Calabresi and Bobbitt (1978) note that when decisions about selection, rationing, and allotment are made, we are making "tragic choices." In reality, these decisions often involve the distribution of scarce resources. Thus, balancing competing claims on these resources determines not only who gets certain goods and benefits, but perhaps even who will survive (for example, decisions involving organ transplants). Rarely do we consider this. And, while basic spiritual principles would seem to be beacons to lead us from this quagmire, Calabresi and Bobbitt (1978) dash our hopes by reminding us that "the agony of the tragic choice reflects precisely the conflict of discrete values to which we are committed" (p. 41).

Therefore, while spiritual principles may embody important values that are so universally accepted that they should be expected to guide social policy decisions, we must still balance the competing claims of various value positions. For example, attempts to weigh the relative importance of sustaining individual liberties versus the protective power of the state emerge in such disparate areas as policies on homelessness, abortion, and child protective services. Allotment decisions that grant goods to one sector of society often must exclude the legitimate claims of another. Thus, while social workers may decry the relative importance placed on defense spending versus social programs, the collective society seems to agree that defensive initiatives make a greater contribution to the overall welfare of society. Furthermore, attempts to effectively redress social injustices (e.g., affirmative action) may by necessity violate some principles of equity by earmarking some benefits to select groups.

Conclusion

Social policy ultimately reflects a mix of claims making, rational planning, trade-offs, and choices. It is ironic that with each decision made, equally perplexing and difficult choices seem to follow. Improved technological developments create policy choices that clearly involve matters of values, ethics, and law. Our improved medical technologies have compelled us to enter into a series of wrenching debates and discussions in which we have struggled with the very definition of life. In more sordid moments, these concerns have pitted friend against friend and have placed us on the brink of massive civil disorder. Spiritual principles alone cannot guide us through such dilemmas.

There can be little question that spiritual concerns and issues are preeminent in the lives of many people. That spiritual matters should be considered in work with individual clients is unquestioned. Commonly expressed spiritual principles strike resonant cords with many social workers and seem to provide an important framework for policy decisions. However, as a loosely organized series of principles, they are difficult to translate into action and are subject to misuse. Furthermore, social policy involves difficult choices that often force us to consider the merits of compelling universal principles in conflict.

Rejoinder to Professor Sullivan
Edward R. Canda and Donald Chambers

Sullivan has done us the service of supporting most of the reasons we have given for incorporating spiritual principles into social policy activity. That he comes to an opposite conclusion from ours seems to result from his missing the nuances of meaning and policy implications in the sources he cites.

In regard to areas of agreement, Sullivan wisely points out that there is danger in allowing religious absolutism and exclusivism to dominate policy making; that vague spiritual views and principles are inadequate to inform social policy; and that rigid or status quo religious doctrines can lead to stale or oppressive policies. All of these points provide support for our position that an inclusive, critical-comparative approach to spirituality in policy is necessary. That Sullivan has not been able to articulate such a solution to his stated problems is not sufficient reason to conclude that there is *no* solution.

Sullivan goes so far as to say, "That spiritual matters should be considered in work with individual clients is unquestioned." Yet he feels that spiritual principles are inadequate for policy analysis. As such, he implies that there is an artificial split between the realms of the personal and the political. If Sullivan recognizes the necessity of dealing with spirituality in individual work, how can he deny it in working with collectivities of individuals (i.e., the policy arena)? Further, Sullivan's difficulty with vague spiritual principles arises from his own vagueness about the meaning and implications of spirituality, not from any inherent reason why spirituality must be vague. In agreement with Sullivan on the problems with vagueness, we have attempted to present a clear rationale and principles for spiritually sensitive policy making and implementation.

There are several factual or interpretive errors that need to be corrected in his analysis. First, Canda's definition of spirituality is inclusive and holistic (not broad and vague) because it honors and respects diversity of religious and nonreligious spiritual positions. The conceptualizations in Canda's writings encompass a complete range of abstraction, from general concepts to practical implications, which is necessary in any comprehensive effort to conceptualize and operationalize. It pays to remember that to be abstract does not mean to be imprecise.

In citing Canda's 1990 article, Sullivan fails to point out that the question "If spirituality is the totality of human life, one must ask why use the term at all?" is not rhetorical. Canda answers this question in the article cited. In reference to the same article, Sullivan notes that Canda suggests that the term "religion" could be used as an alternative to the term "spirituality." But Sullivan incorrectly states that this is because spiritual principles are best reflected in organized religion. Actually, Canda's point is simply that the field of academic religious studies gives one definition of religion that is similar to the social work definition of spirituality, but that this religious studies definition is not helpful in the social work context.

We believe that Sullivan confuses spirituality with institutional religion. First, he identifies spirituality largely with institutional religion (as seen above), then he claims that institutional religion is basically conservative. For example, while he accurately recognizes the tendency of religious institutions to support the social status quo, he does not give adequate account for the many modern and historical instances when spiritual perspectives both within and without religious institutions challenge the status quo in both subtle and revolutionary ways. For example, what of the biblical tradition of prophecy against corruption, the recent development of liberation theology, and the powerful social change work of Mahatma Gandhi and Rev. Martin Luther King, Jr.? Indeed, Sullivan neglects to point out, in his citation of Niebuhr, that the theologian referred to absolutist, uncritical religion as "false religion." Niebuhr's concern, therefore, was to advocate for "true religion" which understands that spirituality and social justice concerns ought to be inseparable.

Sullivan also mischaracterizes Eastern philosophical traditions. It is true that Hinduism and Buddhism, for example, point out that human suffering is significantly the result of egoistic illusions and attachments. However, both of these traditions also make a powerful call to action — they prescribe ways for individuals and groups to break out of these illusions and transcend suffering. This is certainly not "nihilistic." For example, Southeast Asian refugees often reconstitute Buddhist temples and support systems in the United States, drawing on a rich and ancient tradition that links physical, mental, social, and spiritual well being (Canda and Phaobtong, 1992). Although Sullivan's conclusion and reasoning have errors, we should acknowledge the important things he has to say about the need for vigilance regarding the dangers of spiritual vagueness, exclusivism, and conservatism.

REFERENCES

Calabresi, G., & Bobbitt, P. (1978). *Tragic choices*. New York: W. W. Norton.

Canda, E. (1990). Afterword: Spirituality re-examined. *Spirituality and Social Work Communicator* 1(1), 13–14.

Canda, E. (1988). Conceptualizing spirituality for social work: Insights from diverse perspectives. *Social Thought* 14(1), 30–41.

Canda, E., & Phaobtong, T. (1992). Buddhism as a support system for Southeast Asian refugees. *Social Work* 37(1), 61–67.

Chambers, D. (1986). *Social policy and social programs*. New York: Macmillan.

Edwards, D. (1982). *Existential psychotherapy: The process of caring*. New York: Gardner Press.

Imre, R. (1971). A theological view of social work. *Social Casework* 52(9), 578–585.

Klein, M., & Kantor, H. (1976). *Prisoners of progress*. New York: Macmillan.

Niebuhr, R. (1936). The attack upon the social gospel. *Religion in Life* 5(Spring), 176–181.

Niebuhr, R. (1932). *The contribution of religion to social work*. New York: Columbia University Press.

Rein, M. (1984). Value-critical policy analysis. In Callahan, D., & Jennings, B. (Eds.), *Ethics, the social sciences and policy analysis*. New York: Plenum Press.

Rein, M. (1983). *From policy to practice*. Armonk, NY: M.E. Sharpe, Inc.

Siporin, M. (1986). Contributions of religious values to social work and the law. *Social Thought* (Fall), 35–50.

Siporin, M. (1982). Moral philosophy in social work today. *Social Service Review* 56(4), 516–538.

Titone, A. (1991). Spirituality and psychotherapy in social work practice. *Spirituality and Social Work Communicator* 2(1), 7–9.

Walz, T., Sharma, S., & Birnbaum, C. (1990). Gandhian thought as a theory base for social work. University of Illinois School of Social Work Occasional Paper Series I. Champaign-Urbana: University of Illinois.

ANNOTATED BIBLIOGRAPHY

Canda, E. (1988). Conceptualizing spirituality for social work: Insights from diverse perspectives. *Social Thought* 14(1), 30–41.

Five religious and philosophical perspectives from the history of social work are integrated to develop a conceptualization of spirituality and its practical implications.

Canda, E., & Phaobtong, T. (1992). Buddhism as a support system for Southeast Asian refugees. *Social Work* 37(1), 61–67

An ethnographic field study that discusses services provided by Buddhist temples for refugees in the Midwest.

Imre, R. (1971). A theological view of social work. *Social Casework* 52(9), 578–585.

This article explores the relevance of basic existential and Judeo-Christian principles to social work.

Niebuhr, R. (1932). *The contribution of religion to social work*. New York: Columbia University Press.

This book is a critical analysis of the relationship between religion and social work.

Rein, M. (1984). Value-critical policy analysis. In Callahan, D., & Jennings, B. (Eds.), *Ethics, the social sciences and policy analysis.* New York: Plenum Press.

A value-critical policy analysis is presented as an alternative to value-free and value-committed approaches.

Siporin, M. (1982). Moral philosophy in social work today. *Social Service Review* 56(4), 516–538.

This article considers the shift in social work from a moral foundation to a individualist/humanist perspective.

Titone, A. (1991). Spirituality and psychotherapy in social work practice. *Spirituality and Social Work Communicator* 2(166), 7–9.

This article provides a working definition of spirituality.

Is Gay Rights Legislation Necessary for the Well-Being of Gays and Lesbians?

EDITOR'S NOTE: After centuries of oppression, gays and lesbians have campaigned effectively to counteract the prejudice and intolerance which characterizes popular attitudes toward homosexuality. They have sought to educate people about sexual orientation, formed lobbying and support groups, and persuaded legislative bodies, primarily at the municipal level, to enact ordinances that protect their rights. These statutes prohibit discrimination against gays and lesbians in areas such as employment, housing, and education. However, the idea that special legislation is needed to protect gays and lesbians is not universally supported. Indeed, many opponents of gay and lesbian rights would like to use the criminal law to suppress homosexuality. In addition, opponents of gay rights legislation argue that while discriminatory legislation should be removed, no special legislation for gays and lesbians should be enacted. Once gays are given the same protection under the constitution as other citizens, no further legal safeguards are needed.

The case for special gay rights legislation is made by Norman Wyers, DSW, who is Professor of Social Work and Director of the MSW Program at Portland State University. Dr. Wyers has published extensively on clinical practice with AIDS victims, and on social policy and income maintenance programs in leading academic journals.

John F. Longres, Ph.D., takes the opposing point of view, arguing against special gay rights legislation. Dr. Longres is Professor of Social Work at the University of Wisconsin at Madison. He has undertaken research into the use of social services by ethnic and racial minorities, and into adolescence and delinquency. He has authored *Human Behavior and The Social Environment* (1990), Peacock, and has published extensively on social work issues in major scholarly journals. He served on the editorial board for the eighteenth edition of the *Encyclopedia of Social Work,* which was published by NASW in 1989.

YES

NORMAN WYERS

> Dear Friends, whether we like it or not, we are in a war that will determine the values of our community. And just as in any war, the side that is willing to make the necessary sacrifices will prevail. And prevail we must as we are fighting for our rights as law abiding citizens and our right to work and live in peace. The so-called Christians of OCA have declared this war of hatred and bigotry, but it is the gay/ lesbian community who must take the defensive measure to preserve peace and justice for all in Oregon. These bigots have targeted the gay/lesbian community first — who will they target next? (No Special Rights Committee, 1992, p. 1).

Similar calls for gay and lesbian rights have been made repeatedly throughout the United States during the past two decades. Such calls have resulted in the promulgation of only four comprehensive, state-level gay/lesbian rights policies (public and private employment, public accommodations, education, housing, credit, and union practices). Twenty-five states have no legislation or ordinances to protect gays and lesbians from discrimination based on their sexual orientation (Lambda Legal Defense and Education Fund, Inc., 1991). Twenty-one cities and counties have adopted comprehensive gay/lesbian rights polices (National Gay and Lesbian Task Force, 1992). The calls for gay/lesbian rights legislation have been totally ineffectual in obtaining rights policies for gays and lesbians at the federal level. This includes the 1991 Amendments to the Civil Rights Act of 1964 as well as earlier rights bills. This has occurred even though support for gay and lesbian rights does not usually negatively affect the careers of the politicians who sponsor such legislation (Gay Rights National Lobby, 1980).

The fifteen to twenty-five million gay and lesbian persons in the United States are among its most despised and oppressed minorities. As Mohr (1988) points out, they are largely an invisible minority (along with diabetics, assimilated Jews, atheists, and released prisoners). Gays and lesbians are discriminated against both unwittingly and intentionally, and may consequently be in greater need of legal rights than the more visible minorities. Because of their heterosexism and stereotyped perceptions of homosexuality, for many non-gay persons the invisibility of gay and lesbian persons and their culture serves to perpetuate hatred, prejudicial attitudes, and intolerant behaviors.

These attitudes and behaviors have resulted in a society in which discrimination against gays and lesbians, both overt and covert, goes largely unchecked. This discrimination is manifest in the absence of gay and lesbian rights in employment, public accommodations, housing, immigration and naturalization, insurance, custody and adoption, and zoning regulations (neighborhood covenants) that bar access to singles or nonrelated couples (Mohr, 1988). It is also manifest in access to health care, in legally sanctioned love relationships, and in sexual practices. It can be further argued that gays and lesbians are denied protection from assault and other violent behaviors, and from guarantees that their assaulters will be punished. In fact, gays are often blamed for the attacks made upon them.

The Need for Gay and Lesbian Rights

In the face of overwhelming evidence of the extent to which gays and lesbians experience discrimination and prejudice, the need for gay and lesbian rights is striking. If these rights are not granted, gay and lesbian persons cannot attain full citizenship and will continue to encounter the destructiveness of civic, political, economic, sexual, and social injustice.

Civic Rights

Civic rights mandate fairness and equity in the implementation of civil and criminal law, so that one can protect himself/herself from damages to one's person and personal property. If persons are denied civic rights, they are denied full and equal treatment by the judiciary and the legal system. Laws that pertain to other citizens do not pertain to gays and lesbians. At this time, gays and lesbians do not have civic rights in the manner and extent enjoyed by non-gay persons. Therefore, they cannot "turn to the law" when they encounter damage to themselves and/or their property, except in those few states and cities that have passed gay rights ordinances or proclamations.

Political Rights

Without political rights, gays and lesbians are denied the rights to freedom of speech, freedom of the press, freedom to assemble, freedom to petition for the redress of grievances, and especially the freedom to associate (Mohr,

1988). Thus gays and lesbians cannot participate fully in the political dynamics of society. Because gays and lesbians are denied these rights, they are prohibited from speaking out against anti-gay attitudes and behaviors or advocating for improvements in their collective lives. If they do speak out, they risk disclosure of their status and thereby face the possible negative consequences of such a disclosure. Thus, they cannot defend themselves for fear of reprisal and the possible loss of their livelihood and social status.

Economic Rights

If gays and lesbians do not have full civil and political rights, they also cannot enjoy full economic rights. When economic rights are denied, gays and lesbians are subjected to restrictions in access to employment, to the possibility of losing employment because of their sexual orientation, to diminished likelihood of promotion and advancement, and even to the denial of opportunities to prepare for economic well-being and career paths. Since employment and economic well-being are major vehicles for the development of self-esteem and personal identity, the denial of economic rights is tantamount to being denied full citizenship and recognition as a valued member of society. Without political rights, gays and lesbians are also denied the right to associate freely and openly with one another. This occurs because participation with other gays and lesbians generally demands public disclosure of homosexuality, both individually and collectively.

Sexual Rights

Approximately half of all states currently have sodomy laws on their books. Although they are rarely enforced, they hang like the sword of Damocles over the sexual behaviors of gays and lesbians. In essence, these laws restrict the sexual behavior of gays and lesbians, since what they do in private is subject to prosecution. The loss of sexual privacy of gays and lesbians has been upheld by the Supreme Court of the United States.

The AIDS epidemic has further exacerbated the absence of gay and lesbian sexual rights, in that HIV-infected gay males have been blamed for the spread of the disease by virtue of their sexual practices. As such, they have been labeled as the perpetrators of the AIDS horror. The sexual liberation experienced in the 1970s has been identified as the cause of the epidemic, and sexual practices have changed dramatically as a result. Nevertheless, while these changes were needed to curtail the spread of the virus, the sexual freedom experienced during that decade has been inhibited. The loss of sexual freedom has resulted in the slowing down of the momentum for gay and lesbian sexual rights.

Social Rights

The social rights of gays and lesbians are either restricted or nonexistent due to the lack of civic, political, economic, and sexual rights. The lack of social rights is not surprising given the lack of guarantees to employment rights, to public accommodations, to housing, and to other related rights granted to non-gay persons. The rights to dress as one prefers, to express affection in public places, to behave in a manner appropriate to one's culture, and even to frequent bars and restaurants (without possible reprisal) where one's friends and peers are in attendance, are not fully granted to gay and lesbian persons. To be openly gay in public frequently results in the loss of invisibility for gays and lesbians. On the other hand, to become visible as a gay or lesbian is apt to invite negative sanctions (or even worse) from the non-gay society. Visibility is not without its potential costs in the absence of the right to be oneself and to express oneself freely.

Rights and Justice

Without being granted full and equal rights, gays and lesbians will continue to experience oppression and second-class citizenship. Because of the invisibility of most gays and lesbians, the persistent discrimination which they experience will go unchallenged in most instances. For gay men or lesbians to challenge discriminatory actions or prejudicial attitudes, it is necessary for them to "come out" and to face their accusers openly and directly. Since their rights have been denied and they do not have protection under the law, it is frequently more difficult for gays and lesbians than other oppressed subpopulations to challenge the discrimination that they encounter. Once "out," a gay or lesbian is subject to continued or even intensified discrimination, especially since public or private disclosure may transform discriminatory behaviors from inadvertent to purposeful.

Gays and lesbians have made important strides during the past two decades in their demands for equal rights. There is some evidence that homosexuality is better accepted in this society because of the gay liberation movement, but much remains to be done. The acquisition of rights, protected under the law, is clearly a major step in the direction of preserving the gains that have been made. While some states and municipalities have enacted gay and lesbian rights policies and ordinances, most have not. Nor has the federal government. The refusal to recognize gays and lesbians as a legitimate subpopulation continues to have deleterious effects.

The concept of "spoiled identity" (Goffman, 1963) is pertinent to this discussion. If one already has been discredited or is even among the discreditable, self-affirmation and positive self-regard are difficult to achieve. For gays and lesbians, it is frequently impossible to develop a positive sense of who they are if their status is devalued by others and negative sanctions are constantly threatened or imposed. To challenge these sanctions, gays and lesbians must confront those who attack them. They cannot and will not do so unless they are protected by law. Therefore, the need for gay and lesbian rights is requisite to the well-being and improved life conditions of approximately one-tenth of the members of this society. Not only will this aid gays and lesbians, but it will also help strengthen the fabric of society itself.

Rejoinder to Professor Wyers   JOHN F. LONGRES

I certainly have no quarrel with my close friend and associate Norm Wyers's systematic listing of the oppressive circumstances endured by lesbians and gays. As I have suggested, the United States is a society that presently permits and encourages discrimination against homosexuals. We are in agreement on this point: legal discrimination of gays and lesbians must be stopped. We apparently do disagree, however, about the degree of oppression and about ways of overcoming oppression.

We should not exaggerate the extent of oppression experienced by gays and lesbians lest we end up trivializing their circumstances. To assert, for instance, that "gays and lesbians are denied the rights to freedom of speech, freedom of the press, freedom to assemble, freedom to petition for the redress of grievances, and especially the freedom to associate" is a gross exaggeration. If all this were true, gays and lesbians would not presently be enjoying a strong, well-organized civil rights movement. Gays and lesbians have developed a community, including a strong sense of personal attachment through social and leisure time activities and a strong set of self-help agencies and organizations that meet their internal and external social, economic, and political needs. They have done this without the existence of any special legislation. They have simply exercised their rights as citizens in a democratic society. This is, after all, the point I am making. Without protective legislation, homosexual women and men are already making their interests heard and are gaining the attention of politicians and the respect of the populace.

It is also an exaggeration to argue that they are denied economic and social rights, or to make the claim that heterosexuals have these rights by law. Most laws which regulate conduct are mute on the question of sexuality. The Constitution, for instance, does not single out heterosexuals for protection, nor does it single out homosexuals for discrimination. Most homosexuals work and dress as they like without living in terror of being arbitrarily dismissed or beat upon. Although no statistics compare income and wealth, my own observations are that there are probably less disparities based on sexual orientation than on race, gender, and age.

The chief dilemma in the law, and this cannot be exaggerated, is that it incorporates important heterosexual assumptions and advantages. Primarily these exist in the meaning and interpretation of family; adult citizens are expected to join in matrimony and procreate as a major way by which to assure the survival of the society. Homosexuals are forbidden in Judeo-Christian church law and in civil law from entering into marriage with same-sex partners. (As indicated, I would favor the elimination of such restrictions.)

Many normative patterns of social life have their basis in family life, neighborhood leisure activities, school and social clubs, "old boys" and "old girls" networks, and a whole host of other taken-for-granted forms of heterosexual bonding. As a result, not being married to an other-sex partner leads to exclusion from many friendship networks and therefore from economic and social opportunities. Homosexuals, of course, may marry other-sex heterosexual, bisexual, and homosexual partners and many of them do. This in the end is an inadequate solution. It is unfair to unsuspecting partners and may take undo advantage of willing partners. It is also often done for the wrong reasons — insecure homosexually inclined men and women hope a sexual relationship with a member of the opposite sex will "cure" them. Finally, it forces people to live in a closet and always be on the defensive. In short, the oppression of homosexuals stems from the advantages given to people who enjoy marital relations with members of the other sex. Because of these advantages, homosexuals are therefore outsiders always trying to get in by either inventing their own opportunities (gay and lesbian owned businesses) or by figuring out other ways to shorten the social distance between them and heterosexuals. I believe this task can be undertaken without recourse to protective legislation and regulation.

The gay rights movement is having its impact on society. Many friendship circles — admittedly most often among the urban and urbane upper middle classes — are integrated along the line of sexual orientation. The process of coming out socially and giving heterosexuals the opportunity to interact with a known homosexual goes a long way toward eradicating barriers. Homosexuals must take the initiative in normalizing such friendship patterns as part of their strategy for breaking down social distance. Yet, it is heartening that many heterosexuals make positive adjustments given the opportunity. I believe this integrative process, slow and frustrating as it may be, is ultimately the best way to assure equality between homosexual and heterosexual people.

My good colleague and I disagree on how best to lessen the disadvantage. I favor the eradication of existing discriminatory laws, policies, and regulations. He favors this as well and, in addition, seeks special protections. The reader will have to decide.

NO

JOHN F. LONGRES

Special legislation and/or protective regulation may be a good idea for other groups, but it is not a good idea when applied to lesbians and gays. In taking this view, I would like to make the important distinction between the need to decriminalize and the need to institute protective legislation and policies. Although they are two sides of the same coin, each side has different implications.

Defining the Context: Decriminalization versus Protective Legislation

As used here, decriminalization means the repeal of all existing laws, policies, and regulations which permit discrimination against homosexuals or homosexual conduct. Conversely, it also means the rejection of any new anti-homosexual policies and laws which may be promoted. It is absolutely necessary to decriminalize homosexual behavior; the law should not intrude upon sexual relations among consenting adults in the privacy of their homes, as it does now in some twenty-four states. Furthermore, laws and policies should not directly or indirectly limit the participation of lesbians and gays in American society. I include here military regulations that forbid openly homosexual men and women from serving in the defense of their country and religious policies that repress homosexual behavior and forbid homosexuals from serving as religious leaders. I also include any regulations that prevent homosexuals from marrying, adopting, and raising children, or working as educators, counselors, and helpers of children. Gays and lesbians ought to put all their political and moral efforts into the eradication of discriminatory laws, policies, and regulations. It is also necessary to challenge the use of homosexuality as a defense in those cases where rights, such as the right to a home, the right to inheritance, and the right to care for sick and infirm partners, are being threatened. That, in the end, will be the major victory that gays and lesbians will need if they are to receive equal treatment under the law, a basic right of citizenship in a democracy.

Protective legislation refers to those laws, policies, or regulations that specifically identify homosexuals as a category of people whose rights must be assured. Examples include recruitment, hiring policies aimed at assuring a homosexual presence in the work place, or assurances that homosexuals cannot be fired merely on the basis of their sexuality. Housing and educational policies that single out homosexuals as a category for special attention also fit in. Protective legislation also includes "hate crime" laws that make a special crime of physically or emotionally harming someone because of his or her sexuality. I do not believe that gays and lesbians need such special legislation to protect them from prejudice and discrimination because that right—once discriminatory legislation is eliminated—is already granted to them in the Constitution. In short, homosexuals should take aim at repealing discriminatory laws, but not at promoting special protective laws.

The Limits of Protective Legislation: Why It Won't Work

There are a number of grounds on which to defend this position. The first is purely strategic. Homosexuals, at least those who are proudly "out," make up much less than 10 percent of all Americans. If they are to gain their equal rights, they need allies among those more than 90 percent who consider themselves heterosexual or are not fully willing to declare themselves homosexual. While some of these people will support homosexuals through thick and thin, others—those on the extreme religious right—are organized to block their every move. The all-important support will have to come from that significant percent of heterosexuals that are neither particularly for nor against gays. How are these heterosexuals to be wooed? Legislation aimed at decriminalization clearly gives the message that gays and lesbians expect their due, no more or less than any other law-abiding, hard-working citizen. Protective legislation gives a different message; it says gays and lesbians want special treatment and special advantages. Even when this is not the case, the fact that it will be interpreted as such by those who are organized against homosexuals creates enough doubt that the majority of heterosexuals will not go out of their way to support protective legislation.

The second reason is financial or economic. The quest for protective legislation puts an extra financial drain on the lesbian and gay community. All too often, when protective legislation is enacted it is met with organized efforts to either repeal or water down the law. People in the state of Oregon are now going through their second referendum on protective legislation. In Wisconsin, the law has been challenged in the courts by religious groups, by a program for delinquent boys, and by a newspaper that has refused to accept gay and lesbian advertisements. As a result, lesbians and gays, or the

State on behalf of them, have had to spend hundreds of thousands of dollars defending the legislation with no assurance of winning. In a tight economy, these important dollars would be better spent on efforts to decriminalize homosexuality, to reinforce the right of equal treatment or, given present needs, to fund research and services for fighting AIDS.

Third, there is concern about possible unintended consequences. Sometimes the noblest of intentions goes wrong. In our zeal for protection we conjure up the image that once a policy is enacted, everyone rallies around it, and the world automatically changes for the better. Reality is often quite different. For instance, the Civil Rights Act of 1964, surely one of the most far-reaching pieces of protective legislation enacted in this century, fed resentment and helped create an enormous backlash, the results of which are more apparent today than ever. Many otherwise liberal Americans drifted to the right in part because of what they believed, rightly or wrongly, was "reverse discrimination." Conservative values became the political rallying point and reactionary elements could blame America's economic, political, and urban woes on readily available minority scape-goats. As for the protected groups, affirmative action and other reforms have had limited success in improving the lot of African Americans, Latino Americans, and Native Americans and have certainly not led to their greater social and physical integration into American society.

Protective legislation for gays and lesbians may also lead to negative unintended consequences. Allan Berube, in describing the evolution of the anti-homosexual military policy, shows that, in part, it was motivated by well-intentioned psychiatric efforts to exclude people who could not be expected to survive the ordeal of combat. Prior to 1944, while prohibiting homosexual behavior, the military did not prohibit homosexuals from serving their country. It was only after Harry Stack Sullivan, a major figure in psychiatry and himself a homosexual, began to work on ways of protect-ing emotionally vulnerable men and women that the idea of excluding homosexuals, as a category of "psychopathic" people, began to surface. Although some psychiatrists and counselors fought the exclusion and strove to protect homosexuals, many others eagerly set about the task of trapping and dishonorably discharging them.

Unintended consequences may reach down to individual homosexuals and constrain the way they think about themselves. For instance, it forces people to live a completely open life and to make one's identification as a homosexual the central feature. While coming out is an important personal and political process, the level of coming out necessary to take advantage of protective legislation may actually pigeon hole people into categories they may not otherwise choose. In terms of sexual orientation, protective legisla-tion encourages people to be either gay or straight. Yet research from Kinsey to the more recent work of Storms has taught us that sexual behavior and fantasy exist on a continuum. Protective legislation works to divide the world into two polar opposite camps of sexuality. Protective legislation also forces people to make their homosexuality more important than other dimensions of their being; gender, race and ethnicity, religion, education, and occupation tend to become secondary or even incidental.

Protective legislation may also negatively affect the psychological well-being of individual homosexuals. The process of bringing a suit or otherwise calling attention to a personal injustice can leave a scar on one's psyche. It is not easy to become embroiled with the police or with attorneys and the court system as a lesbian or gay person. For every hand that is offered in support, many others will be withdrawn or raised in hostility. And just because attention has been called to an injustice, it does not mean that justice will be served. The police are likely to be indifferent to what they will perceive as just one more crime against a homosexual; they might follow the letter of the law but not the spirit of the law. Priorities within police departments as well as attitudes about homosexuals held by individual officers may create a situation whereby calling attention to the problem may be worse than just having lived with it. Working with (or against) attorneys in civil as well as criminal suits may also prove distressing. Attorneys are driven by evidence and by the professional requirement of advocating on behalf of their client. Putting together a case and defending it before a judge or arbitrator will require withstanding a lot of hostile questioning. If the criminal isn't caught, if the civil or criminal case is lost, or if vindication isn't as total as one might wish, the effects can be personally devastating.

I do not mean to suggest in any way that gays and lesbians should refrain from calling attention to injustice or from bringing suits through the court. Certainly if decriminalization is to take place this will have to be done, and the personal consequences associated with this process endured for better or worse. My argument is more limited and directed only at the issue of special legislation. If a case can be brought on other grounds—grounds not rooted in homosexuality but in more universal principles—victims might get just as much redress and contribute as much to the advancement of homosexual rights, but with less personal consequences. For instance, the special crime of "fag bashing" might just as well be handled as the ordinary crime of "assault." Beating up on innocent and defenseless people is a crime which needs to be prosecuted regardless of the sexual orientation of the victim or perpetrator. Or, being fired unjustly may be better handled on work competence grounds, on seniority rights, or on procedural grounds than on the grounds of homosexual rights. There is no need to invent a special crime or a special right when others already exist to cover the situation. Fighting injustice as a citizen—no different from any other—brings pride and dignity to the group. Fighting injustice because homosexuals should receive special protection suggests homosexuals are inferior to other citizens and cannot make it on their own.

Rejoinder to Professor Longres   Norman Wyers

My friend and colleague John Longres makes a series of interesting points in his rejection of the need for what he calls "protective legislation" for gays and lesbians. For him, decriminalization of homosexual activities and behaviors is sufficient for gays and lesbians to achieve full equality in this society. While I fully support the repeal of sodomy laws and any other laws or policies which discriminate against gays and lesbians, I reiterate the absolute necessity of protective legislation. Heterosexism and other forms of prejudice in this society are so extensive and so deeply ingrained that the decriminalization of homosexual activities represents only the first step in the achievement of full citizenship and equality for gays and lesbians.

For example, imagine that all policies that prevent homosexuals from adopting and raising children, or working as educators, counselors, and helpers of children were suddenly repealed. Longres would have us believe that gays and lesbians could then adopt and raise children or work as helping professionals with children. Is he serious? Is he unaware of the negative attitudes held about gays and lesbians by many well-intentioned members of this society? Does he truly believe that the repeal of these anti-homosexual policies would automatically provide the opportunity for gays and lesbians to adopt children or to provide counseling and educational services to them? Repeal of anti-homosexual policies could create a legal neutral zone. But gays and lesbians would not have their stigmatized and despised status altered by this legal neutrality: the *rights* of gays and lesbians to adopt or raise children or to work with children (in any capacity) would then be needed. The same scenario is true for the repeal of any other discriminatory policy. It is one way to begin the quest for rights, but it is not enough by itself.

Gays and lesbians can either accept their lot and try to find a way to adjust to a hostile society, or they can challenge the status quo and press for equal rights. I advocate for the latter approach in the firm belief that rights are requisite for equality and that collective, positive affirmation of gay and lesbian identity can be achieved only through winning rights.

References

Berube, A. (1990). *Coming out under fire: The history of gay men and women in World War II*. New York: Free Press.

Fay, R. E., Turner, C. F., Klassen, A.D., & Gagnon, J. H. (1989). Prevalence and patterns of same-gender sexual contact among men. *Science* (243), 338–48.

Gay Rights National Lobby. (1980). *Does support for gay civil rights spell political suicide?: A close look at some long-held myths.* Washington, D.C.: Gay Rights National Lobby.

Goffman, E. (1963). *Stigma: Notes on the management of spoiled identity.* Englewood Cliffs, NJ: Prentice-Hall, Inc.

Gould, M. (1974). Statutory oppression: An overview of legalized homophobia. In Levine, M. P. (Ed.), *Gay men.* New York: Harper, 51–67.

Lambda Legal Defense and Education Fund, Inc. (1991). *A national summary of anti-discrimination laws: A listing of legal protections for lesbians and gay men re: employment, housing, and public accommodations.* New York: Lambda.

Mohr, R. D. (1988). *Gays/justice: A study of ethics, society, and law.* New York: Columbia University Press.

National Gay and Lesbian Task Force. (1992). *Lesbian and gay civil rights in the U.S.* Washington, D.C.: National Gay and Lesbian Task Force.

No Special Rights Committee. (1992). OCA letter says we are in a war. *Community News: The Capitol Forum,* January, 1.

Storms, M. D. (1980). Theories of sexual orientation. *Journal of Personality and Social Psychology* 38(5), 783–792.

ANNOTATED BIBLIOGRAPHY

Gay Rights National Lobby. (1988). *Does support for gay civil rights spell political suicide? A close look at some long-held myths.* Washington, D.C.: Gay Rights National Lobby.

This monograph reviews the political impact of supporting gay rights legislation on politicians at the federal, state, and local levels. The monograph maintains that contrary to popularly held myths, support for gay rights legislation does not spell political suicide for those elected officials who sponsor or support it.

Mohr, R. D. (1988). *Gays/justice: A study of ethics, society, and law.* New York: Columbia University Press.

Mohr analyzes the ethics and legal issues pertinent to the strengthening of gay civil rights in the United States. His defense of the need for gay civil rights is compelling and brilliantly articulated. He makes a strong case for civil disobedience on the parts of gays and lesbians as they challenge the heterosexism of this society.

Lambda Defense and Education Fund, Inc. (1991). *A national summary of anti-discrimination laws: A listing of legal protections for lesbians and gay men re: employment, housing, and public accommodations.* New York: Lambda.

A collection of protectionist sexual orientation legislation from throughout the United States. Identification is by state, city, and legislative name, number, and date.

National Gay and Lesbian Task Force. (1992). *Lesbian and gay civil rights in the U.S.* Washington, D.C.: National Gay and Lesbian Task Force.

This compilation of lesbian and gay rights legislation provides current data on the United States. Only four states have complete gay and lesbian rights bills, which include public and private employment, public accommodations, education, housing, credit, and union practices. Altogether, 108 cities and counties have enacted some form of legislation to protect the rights of gays and lesbians.

Do Social Workers Have a Major Impact on Social Policy?

EDITOR'S NOTE: Government agencies are primarily responsible for the formulation of social policies, but these policies also emerge through the efforts of legislative representatives, members of the judiciary, and organized political lobbies and professional associations. Although social workers have also contributed to the process of social policy formulation, the extent of the profession's involvement has been debated. Some argue that social workers are more interested in counseling and private practice than wider social and political issues, and that social workers' commitment to social policy is marginal. Other reject this view, claiming that social work has traditionally been a major contributor to the development of sound social policies. The social work profession, they contend, has always used its influence to promote effective social policies designed to promote the welfare of ordinary people.

In this debate, John T. Pardeck, Ph.D., argues YES, that social workers have made a major impact on the formulation of social policy. He is Associate Professor in the Department of Social Work at Southwest Missouri State University, where he teaches social policy and research. He is the author of a number of books on child welfare and over sixty journal articles.

Roland Meinert, Ph.D., takes the opposite point of view, arguing NO, that social workers have not made a major impact on social policy. He is Professor of Social Work and Head of the Department of Social Work at Southwest Missouri State University, and has written extensively about social work education and international social development. He is one of the founders of the Inter-University Consortium for International Social Development and co-editor of the journal *Social Development Issues.*

YES

JOHN T. PARDECK

The social welfare policy-making process can be viewed as having four distinct phases—formulation, legislation, implementation, and evaluation (Karger & Stoesz, 1990). At the formulation stage, the major systems affecting policy development are foundations and think tanks. During the legislative stage, PACs and advocacy groups play a role. At the point of implementation, social workers in agency settings can help insure that policies and programs are implemented properly. Through evaluation, social workers can provide feedback to the policy creators to help insure a program is effective.

Unfortunately, as noted by June Hopps (1986), social workers have lost a great deal of influence in the area of policy development. Some of this can be attributed to the increasing emphasis on clinical social work, which has resulted in a declining interest in community practice. Obviously, community practice is one of the core methods which teaches social workers how to influence social welfare policy. The trend has been for non-social workers, including urban planners, to fill positions traditionally held by social workers in the area of macro-level practice (Brilliant, 1986).

If we look to our history, however, there are numerous examples of social workers who have had a tremendous influence on social policy development. These include such notables as Jane Addams, Harry Hopkins, George Edmund Haynes, and Wilbur Cohen.

Jane Addams was a highly influential leader during the Progressive Era, a social movement that was popular from the early 1900s to the end of World War I. Through her work with the settlement movement, Addams was able to assist numerous oppressed families and individuals. In 1931, Addams received the Nobel Peace Prize for her work.

Harry Hopkins had tremendous influence during the New Deal era. He was the primary architect of the New Deal social programs, including the Social Security Act of 1935. Not only did Hopkins influence domestic social welfare policy, but he also played a critical role in shaping foreign policy during the administration of Franklin D. Roosevelt.

George Edmund Haynes, the first black graduate of the New York School of Philanthropy, was instrumental in the formulation of the National Urban League. Ultimately, the National Urban League played a significant role in the civil rights movement.

Finally, Wilbur Cohen, a social worker, was the Secretary of the Department of Health, Education, and Welfare during the Johnson Administration. Cohen was a vital force in shaping the Great Society programs and had a critical role in the passage of the Medicare and Medicaid programs.

Presently, there are few social workers who rival the influence that Addams, Hopkins, Haynes, and Cohen have had on social welfare policy. However, this does not mean social workers are not playing an important role in social welfare policy development in the 1990s.

Social Work's Impact on Social Policy

Numerous examples of the significant role social workers play at various stages of the policy making process can be identified. While this influence may not be at the levels it once was, it nonetheless remains significant.

At the formulation stage of policy development, a number of think tanks have emerged that employ social workers. The National Center for Social Policy and Practice (NCSPP), which originated with the National Association of Social Workers (NASW), attempts to influence policy through the development of position papers on critical social problems facing American society. Social workers from the NCSPP are often asked to testify at congressional hearings focusing on legislation that affects social policy development.

The Child Welfare League (CWL) and the Children's Defense Fund (CDF) both attempt to influence the formulation of social welfare policy dealing with children and family issues. A number of schools of social work have also created policy centers that serve as think tanks. A goal of these centers is to influence social welfare policy at both the local and national levels. Nonprofit policy centers have also emerged, such as the Progressive Policy Institute.

At the legislative stage of policy development, a number of social workers play a significant role at the national level. These include Barbara Mikulski, a United States Senator from the state of Maryland. Ron Dellums, a congressman from California, has had an impact on national legislation dealing with critical social problems. Throughout the United States there are numerous social workers who serve in elective positions at the local and state levels. No doubt many of these individuals advocate for sound social policies that positively affect people's lives. In fact, the author of this paper ran for school board on several occasions. Through this activity the author was able to move critical issues to the forefront in the community, including improving services for disabled children, recognizing the need for latchkey programs, and increasing resources to the poorer schools within the district. No doubt social workers throughout the United States are involved in this kind of political social work practice.

Also, during the legislative stage of policy development, numerous social workers have a significant influence on social welfare policy through PACs and advocacy activities. For example, the Coalition for America's Children (CAC), the Child Welfare League (CWL), and other collaborating organizations are actively attempting to influence voters and candidates for elective offices as well as legislators at all levels of government to address social policy issues related to the health, education, and security of America's children. These organizations use forums, polls, media events, and public education projects as ways to inform people who can influence policy related to children. Social workers are an intricate part of these efforts that ultimately influence policy makers.

The point at which social workers have the greatest impact on social welfare policy is during the implementation stage. Throughout the United States, social workers employed within the human services arena do help to insure that social welfare policy works effectively.

Social workers are well aware of the fact that the enactment and implementation of a social policy are two separate issues. In the area of public policy, government often fails to include adequate authority, funding, and personnel to achieve program goals. This is a reoccurring problem in policy implementation. It is also not unusual for a government policy to be enacted but not enforced. Numerous states, for example, have mental health institutions operating under court supervision because judges have agreed with social advocates that the institution is not in compliance with the law (Karger & Stoesz, 1990). Furthermore, if we look back to the 1980s, a concerted effort was made by the Reagan presidency not to enforce the civil rights laws. As advocates, social workers play a critical role in insuring that positive policies are implemented, while negative ones are contested.

An example of this is the role social workers play on a daily basis influencing how the Education for All Handicapped Children Act (Public Law 94-142) is implemented. This law gives parents of disabled children numerous rights; however, they often do not know about these rights. Under PL 94-142, parents can request an independent evaluation of their child at the expense of the school district. Parents also have a right to inspect all school records and test results on their child and to obtain copies of these records. Parents of disabled children can request a due process hearing if they disagree with the school district's decision regarding their child. Most importantly, under PL 94-142, school districts must provide special services to disabled children. Social workers in school and child welfare settings play a major role in insuring that disabled children receive services they are entitled to under national policy.

The most recent disabilities legislation, the Americans with Disabilities Act of 1990 (ADA), will also require strong advocacy to insure implementation. The ADA is constructed in such a fashion that the law will be enforced on a case-by-case basis. Social workers will play a significant role in the enforcement of the ADA.

A final example from the field of child welfare is the active role social workers have in the implementation of the Adoption Assistance and Child Welfare Act of 1980 (Public Law 96-272). This law establishes operational requirements for states receiving federal funds. The basic level at which social workers influence PL 96-272 is through insuring that the law is implemented appropriately throughout the child welfare system. Implementation includes making every effort to reunify children with their families, writing case plans for children and their families, and placing children in the least restrictive, most family-like setting possible.

As is well known, PL 96-272 has not received appropriate funding, among other issues, at the federal and state levels. Social workers have played an intricate role in insuring that the law is properly implemented through lawsuits (Granda, 1992). Over the last decade, 60 cases in 26 states have been filed. Some of these cases have gone all the way to the Supreme Court. In fact, class action and other related law suits may be one of the most effective strategies used by social workers to influence social welfare policy at the implementation stage of policy development. Such a strategy is within the boundaries of traditional social work practice.

Social workers can play a significant role in the final evaluation phase of policy development. During this stage, important feedback is provided to policy makers concerning the effectiveness of a given policy. Throughout the United States, social workers in local, state, and federal agencies provide important feedback on policy effectiveness. An excellent example of how social workers can influence national policy through the evaluation stage involves studies conducted by social workers on the foster care system during the 1970s.

Fanshel and Shinn (1978) conducted an extensive study on the foster care system in the state of New York. They discovered that many beliefs about the foster care system were myths. One critical finding of their study was the relationship between visits by biological parents and children leaving foster care. They found that foster children who are visited by parents exit care earlier. This important finding has influenced the foster care system throughout the United States; that is, visitation by biological parents is an integral part of most case plans of children in foster care.

Shyne and Schroeder's (1978) evaluation of the national foster care system has helped shape state and national policy. For example, all foster children must have a case plan, regular court reviews, and placement in the least restrictive, most family-like environment. Shyne and Schroeder's findings played a major role in mandating these requirements.

Finally, even though social workers have had a greater impact in past decades on social welfare policy, we still play a significant role at various stages of the policy development process. As social workers rediscover the importance of community practice and other macro-level practice activities, our impact on social welfare policy will increase.

Rejoinder to Professor Pardeck ROLAND MEINERT

An examination of the response of Dr. Pardeck to the question of whether social workers have a major impact on social policy reveals a very well-reasoned description of the policy process. He takes us through the distinct phases of policy formulation, legislation, implementation, and evaluation. He also identifies individual social workers and social welfare organizations who have been involved at each level. Professor Pardeck does not, however, make a persuasive case that the impact of social workers has been a major one. That is because he is at a disadvantage in the debate, since there are more compelling reasons to answer the question in the negative than in the positive.

It should be noted that Dr. Pardeck does not accord social workers a major role in the first two phases of the social welfare policy process, which include the formulation of basic social welfare policy and its enactment in legislation. He sees them as more involved in the later phases of implementation and evaluation. I agree with this view. It is clear that social workers have played a limited role in the basic activity of developing policy initiatives and bringing them to fruition. On the other hand, they have been responders to social welfare policy by carrying out policy decisions and by evaluating their worth in organizational settings. In this regard social workers remain in a reactive mode rather than as shapers of the basic directions social welfare policy is to take.

Pardeck does identify several social workers who have had a tremendous influence on social policy development. Indeed, persons such as Jane Addams and Harry Hopkins did have a major impact on social welfare policy in the United States. However, it should be noted that their impact occurred in an earlier era and that they are not contemporaries. The two social workers highlighted as currently active on the social welfare policy scene are both elected political officials. One wonders whether the impact of these two congresspersons arises from their social work roles or their political ones.

It appears to me that Dr. Pardeck would support my dual contention: (1) social workers function primarily as reactors, implementers, and evaluators of social welfare policies; and (2) they engage in this activity at smaller system levels (micro) more so than at larger ones (macro). It appears that Professor Pardeck also agrees with me about the negative effect of the clinical social work movement on social policy formulation, and about the necessity to encourage more social workers to become involved in community practice. Even though it is important that some social workers deal with the private troubles of individuals, if they are to become involved in the early phases of the policy process, they must also become more active in public and community issues. Finally, I think my task of debating how social workers do not have a major impact on social policy was inherently a much easier one than Pardeck's was of arguing how they do. More persuasive arguments are available to debate the con side than the pro side.

NO

ROLAND MEINERT

Cogent arguments can be made for both sides of the question as to whether social work has a significant and measurable impact on social policy. In the main, however, there are many more compelling reasons to conclude that social workers do not have a significant impact on social policy than there are to believe that they do. Undeniably, social workers have strongly held philosophical and value positions that serve as a foundation for policy objectives, and they oftentimes pursue them with vigor. But, their success rate in bringing these efforts to fruition is quite low. Policy analysts from other fields assert that social workers are basically reactors to social policies that have been created and implemented by others, while recognizing that there are a few rare instances in which they have developed them. The arguments in support of the belief that social workers have little impact on social policy development are discussed below.

The Limited Impact of Social Workers on Social Policy

In order to measurably impact social policy, with the emphasis on "social," it would require some tightening of the boundaries of the domain in which social workers function. Social work now cuts across more fields of human service than any other profession, including but not limited to mental health, families, children, health, corrections, developmental disabilities, and substance abuse. While it is recognized that social work exerts some effort to impact policy in each of the discrete fields, the overall influence and impact of the profession in the larger social and political sphere is minimal. Social work has gone through several developmental cycles of philosophical and political convergence, followed by ones of divisiveness and separation. The net result of such fluctuation has been an inability to bring the total resources and influence of the profession to bear on any one issue that cuts across the variable fields.

The modest success that social work has had in affecting social policy change has been at the micro-level (agency and local community), as compared to the macro-level (statewide agencies and federal government). This means, for example, that in a large human service organization, social work is more likely to have an impact on policies affecting day-to-day operational procedures and less so on those pertaining to program development or the basic philosophical and policy orientation of the organization. The major human service organizations in the country—state departments of social service and mental health—in most instances have chief executive officers and top administrators who are drawn from disciplines other than social work. Social workers are frequently found at the second and third administrative levels in these departments, but that distances them from the governor, the legislature, and other state power brokers. This separation prevents social workers from direct and intimate participation in the activities and discussions where fundamental policy priorities and initiatives are decided. As Figure 7.1 illustrates, social workers do have a policy impact on procedural activities in small systems more so than they do on basic policy directions in larger systems (Patti, 1974). As a general rule the impact of social work is more likely to occur in the area below and to the left of the diagonal line than above and to the right of it.

FIGURE 7.1   POLICY IMPACT OF SOCIAL WORK[1]

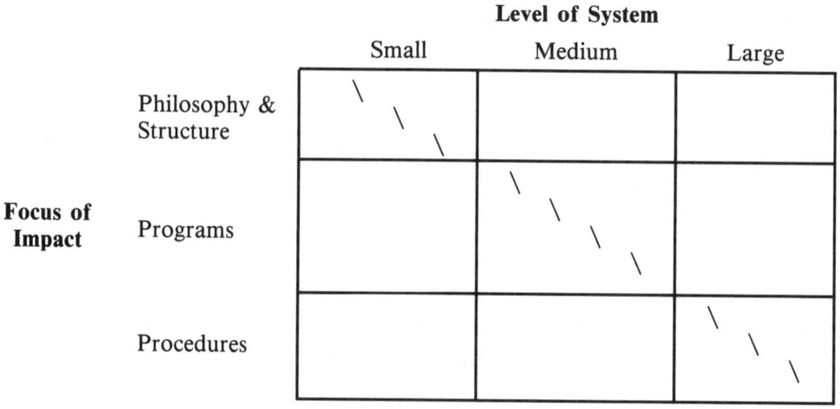

Why Social Workers Don't Have
a Major Impact on Social Policy

It is indisputable that with a membership of over 130,000, the National Association of Social Workers (NASW) both nominally and functionally represents many of the professional social workers in the United States. The association pursues policy objectives, and through its state chapters and national headquarters in Washington, D.C., actively lobbies at the state as well as the national level. When the policy positions NASW has supported and advocated are closely examined, a distinct pattern with two trends is evident. The first reveals that when NASW acts in a policy proactive and assertive fashion, it does so in a manner that is mainly self-serving for its membership and not for its traditional clientele. Over the past decade the two consistently pursued objectives of the organization have been social work licensure and obtaining authorization to receive third-party payments. It is difficult to argue how these objectives are directed to benefit the traditional recipients of social work services and not primarily toward meeting the self-interests of NASW members. In fact, licensure and third-party payments are two of the most recent steps in the fifty-year struggle on the part of social work to achieve full professional status and comparability with other more valued fields such as psychiatry and psychology. While social work has devoted effort to achieve licensure and third-party payments, it has not expended an equal amount of energy to bring about outcomes of more benefit to its clientele such as national health insurance and welfare reform. Social work certainly has associated itself with other groups pursuing these objectives, but reasonable observers would conclude that it has not assumed a primary leadership role in the arena of impacting major social policies such as these.

Few would argue with the assertion that the central elements pervading the process of policy formulation, enactment, and implementation are political in nature. For nineteen of the past twenty-three years the Republican party has occupied the presidency, and over this span of time social work has been aligned with the opposition Democratic party. This alignment includes a total and unquestioned acceptance of the intellectual, moral, and ideological tenets of liberalism. Indeed, throughout the period, the Democratic party has been the political mechanism by which liberal positions have been articulated, and social work has consistently remained politically correct in its adherence to the party's liberal political principles. This induces in social work a condition of bounded rationality in terms of examining the policy positions that might be considered and adopted. It is rare when social work is able to objectively and rationally examine policy proposals for social welfare that emanate from Republicans and conservatives. These simply do not fit into the acceptable conceptual boundaries of social work's institutional mindset, and there are two negative policy consequences because of it. The first is an out-of-hand rejection of policies proposed by the Republican/conservative camp simply on the basis of their ideological origin and not on their merit. The second is that by placing themselves unalterably outside the national presidential party of dominance, social workers have few opportunities to participate in the national policy process. As a result they are not in a position to modify and alter policies in the process of development.

Social work, rather than being a science-based profession, is, therefore, an ideologically based one. Like all professions it is by nature composed of both science and ideology. Most mature professions are, however, more science than ideology, while social work tends more toward ideology than science. As long as the balance is in this direction, it is unlikely that social work will be a serious player on the national policy scene. Even in recent times when the country had liberal presidents as in the Kennedy/Johnson and Carter eras, social workers remained distant from the halls of power. During those times they were not in positions to influence policy and were far removed from Congress and state legislatures. Even when liberalism becomes the ascendent philosophy of power, the generally low esteem in which the public at large holds the profession of social work will keep it relatively powerless. It is also unlikely that social work will become more influential until it becomes more politically adept. In one state NASW provided moral and financial support for a liberal Democratic candidate for a major state office through the chapter political action committee (PACE—Political Action for Candidate Election). After the election NASW expected that she would provide leadership in getting a social work licensure bill passed. Their hopes were dashed when they learned that she was opposed to it as well as any additional licensure in the state.

It has become clear that the interest groups achieving dominance in social work are those in the "clinical" camp. These professionals focus their intellectual and technological resources and skills on the individual client and his/her psychological, behavioral, and interactional adjustment. This focus is supported by the professional education social workers receive at both undergraduate and graduate levels, where students learn more about how to work with the private troubles of individuals than they do about public issues and problems facing the entire society. There is a common way in which policies in the human services develop. In simplest form, a problem is identified, a policy about it is developed, and organizational structures and programs are created to deal with it. If social work identifies concerns related to individual problems, it is reasonable to predict follow-up with policies, structures, and programs that will be oriented to that level. When that occurs, social work does become an actor in the policy process, but the result is not policies that deal with larger social development issues. This induces social work to function as a remedial and residual profession, whereby it deals with the sequela of individual maladjustment rather than with issues of creating a society and environment in which the person can achieve higher and more productive levels of human functioning.

Conclusion

A reasonable and objective analysis leads to the conclusion that social work as a profession has only had a minimal impact on the major social policy issues being formulated and determined in the realm of human services. To argue otherwise would be distorting the reality of the extent to which contemporary social work influences social policy. There are five major reasons for this conclusion:

1. The operational and functional boundaries of social work are very expansive and include more domains of service provision than any other human service profession. This results in social policy efforts in all of them, but only minimal expenditure of resources on a single issue involving them all.

2. The splitting of the profession, with its resultant lack of power, predictably relegates its policy successes to the organizational and community levels and not to the state and nation.

3. The institution of social work is embodied more by the National Association of Social Workers than by any other entity. This group has a long history of pursuing policies mainly of benefit to its membership (licensing and third-party payments), rather than ones benefitting the socially and economically deprived who constitute its traditional clientele.

4. Social work has allied itself with the philosophical, intellectual, moral, and ideological features of modern liberalism. This places it out of the mainstream, which has moved toward the conservative political end. It is politically correct for social workers to remain in the liberal camp at a time when basic social welfare policies are being made outside that tradition. Thus they are prevented from considering policy innovations outside that framework.

5. The majority of social work practitioners, as well as social work students, aspire to clinically oriented careers. Only a minority express interest in social work practice at levels beyond the individual, family, and small group. Given this critical mass of direct service workers, it is unlikely they will become actively involved in policy issues that cut across entire populations and problem areas and that are focused on the social development and human betterment of an entire society.

NOTES

1. The diagram in Figure 7.1 is based on the insights developed by Rino Patti. These insights are then applied to the discussion of social work's lack of impact on social policy development at larger levels. It also explains the success achieved by social work at lower levels.

Rejoinder to Professor Meinert JOHN PARDECK

Professor Meinert and I agree on a number of issues related to the impact that social workers have on social policy. Like Meinert, I feel our emphasis on clinical social work over community practice has weakened our impact on social policy. Furthermore, I agree that the overemphasis on clinical practice has resulted, at times, in very narrow policy efforts, those typically being licensure and third-party payment. However, in order for social work to continue its professional development, these are important short term goals that need to be achieved.

I do part with Dr. Meinert, however, on a number of important points concerning our impact on social policy. Even though social workers are often not the players who originate social policy, we certainly play a vital role in affecting how social policy is implemented. On this point I can speak from personal experience. Throughout my career as a professional social work educator, I have seen countless examples of national, state, and local social policies simply not implemented in the communities in which I have lived. Through personal advocacy efforts in these communities, including working with the OCR (Office of Civil Rights), I have seen dramatic positive changes in the treatment of oppressed people. My hunch is that many of the 130,000 members of the National Association of Social Workers (NASW) are involved in similar efforts throughout the United States.

I also disagree with Professor Meinert that somehow social work's liberal orientation has made us less effective in influencing social policy. Even though the presidency over the last decade was held by conservatives, many members of Congress continue to advocate for liberal social welfare policy. In fact, the Americans with Disabilities Act (ADA) and the new Civil Rights Legislation of 1991 are both policies that are extremely liberal and yet ultimately became national social policy. This occurred even though a conservative president opposed each law.

Finally, Dr. Meinert implies that social work must become more scientific in order to impact social policy. I agree that such is the case. However, to suggest that social policies such as those advocated by the Republican Party are scientific is less than accurate. What conservative social policy has brought us is an increase in poverty, homelessness, and even Ted Turner offering to operate the state of Georgia's prison system based on the premise that he could run it more effectively. The corruption and inefficiency of conservative social policy will pass. In due course, we will grow up as a nation and finally realize that all post-industrial societies need a highly developed social welfare state based on sound social policy. Such an institution provides for all people, including children and families in need at all levels of society. The entire developed world already realizes this; in due course we will also. Social workers will no doubt continue to play an important role in this social development.

REFERENCES

Brilliant, E. (1986). Social work leadership: A missing ingredient. *Social Work* (31), 328.

Fanshel, D., & Shinn, E. (1978). *Children in foster care: A longitudinal investigation*. New York: Columbia University Press.

Granda, M. (1992). Courts of last resort: Litigation and child welfare. *Children's Voice* (1), 26–27.

Hopps, J. (1986). Reclaiming leadership. *Social Work* (31)5, 323.

Karger, H., & Stoesz, D. (1990). *American social welfare policy*. New York: Longman.

Patti, R. (1974). Organizational resistance and change: The view from below. *Social Service Review* (48)3, 367–383.

Shyne, A., & Schroeder, A. (1978). *National study of social services to children and their families*. Washington, D.C.: Children's Bureau.

ANNOTATED BIBLIOGRAPHY

Patti, R. (1974). Organizational resistance and change: The view from below. *Social Service Review* 48(3), 367–383.

Patti contends that social workers occupy low power positions in organizations and that this diminishes their capacity to bring about changes in procedures, programs, and policies.

Schwartz, E. (1977). Macro social work: A practice in search of some theory. *Social Service Review* 51(2), 207–227.

Schwartz argues that the profession of social work has gone through recurring periods of "splitting" and "lumping." In the former, effort is directed toward differentiating and specifying its function and focus, while in the latter it adopts a more generalized and unspecified role. This dialectic-type process has resulted in a sounder theoretical base for direct practice (clinical work), but has left voids at the macro level (larger systems).

Is Privatization a Positive Trend in Social Services?

EDITOR'S NOTE: With the ascendancy of radical right wing ideology, the idea that governments should provide social services for the population has been vigorously attacked. Critics of government involvement in social welfare claim that public social services are bureaucratic and wasteful. Unlike commercial enterprises which must be competitive to survive, governmental organizations have no incentive to be efficient. It is for this reason that citizens everywhere complain bitterly about the quality of public services. Privatization is widely touted as an effective alternative. Although proponents of privatization claim that commercial social service enterprises are more efficient and offer better value for money than government, supporters of government social services contend that the profit motive does not provide a suitable basis for meeting human needs. Social programs should be regarded as collective goods to be provided for all citizens in need, irrespective of their ability to pay. Supporters argue that the government, rather than the business community, is the best agency for providing these services.

The question of privatization is examined by David Stoesz, DSW, who argues YES, that privatization is a positive trend for the social services. Dr. Stoesz is Professor of Social Work at San Diego State University. He has published in leading social work and social policy journals and is the author of *American Social Welfare Policy* (1990), Longman (with Howard Karger); and *Reconstructing the American Welfare State* (1992), Rowman and Littlefield (with Howard Karger).

Howard Jacob Karger, Ph.D., disagrees, arguing NO, that privatization is not a positive trend for the social services. Dr. Karger is Professor of Social Work at Louisiana State University. He has published numerous articles and books including *Sentinels of Order* (1987), University Press of America; *Social Workers and Labor Unions* (1988), Greenwood; *American Social Welfare Policy* (1990), Longman (with David Stoesz); and *Reconstructing the American Welfare State* (1992), Rowan and Littlefield (with David Stoesz).

YES

DAVID STOESZ

Privatization has become an issue in social welfare, although paradoxically, the private sector has been an institutional fixture in the United States since well before the creation of the American welfare state. While critics of the private sector would prefer to characterize it as a nostalgic artifact of noblesse oblige and an obstruction to social justice, in fact many of the most innovative developments in American social welfare are occurring under the auspices of the private sector. Consider the following:

1. *Virtually all social change originates in the private sector.* Social movements that have benefitted labor, women, African Americans, and Hispanics are oriented around such organizations as the AFL-CIO, NOW, the NAACP, and La Raza—all private nonprofit organizations. In those instances where there is insufficient public support to legislate social programs and insufficient profit to lure the commercial sector, the voluntary sector serves an essential function: it allows groups to legitimize and seek redress for their grievances.

2. *The next generation of graduate social workers expect to work in the private sector because it offers superior professional opportunities.* Eventually, most of these students expect to become private practitioners because this form of practice allows them more autonomy and income than conventional settings for social work. Significantly, private practice can be customized to fit the needs of female practitioners who have found the public social services incompatible with their priorities.

3. *In some instances, essential human service programming would not be available had not the private sector undertaken them.* When local government is unwilling to raise taxes to finance needed correctional services — services too expensive for voluntary groups to consider — correctional corporations have been willing to do so. Many American communities are so conservative that abortions would not be available unless commercial ventures were willing to provide reproductive health services.

In a democratic-capitalist political economy, such as the United States, it is as inevitable as it is desirable that the private sector be an active participant in social policy. As a result, a substantial amount of social welfare in the United States is provided under nongovernmental auspices. To that extent, American social welfare has already been privatized. The United Way, for example, has provided important services through thousands of affiliates in virtually every American city for decades. By now we have enough experience to generalize that experiments in governmental service provision have proven less satisfactory than when the same service is contracted through the private sector. Few would argue that Section 8 housing vouchers are superior to the public housing gulags built during the 1950s. Few would argue that the Medicare program's reliance on the private sector affords health care superior to that provided through the Veteran's Administration.

So, what's the brouhaha about "privatization"? Much of the fuss is the result of a rearguard polemic fashioned by liberals who are disappointed about the limits of the governmental welfare state compounded by the irresponsible manipulation of the issue by the far right in order to decimate social programs during the Reagan presidency. Under these circumstances, it is not surprising that "privatization" has come to have explosive implications in the welfare debate. Welfare state liberals would do themselves a favor by acknowledging that government provision of service is not optimal given private alternatives. Few welfare state liberals would choose to live in a public housing project to meet their housing needs, nor would they call the social services division at the local welfare department to get help for a personal problem. For their part, pro-privatization conservatives should recognize that much welfare has already been privatized. It is doubtful that much more welfare could be contracted out to the private sector simply because it doesn't seem profitable. To expect the nonprofit sector to compensate for reductions in governmental welfare effort is impractical to anyone who has looked at the problems closely.

Conclusion

For social workers, the moral of the privatization tale is to become more creative about exploiting the private sector, rather than negatively reacting to it. Social workers would better invest their time conceiving of hybrid service delivery forms than continuing the debate about public social services versus private practice. Let's be real—the public social services are *not* social workers' first choice of employment for very valid reasons. On the other hand, clinical workers must have had a reason for getting into social work in the first place, as opposed to counseling or psychology. Social service administrators would better master the information systems used by the corporate sector than grouse about having poor clients dumped on them. (Tell me, how many administrative social workers could hold their own going nose-to-nose with a peer from the private sector? Anyway, how is it that some private firms do great business off publicly insured clients?) Finally, policy analysts and program advocates could begin to conceive of a more pluralistic response to social problems than assuming that the state is the best instrument with which to remediate problems.

Sorry, folks, but the days of leveraging social programs by making every problem a "federal case" are over. Rumor has it that the model welfare states of Europe are backpeddling on their commitments to social programs, and the collectivist solution fancied by the nations of the second world has disintegrated along with their governments.

If the "privatization" issue is discomforting for social workers, it is probably because it strikes at some vulnerable points. Rather than react defensively—denying a validity that is implicit in the message—social work could use it as an opportunity to fashion creative responses to social problems, to become administratively adept at managing resources, and to become more sophisticated in launching welfare initiatives.

Rejoinder to Professor Stoesz   HOWARD JACOB KARGER

Although I agree on many points with my close friend and colleague, David Stoesz, we part company on the issue of privatization. First, Dr. Stoesz argues that "the private sector has been an institutional fixture in the United States since well before the creation of the American welfare state." I think that perhaps he is confusing the voluntary nonprofit sector with the relatively new for-profit corporate sector. This is forgivable. However, how can he argue that virtually all social change originates in the private sector? Were FDR's work programs (the forerunners of CETA, Job Corps, etc.) a private sector activity? Did Social Security or AFDC originate in the private sector? Where was the private sector when America was languishing in the midst of the Great Depression? Does he forget that the private voluntary sector was one of the most reactionary organizations in the early Depression? In fact, the voluntary sector was so reactionary that the American Red Cross actually returned a million dollar check to Herbert Hoover, saying that it was opposed to federal help for social services. They probably rejected it, muttering something about public relief weakening the moral fiber of Americans.

The problem with Professor Stoesz's argument is that he mixes apples and oranges. For one, he is speaking about the voluntary and for-profit sectors as if they were one entity. The truth is that not only are they separate entities, but their interests are often diametrically opposed. Moreover, it is the private for-profit sector that has been cannibalizing the voluntary sector, especially in important areas like hospitals, home health care, and counseling services.

It is obvious that voluntary nonprofit organizations have made important contributions to the welfare sector, especially in the areas of family therapy, AIDS counseling and hospices, recreation services, and so forth. However, what important contributions have been made by for-profit human service corporations? Have these profit-making corporations eased the pain of the unemployed or single parents worried about feeding their families? Have they helped AIDS or cancer patients inch toward a more dignified death? Have they provided recreation services for poor kids wandering through America's urban junkyards? The answer, of course, is "no." Instead, these for-profit human service corporations extol the virtues of the marketplace while they gorge themselves at the public trough.

Professor Stoesz makes the point that private for-profit corporations have made themselves useful by providing abortions in areas that would not otherwise be served. Where are these exemplary corporations, at least in terms of America's smaller towns and cities where abortions are virtually unavailable? In fact, the areas served by for-profits are mainly in metropolitan areas where women already have a wide range of choices for abortions. One can accuse for-profit corporations of many things, but they cannot be accused of being courageous or being on the cutting edge of social change.

Finally, Professor Stoesz admonishes social workers to exploit the opportunities presented by privatization. Is this not akin to presenting awards to social workers for providing blankets to concentration camp inmates? Making the best out of a bad situation only legitimizes the situation, it doesn't change the essential reality. Perhaps the basic strength and the basic weakness of social work have always been to "make the best out of a bad situation." Dr. Stoesz suggests that we continue that time-honored tradition. I suggest that we fight against privatization.

NO

HOWARD JACOB KARGER

The privatization of social services is one of the most important trends in human services since the inception of the American welfare state in 1935. Moreover, it is an international phenomenon that is occurring in most parts of the developed and developing world, including such diverse places as the

United Kingdom, the Philippines, and the West Indies. At least in the United States, privatization has made important inroads in such areas as mental health (including the growth of private practice in social work), mental retardation, chemical dependency, nursing homes, home health care, hospitals, and even corrections (Stoesz and Karger, 1991).

Before beginning this debate, however, it is necessary to define what is meant by the privatization of social services. The privatization of social services refers to the separation of governmental funding from governmental provision of human services. Specifically, while government continues to fund social services, it absolves itself of the responsibility to directly provide them. Hence, government may choose to solicit bids for the provision of specific services (e.g., chemical dependency treatment, the establishment of a battered women's shelter, etc.), or it may directly contract with a private for-profit or voluntary nonprofit agency. In either case, government retains the responsibility for funding and regulating services, even though it does not actually directly deliver them (Karger and Stoesz, 1990).

Why Privatizing Social Services Won't Work

While on the surface privatizing social services may seem somewhat unimportant, at least compared to deep budget cuts, its implications for the welfare state are profound. Perhaps one of the foremost concerns in privatizing social services is a moral question. Given the American obsession with economic growth and international competitiveness, the moral implications of social policy decisions are often submerged in a cold economic bath. Questions such as "Is it morally correct to allow for-profit companies to make a profit off the hardship of others?" seem almost anachronistic in a society obsessed with creating a cheap public sector. Nevertheless, for some of us the ethics of prospering off the hardships and the problems of others seem parasitic and morally reprehensible. Moreover, the desire to make a profit from mental retardation, mental and physical illness, domestic abuse and so forth, represents some of the most egregious aspects of capitalism. It is greed at its worst.

Some supporters of privatized social services argue that morality has little to do with good economics or good social policy. For them, the adoption of a free market represents the establishment of a natural order that transcends extant moral principles. Others argue that social policy should not only be informed by higher moral principles, it should be led by them. Apart from the knotty moral problems inherent in the privatization of social services, supporters predicate their arguments on several assumptions.

First, most supporters of privatization argue that private is always more efficient than public (Kuttner, 1986). Many of these people also argue that for-profit is always more efficient than nonprofit. Although on the surface this assumption appears to be plausible, it nevertheless remains untested. When the Institute of Medicine of the National Academy of Sciences tested this hypothesis they concluded that "there is no evidence to support the common belief that investor-owned organizations are less costly or more efficient than not-for-profit organizations (Gray & McNerney, 1986, p. 525). Moreover, anyone who has had extensive dealings with IBM, General Motors, or any number of large corporations knows that superior service is not always an intrinsic part of for-profit corporations.

Supporters also claim that privatization will lead to cheaper and better services. This is predicated on the belief that the competition inherent in privatization will introduce better management and corporate efficiencies, which in turn, will result in better services at lower prices. While this philosophy may work in a normal market characterized by elastic demand, the human services are a different breed of cat. First, one is hard pressed to imagine that someone facing serious cardiac surgery will do cost-based comparison shopping when choosing a hospital. Or, that someone recently diagnosed with cancer will defer treatment in anticipation that prices for chemotherapy will fall, or that they'll be able to save enough money to afford treatment later on. Moreover, few people will stave off mental illness until the local clinic runs a "January white sale" on therapy. The economic principles at work in human services are simply not the same principles that dominate the normal marketplace. Unlike the marketplace, decisions about health and human service needs are not made by market savvy "rational consumers." Instead, most decisions about human services are made by clients or families that are in crisis and who have neither the time nor the energy to consult *Consumers Report* to find the best product at the best price. Thus, a major precept of the market—the rational, informed consumer who is able to make leisurely choices among a variety of products—is absent when it comes to human services. Most human service decisions are made by psychologically, emotionally, or economically captive populations. By no stretch of the imagination is social services a marketplace where normal market rules apply.

Second, true competition is based on real competitiveness between and within markets. However, social service agencies (whether for-profit, public, or nonprofit) do not compete directly against each other for the consumer's dollar. In most cases, reimbursement rates and/or per capita client costs are negotiated directly with a governmental unit (federal, state, local) or a voluntary non-profit funding agency such as United Way. Hence, pure competition in the sense of six vegetable vendors each competing against each other for the customer's dollar, simply does not apply to highly complex human service markets. In fact, if market principles actually affected the cost of social services, then we would be able to see real reductions in costs (e.g., the tumbling of computer prices since the late

1980s), at least where social service privatization has been most active. Yet, an examination of social service budgets reveals the opposite: the cost of providing social services and health care has increased dramatically during the 1980s and 1990s. In most instances, this increase has outpaced the relative growth of inflation, especially in the health care area.

Proponents also claim that privatization will give consumers more and better choices. In effect, these proponents argue that the social choice found in normal consumer markets—automobiles, stereos, restaurants, etc.— should be applied to human services. First, clients often have choices between facilities, doctors, treatment centers, and so forth, even in the most rigid state-provided social services. Second, it is questionable whether consumers can or will make appropriate decisions given a plethora of choices in social services. Moreover, the range of social services that are presently available—private, public, nonprofit, religious, secular, and so forth— already form an almost impenetrable maze for many clients. Adding more service providers will only make that maze seem even more impenetrable. Finally, creating more choices is not synonymous with creating better choices. Unlike the private marketplace, more social service vendors does not necessarily mean cheaper prices, more efficiency, or better cost containment.

Thus, if authentic competition and normal market forces are irrelevant, then what is the *raison d'être* for privatizing social services? It appears that the real engine driving privatization is not simply economic efficiency, but ideology. In other words, privatization is congruent with a free market orientation that stresses the maximization of profits across the widest social landscape possible. In that sense, corporate investment in human services represents a secure investment in one of the last untapped markets in America. It also represents capitalism's continuing search for new and expanding markets.

The Dangers of Privatization

Whatever gains that may accrue because of privatization pale in contrast to its negative consequences. For one, privatization may lead to the commodification of human need. In other words, to maximize organizational efficiencies, corporations will be encouraged to treat human need as a commodity. Hence, human need is not simply viewed as a condition warranting concern, attention, and intervention, but a marketable commodity to be exploited and mass marketed to prospective customers. To accomplish this, social services must be commercialized in order to create the perception that the client *must* have their product. The danger of commodification is illustrated by the aggressive advertising campaigns started by some private mental health corporations. These powerful television advertisements hawk everything from bulimia, anorexia, and depression to family violence and alcoholism. All the consumer has to do is call the 800 toll-free number for details and the location of the nearest treatment center.

The second danger in privatization is the problem of "creaming." Specifically, "creaming" refers to the practice of caring for clients who have less serious problems and who have the ability to pay. Clients with chronic problems that are under public sponsorship are referred to governmental agencies. Thus, public hospitals become the social dumping ground for the poor and chronically ill who are not covered by private insurance (Friedman, 1984). As the caseload of difficult patients increases in overcrowded and underfunded public hospitals, the quality of care goes down. This adds to society's perception of public hospitals as hospices rather than hospitals.

The third danger in privatization is the creation of human service oligopolies. Like their cohorts in the industrial sector, human service corporations have a tendency to acquire other firms in order to expand into new markets or to eliminate competition (Stoesz & Karger, 1991). This trend has been especially evident in the nursing home and health care industries. The danger of oligopolies is that they may become monopolies that will eventually control prices and dictate the terms and conditions of service. As their economic power grows, their political power follows suit. Thus, it is not difficult to envision large human service corporations that not only contravene public policy but actually make it. In the context of this kind of political and economic power, the ability of government to regulate services will likely diminish. Moreover, the implementation of expensive regulatory procedures may fade as public budgets become tighter and the middle class becomes resigned to receiving its services through private channels.

Perhaps the greatest danger of privatization is the possibility that it will further exacerbate a dual welfare system. The scenario goes something like this. In a highly stratified welfare system, the middle class will only use private social services while the poor will be relegated to using inferior public services. As human service corporations displace the role of both the public and voluntary nonprofit sectors, they will begin to command the allegiance of the middle class who will then define human services within a corporate context. This trend will further weaken the political and economic support for governmental programs that serve those unable to gain access to corporate human services. The more these governmental services are used exclusively by the poor, the less allegiance they will receive from the middle classes. As more resources are channeled into the corporate human service sector, governmental programs will wither and become more stigmatized. As this happens, vulnerable publicly sponsored social services become an easy target for budgetary cuts. Moreover, as public services deteriorate in terms of coverage and quality, the middle class will avoid them in greater numbers, thereby leading to even more stigmatization. This cycle will eventually culminate in a publicly sponsored social service system that is so desiccated it will simply collapse from its own weight.

While it obvious that there is a need to make social services more accountable, more efficient, and more cost sensitive, privatization is not the answer. In the end, privatizing social services will only lead to higher costs, less accountability, and more insensitivity to the needs of clients for whom the services are most essential. Privatization is an idea whose time has come, and, hopefully, will soon pass.

Rejoinder to Professor Karger David Stoesz

As would be expected, Professor Karger has done us a service by pointing out some of the hazards of privatization; but, like so many die-hard welfare statists, his head remains firmly planted in the sand. What seems to elude so many from the left is that privatization offers considerable promise to a profession that has wallowed in irrelevance for the last several decades. But, recalling an old professor's dictum—"nobody said the client has to get better"—I shall try, one more time, to address Karger's concerns.

Social innovations originate in the private sector. This is because public policy requires the agreement of elected officials, people who are unlikely to subsidize ventures with taxpayers' funds until the ventures are demonstrated to be of value. Behind virtually every public social welfare initiative a private sector predecessor can be found. To be sure, much of what is known as public policy exists because government has adopted private initiatives and extended benefits to the public. In many of the more successful programs, government decides to contract with the private sector rather than provide the services itself. Social Security was modeled after private pension plans. Medicare parallels private health insurance. The Job Corps was influenced by the training experience of private industry.

Such innovations continue today, although they are largely unfamiliar to social workers who remain intellectually dependent on the public sector. For-profit correctional firms are gradually upgrading jails and prisons across the country, and they are doing it by providing more cost-effective and better services. The Los Angeles County workfare program, GAIN, is administered by MAXIMUS, a for-profit firm which, preliminary analysis shows, is doing a credible job. An even more enterprising firm, America Works, has convinced Connecticut and New York to pay $5,300 for each AFDC recipient successfully placed in private employment; the company gets nothing if the placement is not permanent.

Perhaps one reason why social workers have so little influence in such developments is the poverty of their administrative research. The best data currently generated in the United States is about workfare and it is done by the Manpower Demonstration Research Corporation, another private agency. Yet there is virtually no data of comparable sophistication about the costs of social service provision. The best comparisons of costs by agencies of different auspices is being done by the Personal Social Services Research Unit (PSSRU) at the University of Kent in the United Kingdom. If advocates of the public sector are so adamant about the superiority of their mission, why have they failed to generate the data to back their claims? They have, after all, controlled the means of social service administration for the better part of the last century.

But it is in raising the issue of dualism that welfare statists become nothing less than hypocritical. Their fear is that privatization will leave the poor with substandard care. What can be more dualistic than the present arrangement in which the poor must rely on the public sector monopoly of service provision while the more affluent obtain services through the market? The public welfare department is the clearest demonstration of dualism in American social welfare, and it is a creation of the welfare state. On the other hand, privatization, properly implemented, offers the possibility of integrating the poor into the American mainstream.

Finally, the social work profession has much to gain by thinking seriously about the promise of privatization. Because of its association with public welfare, the profession has endured a considerable loss of status. If social work is to be relevant for the twenty-first century, it will have to accept the challenge of privatization and design ways in which the private sector can be put to more socially constructive uses.

REFERENCES

Friedman, E. (1984). The dumping dilemma. *Hospitals* (September 1), 211–214.

Gray, B., & McNerney, W. (1986). For-profit enterprise in health care. *New England Journal of Medicine* 314 (June 5), 1523–1525.

Karger, H.J., & Stoesz, D. (1990). *American social welfare policy*. New York: Longman, Inc.

Kuttner, R. (1986). The private market can't always solve public problems. *Business Week* (March 10), 20–21.

Stoesz, D., & Karger, H. (1991). The corporatisation of the United States welfare state. *Journal of Social Policy* 20(2), 157–171.

ANNOTATED BIBLIOGRAPHY

LeGrand, J., & Robinson, R. (Eds.) (1985). *Privatisation and the welfare state*. London: Allen & Unwin.

This edited book provides a thorough look at the implications of privatization for the welfare state.

Kamerman, S. (1983). The new mixed economy of welfare. *Social Work* 28(Jan/Feb) 1.

The author examines the social welfare sectors that make up the mixed welfare economy of the United States.

Rentoul, J. (1987). Privatisation: The case against. In Neuberger, J. (Ed.), *Privatisation, fair shares for all or selling the family silver.* London: Macmillan.

The author examines how privatization will eventually make the public sector more impoverished as it sells off its assets.

Starr, P. (1986). *The limits of privatization.* Washington, D.C.: Economic Policy Institute.

This is an interesting book that examines the limitations of privatization from an "anti-privativist" perspective.

Stoesz, D., & Karger, H. (1991). The corporatisation of the United States welfare state. *Journal of Social Policy* 20(2), 157–171.

This article examines the growth of the for-profit human service sector since the late 1970s. The authors also provide a scenario of the possible consequences of this growth for the social welfare state.

Has the Time Come for Social Service Vouchers?

EDITOR'S NOTE: Vouchers are an integral part of the trend toward the privatization of the social services. Vouchers are designed to give consumers greater choice when utilizing the social services and this, it is argued, increases competition between social service providers. The end result, supporters claim, is greater efficiency, more account-ability, and lower costs. Despite the appeal of these arguments, the use of vouchers is not universally applauded. Critics contend that the ideas underlying the use of vouchers are fundamentally flawed. Vouchers are antithetical to the humanitarian character of the social services and do not protect the weak and vulnerable. In addition, past experiments with social service vouchers have not resulted in greater efficiency or cost savings. Opponents claim that the current enthusiasm for social service vouchers is ideological rather than rational. They argue that the proponents of vouchers are dogmatic supporters of free market ideas who have little understanding of the unique role of the social services in society.

Lawrence L. Martin, Ph.D., supports the use of social service vouchers, arguing YES, that the time for vouchers has come. He is an Associate Professor at the School of Public Administration at Florida Atlantic University and the co-author of two books on social policy. He is former director of Aging Programs for the state of Arizona and has major research interests in human services administration.

Michael D. Parker, Ph.D., takes the opposite point of view, arguing against the use of social service vouchers. He is Associate Professor and

Chair of the Department of Social Work at Southeast Missouri State University. He has published widely on social work and social policy issues in leading scholarly journals.

YES

LAWRENCE L. MARTIN

Vouchers[1] are coupons issued by a government agency to eligible individuals in need of some service (Hatry, 1983). Eligible individuals "spend" their vouchers at approved provider organizations, which are then reimbursed by the government agency. Rather than cash grants, vouchers are provided in order to insure that resources are expended for the purposes intended (Bendick, 1989).

The Widespread Use of Vouchers

Voucher programs have a long and successful track record in several areas, including food and nutrition, education, health care, and housing. The Food Stamp program is probably the best known voucher program. The Food Stamp program attempts to insure that American families, and particularly families with children, have access to basic nutritional foods. Prior to the Food Stamp program, the only option the poor had was to participate in the Commodity Distribution Program operated by state and local welfare departments that distributed surplus bulk foods (Gilbert, 1983). Today, Food Stamps are accepted just like cash at literally millions of supermarkets, convenience stores, and other outlets nationwide. In 1991, some 23 million Americans participated in the Food Stamp program.

Another large and successful voucher program is the G.I. Bill. Under the G.I. Bill, veterans of the armed forces are provided with the opportunity to have access to higher education. The G.I. Bill has been an important method of upward social mobility for many minorities and particularly for African Americans who tend to use their benefits in greater proportions than other groups (O'Neil, 1977). The Medicare program has demonstrated the viability of voucher programs in the health field. Medicare recipients (the elderly and disabled) are issued an identification card that acts as a voucher. They can access health care services from any Medicare authorized health care provider. In 1988, Medicare served some 33 million elderly and disabled persons (Parker, 1991, p. 44).

Vouchers are also proving effective in the area of housing. With the advent of Section 8 housing vouchers funded by the U.S. Department of

Housing and Urban Development, eligible individuals now have access to the private rental housing market. Prior to the introduction of these vouchers, the only housing alternative available to low income and poor individuals was public housing projects. Under existing federal public housing programs, some 66 cents out of every dollar go for administration rather than housing. Conversely, under housing voucher programs administrative costs are estimated at less than 20 cents on the dollar (Fitzgerald, 1988, p. 38). Some twenty city governments nationally are experimenting with the use of vouchers for elderly housing (Farr, 1989, p. 41).

State and local governments are making successful use of voucher programs for more traditional social services, notably in the areas of specialized transportation for elderly and handicapped, child day care, and food and shelter programs for the homeless (Farr, 1989). The state of New Jersey, for example, reports that its experimental child day care voucher program costs 25 percent less than other types of government-funded day care and has improved client access to services. The state of New Jersey also reports that, according to consumer satisfaction surveys, clients are quite happy with the quality of the services being received (Allen et al., 1989, p. 79). Similar success with child day care vouchers is reported by the state of Pennsylvania. Pennsylvania's voucher program has reportedly reduced the overall cost of child care services by 20 percent and has lowered administrative costs to a meager 7 cents on the dollar (Allen, et al., 1989, p. 30–81). These lower service and administrative costs have allowed Pennsylvania to use the savings to expand its child day care program.

Many city governments also use voucher programs to provide specialized transportation services to the elderly and handicapped (Farr, 1989). Discounted vouchers are sold by city welfare or transit departments to eligible clients who can use them on buses, taxicabs, and jitneys. In some instances, the vouchers can even be redeemed by the friends and relatives of clients when they use their personal cars to provide transportation services.

Using Vouchers

The increased use of social service vouchers would offer several advantages over more traditional methods of service delivery, including the empowerment of clients, expanded service options, and decreased bureaucracy. Clearly the greatest advantage of social service vouchers is client empowerment. Social work has traditionally sought to put the needs of clients first and to assist them in making their own informed judgments. Unfortunately, most social service programs are based on a "one size fits all" mentality. Uniform government programs with uniform standards that result in uniform services do little to address the individual needs of clients or to further their ability to make informed choices.

In a voucher program, clients are free to choose the provider that best meets their own individual needs. This freedom to choose enables clients to "shop for services" in the same fashion as someone from the middle class (Stoesz, 1988, p. 138). If one provider is unable, or unwilling, to deliver the quality that clients want, or to address the cultural or individual needs of clients, the clients can simply take their business elsewhere. With voucher programs new agencies and organizations can easily enter the social services market by agreeing to be certified and to meet governmental standards. This ease of entry means that clients are afforded even greater choice in terms of selecting a service provider.

Conclusion

Given the advantages of voucher programs, why are they so infrequently used in the social services? The answer to this question may be related to another benefit of voucher programs — reduced bureaucracy. The size of the governmental bureaucracy needed to administer and monitor a voucher program is considerably less than that required with other more traditional service delivery approaches. In voucher systems, a lot of the decision making done by government officials and caseworkers is done instead by the clients themselves. The number of government workers needed to advise and counsel clients is consequently reduced. Could it be that the welfare establishment opposes voucher systems because less government bureaucracy means fewer social service jobs?

Rejoinder to Professor Martin   MICHAEL D. PARKER

Professor Martin's argument in support of social service vouchers is one-dimensional and simplistic. Most of his discussion focuses on vouchers as instruments to cut program costs and slim down government bureaucracy. By Dr. Martin's measures, vouchers are successful and effective because they are less expensive than traditional methods of service delivery and because they involve fewer "government officials and caseworkers." For the most part, he cites a few carefully selected, small-scale demonstration programs to support his position.

On another point, I have a great deal of trouble understanding my opponent's attack on the integrity of social service professionals. For Dr. Martin to suggest that social workers and other members of the "welfare establishment" would preserve any social service delivery system against the better interests of clients and society is total nonsense. This line of thinking seems to be more motivated by political rhetoric than facts.

By comparison, Dr. Martin appears to have unsurpassed optimism in the marketplace. He believes that if clients have free choice, their needs will be met because they "can simply take their business elsewhere." At best, Dr. Martin's view is naive, and at worst, it is risky. The free enterprise system that I am familiar with is not nearly so responsive to individual preferences, and consumers have little ability to influence producers. Under these circumstances, vouchers will provide yet another opportunity for critics to "blame the victim." With increased choice, if the clients' condition does not improve, they will simply be blamed for making poor consumer decisions.

Dr. Martin also demonstrates a lack of understanding of voucher theory by ignoring one of its major tenets. He believes the government should set standards and regulate the social service market so that providers can enter the market more easily. Voucher purists would cringe at such a proposal, especially since it threatens the integrity of a voucher system by suggesting that a free market cannot regulate itself. Moreover, voucher proponents believe that government regulations act as disincentives to enter the market, not incentives.

Notwithstanding my previous criticisms, what I find most troublesome about Dr. Martin's discussion is that it is void of ideological concerns. He completely neglects the consequences of vouchers on the values and behaviors that shape the social service system and the trade-offs that must be made to adjust to a free market system. His point that vouchers will empower clients is weak and unsubstantiated. At best, vouchers will empower the best informed consumer, but not necessarily the neediest client. This is because the overriding value of Dr. Martin's position is "caveat emptor" (buyer beware). I refuse to follow this doctrine as the organizing principle of a public social service system.

NO

Michael D. Parker

For more than a decade, our country has been in a conservative mode regarding the design and structure of its social service system. This ideological shift has helped revive interest in vouchers as a strategy for restructuring the provision of public social services. The apparent appeal of a voucher system for social services is worrisome for two reasons: (1) the worth of vouchers has yet to be proven under actual service conditions; and (2) the interests of vouchers run counter to many fundamental values and behaviors that guide the practice of social service professionals.

Lack of Empirical Evidence

Vouchers are used to provide services for three well-known federal programs – the G.I. Bill, the Food Stamp program, and Medicare. Analysis of these programs suggests that vouchers have failed to live up to theoretical expectations. For example, investigations of the G.I. Bill's educational program routinely turn up evidence of program inefficiencies, fraud, waste, and dissatisfaction among veterans. Evaluations of the Food Stamp program indicate that food stamps are both inefficient and ineffective, and that the program has failed to achieve the objectives of increased food purchases and improved diets among the poor. Finally, the Medicare program is plagued with runaway health care costs that increase well ahead of the general rate of inflation. Most of the problems identified in these major federal programs are a direct result of the inherent shortcomings of a voucher system.

Although this information is useful in gaining a practical understanding of a voucher system, it is helpful to look at the results of several voucher experiments to further our understanding. These experiments have been conducted, for the most part, in three service areas – education, housing, and child day care. Results from major studies in each of these areas fail to provide conclusive evidence regarding the merit of social service vouchers.

The most prominent educational voucher experiment is the Alum Rock (California) project. The intent of the experiment was to allow greater parental choice in choosing schools and to encourage competition among schools. On the matter of choice, few parents shopped around for schools. Instead, most made their selection based on geographic proximity and sent their children to the nearest school. Study results indicate that family choice may increase social stratification between white-collar and working-class families. In Alum Rock, wealthier families chose more innovative programs for their children, while working-class and minority families selected more traditional educational programs. After evaluating the experiment, the Rand Corporation (1981) concluded that, at best, the overall effects of vouchers were negligible, and at worst, vouchers worked in a direction opposite from theoretical expectations.

One of the most rigorous voucher experiments to date is the Experimental Housing Allowance Program. A central objective of the study was to assess the impact of voucher subsidies on patterns of housing consumption. Unlike vouchers that can be spent only for specific goods and services, e.g., food and education, housing vouchers could be spent in any way. However, eligibility requirements were established to channel vouchers toward housing consumption. One significant finding is that most participants did not use vouchers to increase housing-related purchases; most vouchers were spent on nonhousing items (Struyk & Bendick, 1991). Put simply, the quality of housing was not improved through the use of vouchers.

The Arizona Department of Economic Security tested a voucher system for child day care services. By offering eligible families greater choice and responsibility in selecting services and promoting competition among providers, it was anticipated that the price, supply, and quality of child care would improve. An evaluative study of the program revealed that, on average, voucher families paid more than non-voucher families for comparable child care services, with the poorest of the poor being at greatest risk for higher prices. Furthermore, there was no indication that the supply and quality of child care services was improved by the voucher program (Parker, 1989). In conclusion, vouchers had a negligible, if not negative, effect on the price, supply, and quality of child day care.

Ideological Concerns

In addition to the lack of empirical evidence, we should forgo a system of social service vouchers on ideological grounds. It is important to point out that the potential consequences of vouchers strike at the heart of the social service system as it currently exists. To better understand this concern, several key issues are addressed below.

Competition

Competition is a fundamental concept of classical economics and of voucher systems. Theoretically, in a competitive social service market, clients will determine the allocation of resources by virtue of their demand, and providers will offer the goods and services clients want in the largest quantity and at the lowest prices.

The possibility of a competitive social service market raises several key questions. For example, will scarce resources be allocated to the most persuasive rather than the most skilled provider? Will marketing skills become more important than professional skills in delivering services? Will name recognition and image become more important than substance? Will controversial and less popular services, such as working with AIDS patients or methadone counseling, be offered at all? How will less visible and frequently underserved clients, such as the rural poor and homeless families and children, get the help they need? Finally, in a competitive market, will the general social service community become segmented, factional, and self-serving?

By creating a competitive market, a voucher system would change the humanitarian nature of the social service system. At a minimum, it would result in a major reordering of relationships between service providers and their clients, with important implications for social service professions.

Information

The marketplace assumes that individuals are rational consumers and that they possess sufficient information to make intelligent choices relevant to their needs. Obviously, without correct or adequate information, individuals cannot make optimal choices. It follows, in a voucher system, that clients must be well informed about market choices.

Therein lies a problem. Traditional social service clients are disproportionately information-poor. They include the ill-educated, the poor, the physically handicapped, the mentally disabled, the aged, the very young, and other disadvantaged individuals and families whose conditions and circumstances impede access to ordinary consumer information or complicate their ability to use information. This problem will be magnified in a social service market, for unlike other market goods, such as toothpaste and shampoo, social services cannot be easily compared and the consequences of a poor choice are often more severe.

There are many unanswered questions concerning access to information in a voucher system. For example, how can potential clients be assured of having all the information they need to select the appropriate provider? What information is appropriate? Will social service agencies have to disclose information regarding their "success rate," their treatment methods, the qualifications of their staff, and their fees? How will information be made available to potential clients? How will potential clients who do not have the ability to make informed choices be accommodated?

Clearly, a voucher system will require clients to evaluate complex social services on the basis of their own observations and judgments. Under these circumstances, a voucher system will empower the best informed consumer, but not necessarily the neediest client.

Regulation

According to classical economic theory, a competitive social service market will be self-regulating. That is, high standards of service will be maintained by consumers selecting superior services over inferior ones. It follows then that social service voucher plans would replace government regulations with the power of consumer choice.

In the social service system, regulations represent society's concern for protecting the welfare of children, the elderly, the mentally and physically disabled, and other groups who are unable to safeguard their own welfare. The necessity for regulating social service programs is also apparent when one considers that social service users are frequently under emotional and environmental stresses that interfere with their ability to make rational decisions that are in their best interest.

The deregulation of social services through a voucher system raises several key questions. For instance, will the market give genuine protection to all those whose welfare is at stake? Will the market provide what the community regards as desired standards? How will the market guard against bias and caprice on the part of the community? Will deregulation lead to abuses by dishonest providers? How will defiance of standards be handled? Who will invoke authority in an unregulated market? How will standards be uniformly enforced from location to location and at different points in time? Will deregulation deflect political and social pressures that should properly be dealt with by a law-making body?

There is no doubt that a voucher system would expose already vulnerable groups to the additional risks and abuses of an unregulated market. Furthermore, it would result in uneven standards from program to program and from community to community. It would also open the door to lower quality services.

Conclusion

In this debate I have discussed a number of limitations of vouchers in meeting social service objectives and have identified many important questions left unanswered about how a social service voucher system would actually work. Clearly, further research is needed to guide policy formulation in this area. For these reasons, I believe a system for social service vouchers is ill advised, and that policy makers must resist the temptation to create voucher programs simply because the idea is politically attractive. To do otherwise would run the risk of strengthening the existing inequalities in society.

NOTES

1. A more detailed version of this paper appeared in the *Journal of Sociology and Social Welfare,* September 1991, (18)3, pp. 39–55.

Rejoinder to Professor Parker   LAWRENCE L. MARTIN

Professor Parker's critique of voucher systems is generally reflective of the welfare establishment's thinking about this form of alternative service delivery. Dr. Parker makes five basic arguments: (1) voucher systems are ideologically impure; (2) voucher systems lead to deregulation; (3) voucher systems are not appropriate for some client populations; (4) voucher systems may lead to competitive social service systems; and (5) voucher systems simply don't work.

Dr. Parker suggests that the social services should forgo voucher systems on "ideological grounds." Apparently, Dr. Parker believes that voucher systems are some sort of clandestine conservative plot to undermine the welfare state. In and of themselves, voucher systems are neither conservative nor liberal policy tools. It is true that some conservative groups promote the use of vouchers. However, I would remind Professor Parker that the three major voucher systems in the United States (G.I. Bill, Medicare, and Food Stamps) were passed into law by a U.S. Congress controlled by liberal Democrats.

Dr. Parker would have us believe that vouchers lead ultimately to deregulation. In actuality, most major voucher systems operate in a regulated environment. Veterans can only use the G.I. Bill at accredited institutions of higher learning or licensed trade schools. Food stamps can only be redeemed at federally certified redemption centers. Medicare cards can only be accepted by federally authorized health care practitioners and facilities. Child day care voucher systems still require that participating facilities be licensed by the state. To participate in most transportation voucher systems, providers must either be government agencies or licensed "common carriers." Finally, private landlords must comply with a host of regulations in order to participate in the federal Section 8 housing voucher program.

Dr. Parker suggests that voucher systems are inappropriate for some client populations. I could not agree more! No one is suggesting that a three-year-old child be given a voucher and sent out to find a day care center or that an Alzheimer patient should be given a voucher and told to shop for a nursing home. Clearly, voucher systems are inappropriate for some client populations. This does not mean, however, that voucher systems are inappropriate for all client populations. Voucher systems are simply *one* alternative service delivery strategy, not the *only* service delivery strategy.

Professor Parker expresses the fear that voucher systems may lead to competitive social service systems where agencies compete for clients and funding. Obviously Dr. Parker and I live on two different planets. I for one have never worked in a community or a state where social service agencies did not compete with each other for clients and funding regardless of the presence or absence of social service voucher systems.

Finally, Professor Parker alleges that voucher systems simply do not work. The problem with Dr. Parker's assessment is that he picks and chooses among several possible criteria—some highly questionable—in making his judgment. For example, he maintains that the Medicare program has not contained health care costs. I am not sure whether this was ever a goal of the Medicare program. And even if it was, no other program we have devised has contained health care costs, so why pick on the Medicare program? Dr. Parker also points out that fraud has occurred in the G.I. Bill program and that the Food Stamp program has failed to achieve some of its objectives. If criteria like these determine the success or failure of social service programs, then it may well be that our society has no successful social service programs.

REFERENCES

Allen, J., et al. (1989). *The private sector in state service delivery.* Washington, D.C.: The Urban Institute Press.

Bendick, M. (1989). Privatizing the delivery of services. In Kammerman, S., & Kahn, A. (Eds.), *Privatization and the welfare state.* Princeton: Princeton University Press.

Farr, C. (1989). *Service delivery in the 90s: Alternative approaches for local governments.* Washington D.C.: The International City Management Association.

Fitzgerald, R. (1988). *When government goes private.* New York: Universe Books.

Gilbert, N. (1983). *Capitalism and the welfare state.* New Haven: Yale University Press.

Hatry, H. (1983). *A review of private approaches for the delivery of public services.* Washington, D.C. The Urban Institute.

O'Neil, D. (1977). Voucher funding of training programs: Evidence from the G.I. Bill. *Journal of Human Resources* 12, 425–455.

Parker, M. (1991). Social Service Vouchers: Issues for social work practice. *Journal of Sociology and Social Welfare* 17, 39–55.

Parker, M. (1989). Vouchers for day care of children: Evaluating a model program. *Child Welfare,* 68(6), 633–642.

Stoesz, D. (1988). A new paradigm for social welfare. *The Journal of Sociology and Social Welfare* 16, 127–150.

Struyk, R., & Bendick, M. (Eds.) (1991). *Housing vouchers for the poor: Lessons from a national experiment.* Washington, D.C.: The Urban Institute Press.

The Rand Corporation. (1981, August). *A study of alternatives in American education, vol. VII: Conclusions and policy recommendations* (Rand Corporation Report R-2170/7NIE). Santa Monica, CA: The Rand Corporation.

ANNOTATED BIBLIOGRAPHY

Allen, J. et al., (1989). *The private sector in state service delivery.* Washington, D.C.: The Urban Institute Press.

This work details the use of alternative service deliveries, including vouchers by state governments. Programs include corrections, employment, training, and transportation, among others.

Farr, C. (1989). *Service delivery in the 90s: Alternative approaches for local governments.* Washington D.C.: The International City Management Association.

This publication focuses on alternative service delivery strategies — including vouchers — at the local (city and county) government levels. A section deals with health and human services.

Fitzgerald, R. (1988). *When government goes private.* New York: Universe Books.

This work is a collection of successful privatization case studies (including some dealing with vouchers) implemented by government agencies in the United States, England, and other countries.

Friedman, M. (1962). *Capitalism and freedom.* Chicago: The University of Chicago Press.

This classic work is one of the first attempts to present a theoretical model for social service vouchers. This model is then applied to public education.

Hatry, H. (1983). *A review of private approaches for the delivery of public services.* Washington, D.C.: The Urban Institute.

This classic work is one of the first systematic attempts to understand and classify various privatization strategies, including vouchers.

Parker, M. (1991). Social service vouchers: Issues for social work practice. *Journal of Sociology and Social Welfare* 17(3), 39–55.

This work reviews major voucher programs and experiments. It also discusses potential consequences of social service vouchers by identifying issues that are of concern to social work.

Are Shelters for the Homeless Doing the Job?

EDITOR'S NOTE: In recent years, the problem of homelessness has become more acute. Cutbacks in government support for low-income housing, the rise in unemployment, deinstitutionalization, reductions in social service expenditures, and other factors have contributed to the growing numbers of persons who have no place to live. In the absence of effective housing policies, many new shelters operated by voluntary social service agencies have been established. Supporters of these organizations argue that shelters do a good job caring for the homeless, providing medical and other services and offering protection against inclement weather, violence, and crime. Opponents of the shelter movement claim that shelters are an inefficient and haphazard response to a housing problem that should be addressed at the national level through adequate government intervention. These critics argue that although shelters do provice the immediate necessities of homeless people, they detract from the urgent need for comprehensive, radical solutions.

Developing these arguments, Larry W. Kreuger, Ph.D., argues YES, that shelters are doing a good job. Dr. Kreuger is Associate Professor of Social Work at the School of Social Work, University of Missouri-Columbia. He has published extensively on the issue of homelessness and works with homeless people in St. Louis. He has undertaken numerous research studies into the problem of homelessness and has served as a consultant to various federal and state agencies.

Dr. John J. Stretch, Ph.D., argues NO, that shelters are not doing a good job. He is Professor of Social Policy and Social Research at the School of Social Service, Saint Louis University, St. Louis, Missouri. He has served as an expert witness and consultant on homelessness to the House Select Committee on Children and Youth, and The Homeless Task Force for the Secretary of the Department of Housing and Urban Development. He has published numerous articles on homelessness in various social work journals.

YES

LARRY W. KREUGER

A Scenario of Homelessness

It's almost 6:00 P.M. and only 30 degrees outside. Your fingers are about numb and your feet ache. You are standing on the doorstep of We Care, a shelter for homeless families in a large urban area. You stand on the threshold of disappointment, as you are likely to be told the shelter is full, and that you and your two children will have to look elsewhere. Looking elsewhere is not a new experience for you as a 26-year-old African-American unmarried head of your family. Four days ago the three of you were forced to move from your apartment on 60th Street because your building is to be condemned. The whole block is being torn down to make way for a sports complex. Trying to make ends meet on AFDC and food stamps is not easy and you cannot afford most of the apartments which are available. Many apartment owners and operators don't lease to families on AFDC; many don't rent to African Americans.

You and your children have reluctantly joined the ranks of anywhere between 300,000 to 3,000,000 homeless individuals and families living in shelters, missions, settlement houses, and welfare hotels; and in cardboard boxes, under bridges, and on park benches. Homeless women fortunate enough to reside temporarily in shelters will probably live through particularly cold nights like this one and some will see brighter and warmer days ahead. Some who are not so fortunate will be raped, beaten, and robbed. Others will likely either be driven to depression and suicide, alcohol or substance abuse, and prostitution, or they will be murdered.

Some shelters have already turned you away because they only provide services to men, to those who are mentally ill, or to single women or women unaccompanied by children. Shelters such as these often do little more than provide a meal or two and a cot. Some shelters require that you provide proof of prior hospitalization for mental illness. Some shelters provide police a place to drop off alcoholic men in need of detoxification treatment. Taking the homeless alcoholic to a hospital usually takes a great deal of time and paperwork.

If you could just get someone to answer the doorbell, you and your children, ages four and two, would discover that the We Care shelter is really an old church building. Just inside the door you would find a reception area occupied by an old worn out desk with a small lamp providing the only illumination for an elderly but friendly African-American woman who manages the comings and goings of the only regular entrance.

After you completed the necessary paperwork at the front desk, and assuming you were found eligible to receive services, you would make your way into the living area, which is nothing but the main church hall made over into a dormitory room. This looks like the place people would have slept during an air raid. The pews are gone, and there are clusters of cots spread around the floor with women about your age seated on some of them. There are sounds of a television and people talking in the distance. Children are running here and there. In time you will learn that other families staying here are just like you. A few women are transient, persons who got stranded passing through town on their way to somewhere else. Most homeless women, like yourself, were born and raised locally. Many are abused women who have found a safe haven. Almost all come from poorer neighborhoods, and many are homeless because of what seems like random and unpredictable events such as natural disasters, floods and fires, and political and economic disasters such as condemnations caused by gentrification.

At this hour the kitchen area in the church basement is quiet and the downstairs dining hall is abandoned. Ordinarily, only women and their children are allowed to stay in this shelter. Men and adolescent boys over twelve are unwelcome. Everyone pitches in with housekeeping, cooking, washing clothes, and other chores. During the day the children who are old enough will be bused to a nearby school. If a volunteer babysitter shows up to watch the young children, you will be expected to look for work or perhaps take GED classes to complete your high school degree. In any case, you will be allowed to remain at We Care for up to 60 days.

Finally the door opens and someone lets you into the warmth of We Care shelter. You and your children will be safe tonight and for many nights to come. Soon you will meet the shelter operators. On the staff at We Care are highly trained social workers who have developed a wide range of specialized services to help you, and others like you, complete your education, learn to manage your money, locate an apartment, find help, deal with landlords, find and keep a job, take better care of your children by recognizing illnesses, and a host of other life skills. In addition, if you are lucky, every week or two the shelter will be visited by a volunteer physician and nurse who perform checkups, provide immunizations, and make referrals for further care if needed.

The Need for Homeless Shelters

There are no good reasons for living in shelters. But, there are certainly good reasons for providing access to shelters for the millions of people who find themselves without residence or resources (Jahiel, 1987). Shelters are needed now more than ever for many reasons. For one, shelter residences are better than sleeping in harsh conditions under bridges or in cardboard houses. They provide nighttime sleeping arrangements for the truly help-less, homeless street people who are mentally ill, disoriented, and unable to care for themselves. Second, shelters provide temporary emergency living quarters for low-income (often minority) families who cannot afford other living arrangements and who suffer from random and unpredictable natural events such as fires and disasters, or from largely unpredictable political or economic events such as foreclosures, evictions, or condemnations. Shelters also provide short-term solutions to the immediate survival needs for food, clothing, and bedding for people who lose their place of residence (Kreuger, 1987).

Shelters offer some protection for potential victims of crimes of street violence, such as rape, drive-by shootings, and other environmental trauma. They also offer security and stopping-off havens for low-income persons passing through, and for transients who would otherwise be sleep-ing on park benches. Shelters offer the last line of defense for persons of color who have been systematically discriminated against in the search for apartment rentals. They also provide a defense for those discriminated against in mortgage and home repair loans, and who have been the victims of bank redlining. Furthermore, shelters provide safe destinations for abused women and abused or neglected adolescents who are contemplating seeking help.

Shelters can also offer a mechanism for getting better housing through placements, subsidies, and vouchers, and they offer a relatively more effi-cient organizational mechanism through which an array of social services (counseling, job training, education, health care, etc.) can be provided to those unfortunate few who have lost their place of residence. Shelters also offer a minimal last line of defense against the harsh economic and political reality of mean-spirited politicians whose economic policies cause loss of low-income housing, gentrification, and the various economies of greed. And, shelters provide some support for law enforcement officers who are able to drop off drunks needing a place to sleep it off, rather than using up hospital or jail space for these people. Finally, there is an economy of scale involved when using shelters rather than trying to provide such services on a one-on-one basis.

Given the political and social realities of poverty in the United States at the turn of the twenty-first century, shelters continue to solve a host of immediate survival and longer term community rerouting functions for homeless individuals and families (Bassuk, 1991).

Rejoinder to Professor Kreuger   JOHN J. STRETCH

Professor Kreuger's arguments, although laudable, are misplaced. He bases his entire justification for shelters on their pragmatic necessity. As such, he fails to address the core issue. The question is not whether shelters do some good; they certainly do. The central debate is why should we have them at all?

As long as we are tolerant of a basically inequitable and inefficient economic system that perpetuates the causes of homelessness, we will continue to justify wasteful and ineffective responses such as shelters. Furthermore, when we permit our social values to deteriorate to the point where individuals feel no responsibility for their lives, and when we do not educate citizens on how to cope with the stresses of modern society, we will seek false solutions through endless social engineering and intrusive social fixings.

Professor Kreuger tugs at our heart strings but insults our intellect. He would lead us to believe that the case example he so maudlinly presents is typical. He further tries to lead us to believe that shelters provide all people with a silver lining and a happy ending. He implies that "shelters know best" and that the woman in his vignette was guided by an unseen hand to better days. Come on, Dr. Kreuger, where is your data?

He goes on to convince himself of the unassailable rectitude of his own position. He leads us to believe there are many strong arguments in favor of shelters, but comes up with only twelve recursive statements which fail to convince.

Finally, he cops out by begging the issue. Professor Kreuger's statement about "the political and social realities of poverty in the United States at the turn of the twenty-first century" is the most telling argument of why shelters have and will continue to aid and abet a me-generation-centered society which has abandoned the poor.

NO

JOHN J. STRETCH

Since the time of organized social services under the Elizabethan Poor Law, there have always been shelters and shelter-type services. They have not worked as substantive approaches to serious and intransigent societal problems. The English Poor Laws of the early eighteenth century were more straightforward than the modern United States Poor Laws of the twentieth. The poor house and the alms house were meant to get the homeless out of sight. They were also designed to provide the least amount of support for the greatest number of poor people. Even then, efficiency was king in serving the homeless.

Today we engage in endless policy debates on how many and what kind of worthy and unworthy homeless inhabit our cities and countryside (Weigard, 1985). This debate between the soft-hearted and hard-headed serves no humane objective. The Census Bureau, certainly a major hard-head, lends scientific support to the notion that there are very few true homeless individuals and families; moreover, most of them are to be found in urban shelters (Wright, 1989).

It is comforting to conservative policy makers to terminologically diminish or do away with large segments of the unhoused and ill-housed. Mean-spirited policy makers narrow and twist definitions to exclude hundreds of thousands of homeless individuals, families, and children (Stretch, 1985). Using these arbitrary policy parameters, these people simply do not exist. Thus, out of sight definitionally is out of mind programmatically.

Added to this deliberate definitional confusion is the lack of clarity in policy objectives. The new glories of privatization have taken their toll. The federal government sees homelessness as primarily a state issue. The states, in turn, obligingly see homelessness as a local issue. To ease the social conscience of the body politic, a new chimerical beast has been invented. The new social chimera is public-private partnerships. Public-private partnerships are a facile neologism for dumping responsibility on churches, United Ways, and other more eleemosynary enterprises.

Why Shelters Don't Work

Too many shelters are unstandardized, unlicensed, unregulated, unsafe, and unsanitary. Many are fire traps. Many lump the mentally ill, the substance abuser, the chronic hoboes, bag ladies, abused women, and intact families with young children and infants into warehousing accommodations. Some shelters have developed specializations in serving the range of homeless populations. Some have even developed elaborate medical, dental, psychiatric, and social services to meet basic needs. Other shelters have provided a full range of rehabilitation services which include community placement, follow up, and subsidized housing and other care. At first blush the shelter movement, at least for some, appears to be doing the job. The fact is that there is a tremendous backlash against expanding these types of expensive approaches (Bidinnotto, 1991). Furthermore, the number of enlightened shelters that actually deliver and produce solid outcomes is unknown. Little empirical support exists for the effectiveness of even the best shelters. The most damning aspect of shelter provisions is that homeless persons who seek them out have absolutely no entitlements to their services and no redress if they are turned away.

With no clarity of social purpose and no criteria for assessing social impact, the shelter "non-systems" make do and limp along with crumbs from uncertain and inadequate federal and state appropriations. The shelters are unrepresented as a professional group when it comes to presenting a unified voice for addressing the burgeoning increases in all segments of the homeless population or rationally devising a true system for dealing with the overwhelming issues presented by the complexity of homelessness in a modern post-industrial society. At best, shelters are muddling through. The sad commentary is that as a society we feel good about it. HBO specials and network tearjerkers make us entertainingly aware that something is wrong. We salve our collective social conscience by donating a few more dollars to our local charities who oblige us by assuring us that they are taking care of the real problems of the worthy homeless.

Conclusion

On balance, given all of the above, shelters and shelter services are in the main performing a disservice to the fundamental needs of the homeless. Shelters obscure the fact that we must commit both resources and professionals to forcibly eradicate the absolute shame of homelessness and its grinding up of human potential. It is mind boggling that we have an epidemic of homelessness in the United States, one that has become acceptable because we are hiding the homeless from public view in shelters. I therefore place a good deal of the blame for fooling the public that something substantive is being done about homelessness, squarely on a policy-naive, local, and fragmented shelter "non-system." The shelters give unwarranted social comfort to the rich. They also continue to perpetuate the myth that by going through a shelter most of the homeless, through good old American bootstrapping, can return as better people to their communities . . . as long as they don't move next door.

Rejoinder to Professor Stretch LARRY W. KREUGER

The best way I can think of to respond to Dr. Stretch's poorly disguised conservatism is to take him on point by point. First, he is simply wrong in his claim that shelters don't work. It is unfortunate that shelters have been an integral part of our society's response to the homeless, transients, and immigrants since day one. For different populations in our history, shelters have temporarily but successfully provided one of the last defenses against the perils of industrial capitalism.

Professor Stretch is misguided in characterizing the attempts by dedicated social workers to rally local, regional, and national support for the homeless as an "endless policy debate" followed by televised "tearjerkers." His garbled and simplistic solution is utopian. Yes, if we had an adequate federal housing policy to help low-income families, there would be no need for charitable social movements to engage in services for the homeless. Perhaps Dr. Stretch has a quick and easy policy solution to make everyone middle class and thus eligible for favorable subsidies (i.e., interest deduction for home mortgages, child care deductions, and other favorable tax breaks). In the meantime, a segment of the poor will predictably be homeless and thus have a need for shelters.

Dr. Stretch's claims about a lack of standardization and regulations are simply unfounded and constitute a cheap shot. I have never worked with shelters that fit his damning descriptions. Shelters for the homeless are subject to the same sanitary regulations as hotels and restaurants.

Finally, if shelters are performing a disservice as Professor Stretch claims, what would be the substitute? Does he know of a few million low-income apartments he would be willing to rent to the homeless individuals and families awaiting a place to live? Get with it, Dr. Stretch, and also get real.

REFERENCES

Bassuk, E. (1991). Homeless families. *Scientific American,* 66–74.

Bidinnotto, R. R. (1991). Myths about the homeless. *Readers Digest,* June, 99–103.

Jahiel, R. I. (1987). The situation of homelessness. In Bingham, R. D., Green, R. E., & White, S. B. (Eds.), *The homeless in contemporary society.* Newbury Park: Sage Publication.

Kreuger, L. W. (1987). Tracking health services for the homeless: Issues in information management. Paper presented at the Annual Program Meeting of the National Institute for Information Technology: Health Related Services. Myrtle Beach, SC.

Stretch, J. J. (1985). Children of the homeless. Paper presented at the Annual Program Meeting of the Third National Social Work Conference, New Orleans, LA.

Weigard, R. B. (1985). Counting the homeless. *American Demographics* (December), 34–37.

Wright, J. D. (1989). *Address unknown: The homeless in America.* New York: Aldine De Gruyter.

ANNOTATED BIBLIOGRAPHY

Bassuk, E. (1991). Homeless families. *Scientific American,* 66–74.

An excellent summary presentation of the problem of homeless families in the United States.

Bidinnotto, R. R. (1991). Myths about the homeless. *Readers Digest,* (June), 99–103.

A conservative discussion of facts and fallacies relating to homelessness.

Burt, M.R. (1992). *Over the edge: The growth of homelessness in the USA.* New York: Russell Sage Foundation and the Urban Institute, Washington, D.C.

An empirical study of the rise of homelessness in the 1980s.

Jahiel, R. I. (1987). The situation of homelessness. In Bingham, R. D., Green, R. E., & White, S. B. (Eds.), *The homeless in contemporary society.* Newbury Park: Sage Publication.

A concise conceptual review of types of homeless individuals and families.

Kreuger, L. W. (1987). Tracking health services for the homeless: Issues in information management. Paper presented at the Annual Program Meeting of the National Institute for Information Technology: Health Related Services, Myrtle Beach, SC.

A description of the methodological aspects of several programs for delivering coordinated services to homeless individuals and families.

Stretch, J. J. (1985). Children of the homeless. Paper presented at the Annual Program Meeting of the Third National Social Work Conference, New Orleans, LA.

An early empirical discussion on characteristics of sheltered homeless families with children.

Weigard, R. B. (1985). Counting the homeless. *American Demographics* (December), 34–37.

A thorough review of methodological and conceptual issues regarding efforts to enumerate homeless populations.

Wright, J. D. (1989). *Address unknown: The homeless in America.* New York: Aldine De Gruyter.

An examination of national data on homelessness, with excellent summary statistics and trends.

Is the Social Welfare System Inherently Sexist and Racist?

EDITOR'S NOTE: Although sexism and racism still permeate our society, much has been done to expose these problems and to educate people about the evils of prejudice. Institutionalized procedures that reflect deeply rooted racist and sexist attitudes have been uncovered in many places, and it is a matter of concern to social workers that the profession has not been immune from these tendencies. Equally disturbing is the claim that social service programs give expression to racist and sexist sentiments. Critics argue that the welfare system inevitably reproduces the dominant value ethos of society and that social policy is based on beliefs and institutions that contain strong race and gender biases. Opponents contend that this claim overstates the case. While they acknowledge that racism and sexism do exist in society, they believe that the welfare system operates to counteract these influences.

This important issue is addressed by Mimi Abramovitz, who argues YES, that the social welfare system is inherently racist and sexist. Dr. Abramovitz is Professor of Social Policy at the Hunter College School of Social Work in New York. She is the author of *Regulating the Lives of Women: Social Welfare Policy from Colonial Times to the Present* (1988), South End Press and the co-editor of *Journal of Progressive Human Services.* She has published in leading scholarly journals and is regularly invited to speak at national and international meetings.

Howard Jacob Karger is Professor of Social Work at Louisiana State University. He has published numerous articles and books including *Sen-*

tinels of Order (1987), University Press of America; *Social Workers and Labor Unions* (1988), Greenwood; *American Social Welfare Policy* (1990), Longman (with David Stoesz); and *Reconstructing the American Welfare State* (1992), Rowman and Littlefield (with David Stoesz).

YES

MIMI ABRAMOVITZ

Race and gender domination structure society and its institutions, including the social welfare system. Despite numerous victories, the civil rights and women's movements (joined by many social workers) could only mute these injustices. It is clear that sexism and racism remain deeply ingrained in the social welfare system, especially after looking at (1) the race and gender structures of wider society, (2) the biases found in the conceptual underpinnings of the social welfare system, (3) the stereotypes embedded in the rules and regulations of social programs, and (4) the impact of social policies on social problems.

Defining Racism and Sexism

For the purpose of this debate racism and sexism are considered together. But this does not mean they are the same. Whites have more power than persons of color, regardless of gender, and within racial groups men dominate women. Racism and sexism refer to a belief that socially acquired differences in intelligence, morality, family structure, culture, behavior, etc., are intrinsically related to the biological characteristics of race and gender. Racism and sexism also signify a belief in the superiority of the characteristics of socially dominant groups. These beliefs justify the marginalization of the allegedly inferior groups, excluding from the community of equals, and rationalizing the violence, the denial of rights, and the dehumanization that lies at the heart of racism and sexism.

Racism and sexism appear in both individual and institutional forms. *Individual* racism and sexism refers to the overt attitudes and behaviors of persons. It includes prejudiced thinking that prejudges others and leads to the differential treatment of persons based on group association. *Institutional* racism and sexism, our topic here, refers to processes by which societal institutions systematically create and enforce prevailing racial and sexual inequities. If racist or sexist consequences accrue to laws, customs, policies, or practices, the institution in question is, in effect, racist or sexist. This is so whether or not the individuals involved have racist or sexist intentions or are even aware of these outcomes.

The Wider Society

The racism and sexism embedded in the social welfare system reflects the racial- and gender-based distribution of power in the wider society. Socially, economically, politically, and ideologically, the "isms" act to enforce both the power of dominant groups and the societal conditions supportive of capitalism, patriarchy, and racism. Socially, racism and sexism control the behavior of subjugated groups by rewarding people who conform to norms based on white, male, middle-class, heterosexual standards, and penalizing those who do not. Economically, the "isms" marginalize women, persons of color, and the poor by keeping them available as sources of low-paid market and unpaid domestic labor. Politically, the "isms" protect the status quo by camouflaging the real power of those who benefit most from the current arrangement. The "isms" also divide similarly oppressed groups who might otherwise fight together for a bigger share of the proverbial pie, or who might struggle to create a new and better one. Ideologically, institutional racism and sexism rationalize inequality. They justify the inequities that are intrinsic to capitalist, patriarchal, and racist societies by defining the uneven distribution of resources, chances, and privileges as biologically based, "natural," and therefore difficult to change.

But haven't anti-discrimination, social welfare, and labor laws improved the situation? Yes, but the historical record reveals that while legislation has reduced barriers, opened doors, improved conditions, and otherwise attacked racism and sexism, it has not prevented the "isms" from repeatedly resurfacing in new forms. For example, the post-Civil War laws of Reconstruction (which extended rights to blacks) were quickly overthrown by the segregationist laws of Jim Crow. The hard-won civil rights gains of the 1960s gave way to Supreme Court conservatism in 1991, albeit modified somewhat by congressional redress. Sexism was also encouraged by the refusal to grant women the vote until 1920; by the failure of the Equal Employment Opportunity Commission to enforce the anti-sex discrimination provisions of the 1964 Civil Rights Act; and by the current attack on women's right to choose. The liberalism of social policy is directly affected by the political climate, the pressures exerted by popular movements, and the need for elites to preserve the status quo. However, for anti-racist and anti-sexist reforms to succeed, they cannot be perceived as posing too great a threat to white and male supremacy. The wider society remains sexist and racist because undue challenges to dominant interests risk defeat or resistance via lax enforcement, obstructive rules, ideological backlash, or outright reversal.

Conceptual Underpinnings

The social welfare system is inherently racist and sexist not only because it inevitably reproduces the racism and sexism of the wider society, but also because its conceptual underpinnings — research methods, social theories, and democratic principles — contain strong race and gender biases.

Biased Research Methods

Since its emergence in the nineteenth century, social science research has accepted the marginalization of disenfranchised groups, denied their representatives a place on research teams, and deemed their life experiences less worthy of study. Social scientists uncritically formulated research questions that excluded the interests of women and persons of color, among others. This research also used samples composed of white males, many of whom were college students readily available to researchers. Not surprisingly, findings were uncritically and inappropriately generalized to other groups as if no differences existed. Social science theory also harbors stereotypes of women, persons of color, and the poor. The most widely critiqued include Freud's theory of female sexuality, Parson's instrumental and expressive family roles, Moynihan's analysis of the African-American family, Oscar Lewis's culture of poverty, and recent concepts of the model (Asian) minority. More inclusive, multicultural research should benefit the social welfare system.

Individualist Explanations of Social Problems

The racism and sexism found in social welfare programs is also rooted in the individualistic explanations of personal and social problems that inform social policy. Mainstream social science typically explains social problems in terms of personal characteristics, often evoking the nature/biology paradigm which, as noted above, underpins racism and sexism. Although portrayed as simplistic and outdated, this paradigm periodically reasserts itself in more sophisticated forms that mask earlier and cruder claims of racial and gender inferiority. In the context of the rapid industrialization and high rates of immigration that marked the turn of the century, eugenic and Social Darwinist theories attributed rising rates of poverty, alcoholism, mental illness, and most social problems to inferior genetic or intellectual endowments. As such, only the fittest (e.g., those who were native born, white, and middle class) could and should survive. In the 1940s and 1950s sociologists blamed criminal behavior and other social problems on the individual's inferior environment (bad companions, broken homes, improper socialization), while the schizophrenigenic mother took the rap for serious mental illness. Today's "underclass" theory continues to link poverty and social problems to morally deficient attitudes, behaviors, and a culture of poverty. By suggesting that welfare mothers, poor persons of color, school drop-outs, and drug users and criminals violate traditional American values (e.g., individualism, self-reliance, discipline, hard work, and proper family life), this social theory thinly disguises old notions of individual and group inferiority and blames the victim. In doing so, the "underclass" theory has rationalized deep cuts in social welfare and justified recent "reforms" that tie the receipt of benefits to behavioral change by the poor (see the Mark Lusk and Diana DiNitto debate in this volume). The theoretical emphasis on the behavior of the poor also obscures the relationship between the declining standard of living and the profit-driven decisions of the business sector and the state. In a society where women and persons of color are heavily overrepresented among the poor, it becomes inherently racist and sexist to blame the decay of the social fabric on the decisions of those at the bottom, while ignoring those decisions made at the white and male-dominated top.

Equal Opportunity

The principle of equal opportunity is rooted in the notion of a fair and open race in which competitors have the same chance to succeed. This cornerstone of liberal social policy has not undone U.S. racism and sexism because the similar treatment of people with different backgrounds, resources, and capabilities usually reproduces inequality. Designed to facilitate personal mobility by increasing skills or reducing discriminatory barriers, programs such as fair housing, equal employment, and open admissions create formal equality under the law. But the results continue to be unequal because the entrants to the race for jobs, housing, and education possess unequal amounts of the resources needed to compete effectively. In effect, this process favors those who enter the "free competition" with greater command over resources and perpetuates the disadvantages of those handicapped by a prior lack of social and economic opportunities. Because equal opportunity programs often reproduce pre-existing race, gender, and class inequities, the underlying structures of racism and sexism remain intact. According to John Rawls, genuine equality of opportunity requires society to give more attention to those with fewer assets and to those born into less favorable social positions. This "principle of redress" suggests that equality of result flows not only from enhanced opportunities, but also from social compensation for past inequities.

Social Program Rules and Regulations

A full assessment of the racism and sexism built into the social welfare system requires an examination of the internal regulations of social programs as well as their external contexts. Examples from two major social welfare policies are used to illustrate how seemingly neutral provisions result in racist and sexist outcomes. Similar patterns can be obtained in the many other social programs not discussed here.

Coverage

Despite its many accomplishments, the landmark 1935 Social Security Act (SSA), still the core of the modern welfare state, reproduced rather than eradicated sexism and racism. It did so by accommodating to racial exclusion and the economic dependence of women on men. For many years, the Social Security Retirement and Unemployment Insurance programs covered only industrial occupations, which happened to employ mostly white, working-class men. The decision, which excluded the large number of women and persons of color employed as agricultural and domestic workers, casual laborers, or employees of governmental, nonprofit, religious, charitable, scientific, literary, and educational organizations, was defended by arguing that the inclusion of industries outside of interstate commerce would render Social Security unconstitutional. It was also argued that universal inclusion would increase the complexity of tax collections from such decentralized occupations.

The origins of federal housing policy also fueled long-lasting racist and sexist policies. Housing officials favored restrictive covenants until 1948; used mortgage loan practices that led to the current racial divide between the suburbs and the inner city; located public housing projects so as to avoid racial integration; and failed to fully enforce the 1968 fair housing law. The legacy of polices that permit segregated residential patterns continues in current governmental rules that allow federally subsidized private landlords to refuse housing vouchers, to reject children, and to impose stringent income tests on applicants.

Work Tests

From the outset, the Social Security and Unemployment Insurance Programs defined individuals as deserving and undeserving of aid based on their employment record. By favoring individuals with steady jobs, long work histories, and higher wages, such "work tests" automatically penalize workers who face race and sex discrimination. Work tests further disqualify women by not defining their domestic labor as work, by ignoring how their family responsibilities limit their labor force participation, and by otherwise failing to account for gender differences in work patterns. Because of wage-based benefit formulas, low-paid workers (who are overwhelmingly women and persons of color) receive smaller pensions and unemployment compensation checks. Given their shorter life span, persons of color often receive less in benefits than their white counterparts, although they pay into the system for the same length of time.

The devaluation of women's work has also led to sexist housing policies. Until 1973, Federal Housing and Veteran's Administration mortgage loan programs discounted a women's income when calculating a family's loan–income ratio. The argument was made that women's irregular labor force participation made their income unpredictable. This practice effectively denied home ownership to thousands of working-class households that depended heavily on women's income. It also virtually ruled out home ownership for women except through inheritance or a divorce settlement. The ramifications of this policy fell heavily on African-American women who have always worked and contributed significantly to family income.

Family Test

Many social policies contain what might be called a "family test." The idealized version of the family — based on the traditional two-parent, male-breadwinner, female-homemaker household — is deeply encoded in the welfare state, whose programs treat women differentially according to their marital status. Married women, and previously married women who lack a breadwinner through no fault of their own (e.g., widows and wives of sick, disabled, or temporarily unemployed men) receive better services than single mothers, abandoned wives, and women whose breadwinner does not provide adequate support. The latter are more likely to be poor white women and women of color, whose poverty or other life circumstances prevented them from complying with the family ethic. They must then turn to the meager and stigmatized Aid to Families with Dependent Children (AFDC) program, which upholds the family ethic by promulgating rules and regulations that punish poor women for departing from prescribed wife and mother roles.

Social Program Cutbacks

The past decade of domestic program cutbacks has also led to racist and sexist consequences. Now widely acknowledged to have redistributed income upwards from the "have-nots" to the "haves," the Reagan–Bush cuts fell especially hard on women and persons of color. Informed by the "underclass" theory, programs which serve mostly women and persons of color, such as AFDC, Food Stamps, and public housing, received the deepest cuts. Larger programs that benefitted more white persons, such as Social Security, Medicare, and Veteran's Compensation, tended to be spared even though they consumed more government dollars. Due to the relentless attack on the welfare state, the numbers of hungry, homeless, and jobless persons rose sharply as did rates of crime, drug use, and school drop-outs. Fueled by sexism and racism, many now inaccurately link these rising social problems to the behavior of welfare mothers and Willie Hortons rather than to the actions of the business sector and the state.

Program Outcomes

It has been argued so far that the social welfare system is inherently racist and sexist owing to external social forces, conceptual underpinnings, and program regulations. A look at the social conditions addressed by social welfare policies reveals continued differentials based on race and gender. For example, poverty rates still vary sharply by race and gender despite social policies that promote equal pay, compensate for joblessness, and distribute income. Likewise, the development of more responsive health education and housing policies has not ended unfavorable racial variations in health status, public school expenditures, college enrollments, residential patterns, and labor market structures. Sexist outcomes remain in health research agendas; laws against rape, sexual harassment, and family violence; and the strong resistance by business and government to child care, family leave programs, and abortion.

Conclusion

Despite twenty-five years of anti-discrimination and affirmative action laws, women and persons of color have not caught up with white men. Now that the leaders of business and government have decided that disinvesting in labor and social welfare programs is the best way to maximize profits and weaken popular movements, hard-won affirmative action and redistributional gains have been lost. In the final analysis, despite good intentions and numerous exceptions, social welfare policy has reproduced rather than eliminated societal racism and sexism. As a result, many of the welfare state's major achievements have not been equally shared by all. The social welfare system can be freed of racism and sexism only if we reject the social construction of differences based on race and gender. In effect, race, gender, and class equality should be made national goals. To reach these ends we will have to build mass movements that transform society.

Rejoinder to Professor Abramovitz

Howard Jacob Karger

My opponent's debate suffers from several problems. For one, she rightfully bemoans the gaps in the early Social Security Act of 1935. The hardship of the early exclusions obviously caused great distress for millions of workers who fell through the cracks, especially low-income workers, many of whom were black or female. However, Professor Abramovitz fails to compliment the federal government for eventually correcting these oversights. It seems that glaring policy faults are emphasized while their remedies are glossed over.

Professor Abramovitz also accuses federal housing policies of failing vulnerable families (mother-only and families of color) by allowing landlords who receive federal subsidies to discriminate by rejecting families with children, and by requiring applicants for subsidized private housing to pass stringent income tests. While I agree that this situation is deplorable, I do not agree that it is solely the fault of federal policy. The blame should be placed squarely where it belongs: on the shoulders of landlords. In a free market economy social institutions are able to put only limited demands on the private sector. The real solution is to encourage the federal government to build more public housing for which it can set rules, not to criticize the social welfare system for not being able to enforce its will on the protected private sector.

My opponent goes on to criticize welfare programs which treat married women (or previously married women who lack a breadwinner through no fault of their own) better than single mothers or women whose breadwinner does not provide adequate support. Although Professor Abramovitz correctly maintains that the latter category contains more poor white women and women of color, her argument contains several contradictions. For one, if the social welfare system is sexist, why does it treat middle-class women better than poor women? If the welfare system contains an innate antipathy for women, should this not extend to *all* women? It seems that my opponent is confusing the harsh restrictions of needs-based programs with the more liberal benefits of social insurance programs. While this situation is clearly inequitable, it is more a product of the value society places on labor-force-related benefits than an indictment of the sexism of the social welfare system. This is especially true since poor white males who request the same non-workforce-related benefits receive the same shoddy treatment as poor white women.

There is a deeper contradiction in my opponent's argument, one that seems to be endemic to a Left analysis of the welfare system. While on the one hand Professor Abramovitz criticizes the welfare system for oppressing women and blacks, on the other hand, she bemoans the cuts in services that characterize the Reagan and Bush years. She cannot have it both ways — either the welfare system is deleterious to women and minorities or welfare benefits are positive and help sustain economically vulnerable populations. To tear into the welfare system as racist and sexist and then to demand that it provide more benefits is inconsistent. In the final analysis the only thing that stands between many of the poor and starvation is an embattled social welfare system.

NO

HOWARD JACOB KARGER

The argument that American society is both sexist and racist is virtually indisputable. For example, women earn anywhere between 65–70 percent of the wages of men, and few places have fully instituted comprehensive Affirmative Action policies or active strategies for achieving comparable worth. Moreover, women's rights under the law are more tenuous than those of men (National Commission on Working Women, 1982). Perhaps even more telling is that after fifty years of legislative activity, there is still no Equal Rights Amendment to guarantee women the same legal rights as men. The economic and social situation for minorities is equally as bleak. Despite the fact that blacks make up almost 12 percent of the population, they account for 44 percent of all AFDC recipients. Moreover, although education improves the relative economic standing of blacks, 40 percent of blacks in 1984 with four or more years of college earned $20,000 to $40,000 a year; the same percentage as whites with only a high school education (Council on Interracial Books for Children, Inc., 1984). These inequalities exist despite several decades of Affirmative Action and Equal Employment Opportunity policies instituted at the federal level.

Despite the preponderance of evidence suggesting that American society is both sexist and racist, the question remains as to whether the social welfare system suffers that same fate. While it would appear on the surface that all social institutions would be infected by the same sexist and racist germ as the general society, the evidence is more circumstantial when it comes to the social welfare system. It is the author's position that in democratic capitalist societies it is possible for programs and institutions to exist that are inimical to other social institutions. Democratic capitalist societies are full of such contradictions. Thus, while society itself may be racist and sexist, it is possible for certain institutions, including the social welfare system, to exist in contradiction to the prevailing social ethos.

Racism and Sexism in Social Services: Where's the Evidence?

The argument that the social welfare system is inherently racist and sexist goes something like this: Because of structural inequalities (i.e., the ownership and control of the economic, social, and political resources by a relatively small cadre of well-off white males), American society is by definition both racist and sexist. Thus, if the structure of society is both sexist and racist, then its institutions must by definition reflect the same trends. Since the social services comprise a major social institution, they must also by nature be racist and sexist. Therefore, if the social welfare system is inherently racist and sexist, it stands to reason that this ubiquitous discrimination should be reflected in all social service programs.

Despite the apparent cogency of this argument, it breaks down on several levels. First, institutional racism and sexism denotes an exclusionary process, one that usually involves the denial of rights, benefits, or privileges to a group deemed unworthy of receiving equal treatment. In the case of labor force participation, this discrimination is evident in the salary differentials of women and minorities compared to white males. However, if the social welfare system is indeed racist and sexist, then how is this invidious prejudice manifested? Do social service agencies or programs overtly discriminate based on race or gender? More specifically, are social services denied to women and minorities *because* of their race or gender? The answer to this question is a resounding "No!" At least with regard to income maintenance services such as AFDC, Food Stamps, housing assistance, and so on, women and blacks are over- not under-represented in the ranks of those receiving assistance. Do women and minorities receive less statutory-related benefits (i.e., income maintenance, in-kind benefits, or social services) than similarly eligible white males? Even ardent welfare advocates would be hard pressed to prove that, all things being equal, women and minorities receive fewer welfare benefits than white males eligible for the same programs. In fact, some entitlement programs such as AFDC discriminate in the reverse direction; that is, they reward benefits based on gender-related criteria such as dependent children living at home. Thus, while able-bodied women with children are considered worthy of assistance, many places deny that same assistance to able-bodied men without children. In short, there appears to be little evidence to suggest that the social welfare system is either racist or sexist in the way it provides services and cash benefits to women and minorities as compared to white males.

Second, if social service and income maintenance programs were both racist and sexist, it would stand to reason that poor white males would receive better treatment and more generous benefits than women or minorities. Again, even the most fervent welfare advocates would be hard pressed to argue that poor white males receive more benefits or better services than female or minority clients. In fact, public welfare regulations that impact upon poor males are more exclusionary and stringent that those targeted toward women. Moreover, the fact that no federal legislation exists that addresses the needs of poor, long-term unemployed single males is indicative of how society views men who appear on the surface to be able-bodied. With few rights-based entitlement programs for poor single males, most are relegated to the capricious and often highly politically sensitive General Assistance (GA) programs. The recent GA cuts in Michigan and California illustrate the vulnerability of poor unemployed males not covered under a strong statutory umbrella.

Some welfare advocates argue that the inherent sexism in the social services is illustrated by the anemic AFDC grants awarded to single women as compared to the more generous benefits given to Social Security recipients. Although initially convincing, this argument is spurious since comparing Social Security to AFDC is like comparing apples to oranges. Specifically, Social Security was designed as a social insurance, not a needs-based program. Because of this important distinction, Social Security payments, which are based on social insurance concepts rooted in labor force participation, will naturally be higher than benefits awarded because of need. While this may not be fair, it is an inequity based mainly on labor market conditions and capitalist ideology, not on gender or racial criteria.

Blaming Social Services

Because of its close proximity to the poor, the social welfare system is a logical target for the frustrations of an increasingly stratified class society. For many conservatives the welfare system represents a system of excesses and "overcoddling." For the poor it represents an economic system that has failed to adequately meet even their most basic survival needs. And for progressives, the welfare state symbolizes a social policy that has been arrested as a result of over two decades of conservative dominance. Embattled and embittered, welfare administrators have been increasingly forced to vigorously defend programs and services to a hostile audience of taxpayers and recipients.

On the other hand, there is little doubt that social services, and in particular income maintenance services, are fraught with inequities and serious problems. Cash benefits are appallingly low, and little is being done to give its main adult beneficiaries — single women with children — a chance to fully participate in the primary labor market. Nevertheless, the question remains as to whether the roots of this injustice are to be found in attitudes related to gender and race or to other factors.

It is my contention that the stinginess of the welfare state is not due to an innate hostility toward women and minorities, but to a general hostility toward needs-based welfare programs that are seen as anathema to the spirit of free-market capitalism. Moreover, this deep-rooted antagonism to social welfare programs is based primarily on class discrimination rather than on gender or ethnicity issues.

Feminist and minority advocates who base their critique of the social service system on issues solely related to race and gender miss the important point made by William Julius Wilson (1987), a University of Chicago sociologist. Namely, the current causes of poverty are rooted more in class discrimination than in race or gender issues. For example, despite the economic handicaps of gender, many educated, middle-class white women are able to construct an economically viable life, even if they are single mothers. Moreover, the same is true for many educated black women. This statement is not meant to imply that racism and sexism do not exist. They do exist, and their effects upon women and blacks are pernicious. However, at this point the adverse effects of class discrimination are far more salient in determining the economic life of women and minorities than are the issues of gender or race prejudice.

Conclusion

To label the social welfare system as a sexist and racist institution is counterproductive. For one, the social welfare system does not for the most part create policies or programs — it implements them. Thus, if the welfare system fails to meet the basic needs of the poor, it is not the fault of the system but of policy makers and legislators who appropriate inadequate funds to social programs. For example, if legislators suddenly decided to increase all AFDC grants to $2,500 a month for a family of three, the sexist and racist critique of the welfare system might well evaporate overnight. In that sense, the problem with welfare is not a philosophical one, but one of resources. Therefore, welfare does not fail the poor because it is racist or sexist; it fails them because it doesn't give them enough money. To focus one's critique of the welfare system on racism or sexism is to help obfuscate the real welfare debate.

The major task of the social welfare system is not to create a utopian society, but to rectify the excesses of capitalism and to remedy the more egregious aspects of economic displacement. It is that goal upon which the success or failure of the welfare system should be judged. To otherwise accuse the social welfare system of encouraging racism and sexism by its institutional policies is akin to blaming the weatherperson for the weather. Neither will change the temperature.

Rejoinder to Professor Karger   Mimi Abramovitz

Professor Karger acknowledges that American society is both racist and sexist. But he wrongly concludes that it is possible for certain institutions, such as the social welfare system, to escape the taint. His argument is built using a definition of institutional racism and sexism that is too narrowly confined to acts of legal discrimination. This definition misses the point about institutional racism and sexism, which speaks to the more subtle ways in which societal institutions systematically enforce prevailing racial and sexual inequities. To be institutionally racist or sexist, a societal institution does not have to overtly discriminate against women and persons of color *because* of their race or gender, as my worthy opponent claims. Rather, institutional racism and sexism refers to the fact that societal institutions produce racist and sexist outcomes *regardless* of the intentions or even the awareness of the individuals involved. Institutional racism and sexism goes beyond prejudicial attitudes and acts of discrimination to the consequences of institutional organization and structure.

With "the isms" defined as exclusion due to discrimination, Karger asks, "how can social welfare programs be inherently racist and sexist if women and persons of color are over-represented on the rolls of means-tested public assistance programs?" Women and persons of color *are* over-represented in these programs. But relative to Social Security and Unemployment Insurance — which include more whites and men — the means-tested programs are highly stigmatized, stunningly meager, and increasingly punitive. The differential treatment of people by public assistance and social insurance programs cannot be simply dismissed as a matter of comparing "apples and oranges," as Professor Karger suggests. Rather, this differential describes the development and acceptance of a two-tiered income support system that is stratified by gender and race as well as class. Because the entire system links benefits with employment experiences (which Karger correctly notes), the social welfare system invariably reproduces the racism and sexism of the labor market. Rather than being evidence of the absence of racism and sexism, the over-representation of women and persons of color in the most mean-spirited income maintenance programs reveals the inability of the income maintenance system to escape the "isms." The social welfare system could be organized to mute the impact of racist and sexist labor market patterns. For example, women could be given Social Security credit for years out of the labor force, which some European nations do. But to expunge the system's racism and sexism would elicit enormous resistance and expose capitalism's dependence on the welfare state to undercut wages, to enforce the traditional nuclear family, and to supply industry with low-paid workers.

Professor Karger's statement that the caseload composition of AFDC may even represent reverse discrimination is simply wrong. Although most adult AFDC recipients are mothers (caring for children), to qualify for aid a child must be deprived of parental support due to the absence or death of the breadwinner (who can be male or female). Single fathers with children can and do receive aid. But so many more mothers are on the rolls because our sexist society assigns to women near-exclusive responsibility for children's daily care, and only a few men contest this arrangement. Not only has the AFDC program failed to escape the wider society's sexist definition of gender roles, but its harsh and punitive rules and regulations reinforce them by punishing husbandless women, who are viewed as departing from prescribed wife and mother roles.

Professor Karger usefully reminds us that the organization and structure of social welfare reflect deep class biases. But the argument that class is *more significant* than race (and by implication here, gender), made by William J. Wilson remains highly controversial, hotly debated, and unresolved. Moreover the effort to rank the impact of class, race, and gender actively denies the inseparability of the these demographic variables, especially among the poor. In discussing Wilson, Karger shifts from social welfare issues to Wilson's analysis of poverty. In so doing *he* mixes "apples and oranges." Eligibility for Social Security and other social programs is not linked to poverty. To then show that single mothers of all races can enter the middle class, as Karger maintains, does not speak to the racism and sexism of the social welfare system at all. While recognizing that we have made gains in civil and women's rights, Karger fails to mention that due to the intensified racism and sexism of the past fifteen years, many of these hard won victories have been lost.

Much of Professor Karger's discussion focuses on the AFDC program rather than the entire social welfare system, which is the subject of this debate. This is especially true when he suggests that if AFDC awarded $2500 a month, the sexist/racist critique of it would fade. This elicits various responses. Suffice it to say that due to institutional sexism, racism, and classism, and the need to enforce traditional family forms, the work ethic, and low wages, it is unlikely that we will ever see such a large AFDC grant, much less a more generous welfare state. Karger concludes by saying that the task of social welfare is to rectify the excesses of capitalism. One could add the excess of patriarchy and racism as well. While it is not possible to fully cleanse the social welfare system of the "isms" without transforming the wider society, we cannot let them stand. We must challenge the inherent racism and sexism of the social welfare system by reviving the commitment, the liberal political climate, and the movements for women's and civil rights. To be successful, the resulting struggles must also include challenges to ageism, classism, heterosexism, disablism, and other sources of oppression.

REFERENCES

Council on Interracial Books for Children, Inc. (1984). *Fact sheet on institutional racism.* New York: Council on Interracial Books.

National Commission on Working Women. (1982). *Women's work: Undervalued, underpaid.* Washington: National Commission on Working Women.

Wilson, W. J. (1987). *The truly disadvantaged: The inner city, poverty and the underclass.* Chicago: University of Chicago Press.

ANNOTATED BIBLIOGRAPHY

Abramovitz, M. (1991). *Regulating the lives of women: Social welfare policy from colonial times to the present.* Boston: South End Press.

The author presents a description and analysis of the impact of sexism and sexual stereotypes in the development of the welfare state from the colonial poor laws to Reaganomics. Special attention is paid to income maintenance programs, poor white women, and poor women of color.

Eisenstein, Z. (1984). *Feminism and sexual inequality: Crisis in liberal America.* New York: Monthly Review Press.

This is a collection of essays, several of which are focused on women and the welfare state.

Gordon, L. (Ed.) (1990). *Women, the state and welfare.* Madison: The University of Wisconsin Press.

This useful collection of articles reflects new feminist scholarship on the welfare state. It includes articles on gender and social policy; women and politics; race, gender, and social welfare; family violence; the women's movement; and the War on Poverty and AFDC.

Lee, T. (1990). "Trapped on a pedestal: Asian-Americans confront model minority stereotype." *Dollars and Sense,* March, 12–15.

This useful short article raised the issue of the model minority as it affects Asian Americans.

Orfield, G. (1988). "Race and the liberal agenda: The loss of the integrationist dream, 1964–1974." In Weir, M., Orloff, A. S., & Skocpol, T. (Eds.), *The politics of social policy in the United States.* Princeton: Princeton University Press, 313–356.

This chapter examines how race was removed from the liberal political agenda. As such, the chapter reviews the history of the battle for integration as well as the civil rights and black power movements.

Slessarev, H. (1988). "Racial tensions and institutional support: Social programs during a period of retrenchment." In Weir, M., Orloff, A. S., & Skocpol, T. (Eds.), *The politics of social policy in the United States.* Princeton: Princeton University Press, 357–388.

This chapter provides a comparative analysis of the impact of budget cuts on Medicaid and subsidized housing programs.

Are False Allegations of Child Sexual Abuse a Major Problem?

EDITOR'S NOTE: Child sexual abuse has become a major public issue today. Sensational news media reports about child sexual abuse are now commonplace and demonstrate a greater concern for the problem. Law enforcement agencies and the child protective services have become more vigilant. Allegations of child sexual abuse are now treated more seriously than ever before, and intervention is likely even when firm evidence is not available. This has led to a concern that false allegations of sexual abuse may be made by children, their parents, or other adults, and that innocent people may be prosecuted without proper evidence or due process. Some child welfare experts now believe that false allegations are a major problem, and they advise that great caution be exercised when investigating child sex abuse cases. Other experts disagree, noting that scientific studies of the incidence of false allegations of sexual abuse have shown that the problem is very small indeed. In addition, they claim that children very rarely lie about sexual abuse. Although they do not deny that false allegations occur, they are convinced that the problem is minor one and that innocent people are adequately protected by the investigative process.

In this debate, Michael Robin, MSW, MPH, argues YES, that false allegations of child abuse are a major problem. Mr. Robin is a doctoral student at the University of Minnesota and a medical social worker serving children with epilepsy. He has published several articles on child welfare issues and is editor of *Assessing Child Maltreatment Reports: The Problem of False Allegations* (1991), Haworth Press.

Peter J. Pecora, Ph.D., argues NO, that false child abuse allegations are not a major problem. Dr. Pecora is Associate Professor at the School of Social Work, University of Washington, and Manager of Research for the Casey Family Program in Seattle. His books include *Managing Staff Development Programs* (1984), Nelson Hall; *Managing Human Service Personnel* (1987), Sage; *Families in Crisis: The Impact of Family Preservation* (1991), Aldine de Gruyter; and *The Child Welfare Challenge* (1992), Aldine de Gruyter.

YES

MICHAEL ROBIN

False allegations of child sexual abuse have become one of the most controversial issues in the child welfare field today. This issue has become polarized between advocates who have made numerous claims and counterclaims about the nature and extent of the problem. According to many professionals who work in the child protective service system, the problem is greatly exaggerated. But for those who claim to be "victims," false allegations of child sexual abuse are a serious and extensive problem that deserves greater public attention.

Defining False Allegations

Much of the controversy about false allegations is based on the several meanings of the word "false." *False* refers to that which is simply wrong or untrue, but it also includes the narrower definition of a person who is intentionally deceitful or dishonest. Unfortunately, most discussions about false allegations of child sexual abuse tend to ignore the distinction between the moral domain of the word "false," which refers to whether or not one is lying or telling the truth, and the larger domain of truth and falsity in general (Bok, 1978).

Therefore, the nature and extent of the problem depend on how the term "false allegation" is used. A broad definition of false allegations of child sexual abuse includes any reports or claims about abuse where abuse did not occur. This may include reports that are based on reasonable concerns but have alternative explanations, reports that are based on misunderstandings or misperceptions of events, or reports that involve "inappropriate" child care that fall short of accepted legal definitions of child sexual abuse. On the other hand, there are many who consider false allegations only to be those reports that are intentionally falsified.

Many discussions of false allegations of child sexual abuse rely on a study by Jones and McGraw (1987). These authors reviewed 576 reports of child sexual abuse made to the Denver Department of Social Services in 1983. They found that 53 percent of the reports were substantiated and 47 percent were classified as unfounded. Among the unfounded reports, 22 percent had insufficient information to be substantiated, 17 percent were made on the basis of a legitimate concern but had other explanations than abuse, and 8 percent involved "fictitious" cases which were defined as deliberate falsifications. Most of those who comment on this study use the 8 percent figure regarding the incidence of false allegations rather than the larger 47 percent of cases where there was little or no evidence that abuse occurred.

Children's Statements

Much of the controversy about false allegations of child sexual abuse centers on the credibility of children's accounts of abuse. For many years, our society has had difficulty accepting the inherent possibility that children could be sexually abused by trusted adults. It was widely believed that children's accounts of abuse were unreliable because of their tendency to fantasize about sexual events and their difficulty in differentiating between fact and fantasy.

To counter this historical denial, child abuse professionals argued that most children lack the motivation and experience necessary to fabricate detailed accounts of sexual abuse. It became a common belief among professionals that "children don't lie about sexual abuse." As Faller (1984) wrote, "we know that children do not make up stories asserting they have been sexually molested. It is not in their interest to do so. Clinicians and researchers in the field of sexual abuse are in agreement that false allegations by children are extremely rare" (p. 475). To many in the child welfare field, a child's credibility is a matter of faith, you either believe the child when he or she claims to be abused or you do not (Sgroi, Porter, & Blick, 1982, p. 69).

But statements that children don't lie about sexual abuse are overly simplistic and fail to capture the enormous complexity in assessing children's statements about sexual abuse. The notion that children don't lie about sexual abuse also fails to take into account the distinction between truth and truthfulness. While it is true that most children do not intentionally lie about being sexually abused, their statements often contain inconsistencies, inaccuracies, and misperceptions. It is certainly possible that a child can make a believable statement without the statement being accurate. The crucial point is not that children's statements should be believed or disbelieved, but that they should be critically assessed rather than taken at face value.

When false allegations are initiated by children, they most often involve older children who may have been previously abused, who are emotionally disturbed, or who seek some type of secondary gain by claiming to be abused. In their study, "False Allegations of Sexual Abuse by Children and Adolescents," Everson and Boat (1989) found that adolescents who deliberately fabricated an account of abuse usually were motivated by a desire to change placement or living arrangements, were retaliating against parental figures for perceived mistreatment, or were desiring greater responsiveness from significant adults in their lives. There were some situations where it appeared that youths were influenced or encouraged by others to make a false report.

Faulty Evaluations

According to Schetky (1989), the basic problem is not that children are frequently making false disclosures, but that faulty evaluations are leading, in some cases, to the misdiagnosis of abuse. Many of those who are responsible for interviewing alleged victims of child sexual abuse have received little, if any, formal training on how to conduct an investigation.

One of the most common errors in child sexual abuse investigations is prematurely concluding that abuse did in fact occur. As Schuman (1986) has written, "in some quarters there is such a degree of sensitivity or outrage about possible child abuse that a presumption exists that such abuse has occurred whenever it is alleged" (p. 1). In fact, in much of the literature on interviewing alleged victims of child sexual abuse, no mention is made of the possibility that the child may not have been abused. Investigators who conduct their work from this perspective are much more likely to interpret data in a manner that reinforces their bias. They are less likely to explore alternative explanations, search for disconfirming data, or correctly identify false allegations. According to White and Quinn (1987), the most counterproductive interview style occurs when the interviewer has strongly held beliefs about what is supposed to have occurred and attempts to get the child to confirm those beliefs. Ideally, child abuse investigators should always maintain a neutral, fact finding orientation and be willing to consider any plausible explanation for the alleged events.

Many persons accused of child sexual abuse complain that investigations are conducted in an atmosphere of implied guilt from the moment the accusation is made. While many investigations are handled sensitively, accused persons are often frustrated by the inability to remove the "stain of accusation" that lingers over their reputation, even when the case is unfounded or there is an acquittal in a criminal trial. To be labeled a potential abuser has enormous consequences which can result in financial and job losses, family disbandment, and social isolation. Symptoms of psychological distress are also found among many of those involved in protective service investigations. They include: anxiety, fear, angry outbursts, loss of self-confidence, fear of losing their children, obsessive thoughts about the events, and difficulty resuming normal activities (Faller, 1985; Tyler & Brassard, 1984).

Another aspect that is not fully appreciated is the extent to which children can suffer when family relationships are strained or disrupted during a child abuse investigation. As Faller (1984) has written, "the protective service investigation itself can increase the level of stress in the home and place a child at greater risk than before" (p. 65). Children can be harmed emotionally when they have to go through extensive medical and psychological examinations or when they are unnecessarily placed into foster care for protection from abuse that never occurred.

Conclusion

It is my contention that the nature and extent of the problem of false allegations of child sexual abuse depend on how the problem is defined. While there is little good data to support the various claims that have been made about the extent of the problem, there is growing anecdotal evidence that false allegations of child sexual abuse are indeed a serious problem. As indicated in this discussion, false allegations have profound consequences for children, their families, the child protective system, and the public. Our society certainly has an abiding interest in protecting children from sexual abuse. But in carrying out this mission, we must also give due regard to the rights of the accused. This includes due process of law and protection from those who might bear false witness. I believe that professional inattention to the problem of false allegations risks alienating the public trust in the child protective system.

Rejoinder to Mr. Robin
PETER J. PECORA

There can be no doubt, as my colleague Michael Robin points out, that to be falsely accused of child sexual abuse must be enormously stressful. I would expect that most of those who work in child welfare would agree that we should work to minimize such occurrences whenever possible. But from my perspective, the central question that needs to be addressed is whether or not the problem of false allegations of child sexual abuse is as extensive as some have stated. It is my position that there have been many exaggerated claims, based on personal anecdotes, reports by advocacy groups such as Vocal, or studies using small unrepresentative case samples that have produced a distorted and misleading impression of the extent of the problem.

For example, some commentators have implied that sexual abuse accusations initiated by vindictive mothers against their ex-husbands have become routine in the context of child custody disputes. One consequence of this claim is that an air of suspicion has arisen regarding any claim about abuse that occurs in these situations. However, one of the few studies to draw upon a national sample of custody disputes concludes that: (1) only a small proportion of custody disputes involve allegations of abuse, (2) false allegations are not disproportionally higher in custody disputes than in the general population, and (3) most unfounded cases are not made maliciously. In fact, most allegations that do arise in the course of these disputes are considered valid (Thoennes & Tjaden, 1990).

Some advocates have also equated "unfounded" reports, which account for between 40 and 53 percent of all abuse reports (Pecora, et al., 1992, pp. 103–105) with false allegations. While it is true that some undefined proportion of unfounded reports does include false reports, there are actually many explanations for cases that are designated as unfounded. For example, in some cases a child victim may be too young to give a credible account, a perpetrator may have been able to cover up an abuse incident, the available information may be strongly suggestive of maltreatment but sufficient evidence is not available, or perhaps a worker lacked the investigative skills necessary to assess the case. Most child protective service workers define unfounded cases as those where they are unable to find enough evidence to confirm the allegation. When unfounded reports are equated with false allegations, it gives a distorted and misleading impression of the problem and contributes to our societal denial about child sexual abuse.

NO

PETER J. PECORA

For centuries, children have been sexually abused, but it is only in recent years that society has begun to appreciate this problem. In 1984, a cover story in *Newsweek* (May 14) described child sexual abuse as a "hidden epidemic" and far more prevalent than many people realized or were willing to admit. With increasing social awareness of the sexual abuse of children, there has been a significant increase of case reporting to local authorities. Nonetheless, despite the fact that reports of abuse have increased dramatically in recent years, there is considerable evidence that underreporting of sexual abuse still remains a serious and extensive problem.

Underreporting from Victims

Most children who have been sexually abused experience enormous pressure, both internally and externally, to deny their victimization. Consequently, what Summit wrote nearly ten years ago still remains valid to some extent, even with the significant increases in reporting rates. Summit (1983) observes that "Most ongoing sexual abuse is never disclosed, at least not outside the immediate family. Treated, reported or investigated cases are the exception, not the norm. Disclosure is an outgrowth either of overwhelming family conflict, incidental discovery by a third party, or sensitive outreach and community education by child protective agencies" (p. 186).

There are many factors that account for the difficulties children have in talking about sexual abuse. In some cases, the child will not know that what is happening to them is wrong, or they may have a vague sense that it is wrong but blame themselves for the abuse. Many children cope with their abuse by repressing it from consciousness, for to acknowledge the abuse would be too stressful and anxiety provoking. Retrospective studies of adults abused as children show that many children do not report the abuse at the time it is occurring. Many will wait years before talking about their experience and, in some cases, a researcher is the first to be told about the sexual abuse (Berliner, 1989; Sauzier, 1989a; Sorensen & Snow, 1991).

Many children fear the consequences of revealing the abuse, as this can be as stressful as the abuse itself. Some children fear they will be disbelieved and will be punished for lying, or that adults will take no action to protect them from retaliation and further abuse. The child also may fear the family disruption that often accompanies the child protective service investigation. They may be blamed, or blame themselves, for the arrest of the offender. Or they may feel they are being punished when they are placed in out-of-home care. In addition, some children have been threatened with dire consequences, even death, should they reveal the abuse (Sauzier, 1989b).

Even when children overcome their fears and do disclose the abuse, they are often pressured to retract their statements. According to Summit (1983):

> Whatever a child says about sexual abuse, she is likely to reverse it . . . In the chaotic aftermath of disclosure, the child discovers that

the bedrock fears and threats underlying the secrecy are true. Her father abandons her and calls her a liar. Her mother does not believe her or decompensates into hysteria and rage. The family is fragmented, and all the children are placed in custody. The father is threatened with disgrace and imprisonment. The girl is blamed for causing the whole mess, and everyone seems to treat her like a freak (p. 188).

Summit concludes that "unless there is special support for the child and immediate intervention to force responsibility on the father, the girl will follow the 'normal' course and retract her complaint" (p. 188).

Societal Denial

People have a need to believe in a rational, reasonable world. To acknowledge that large numbers of children are molested and abused violates our most cherished notions about ourselves, our families, and our society. It calls into question our belief that ours is a child-centered society. As Summit (1988) proclaims, our society has a profound "blind spot" when it comes to acknowledging the ubiquity of child sexual abuse.

Anyone proclaiming . . . [the reality of child sexual abuse] imposes a dismal flaw in our hope for a just and fair society. All our systems of justice, reason and power have been adjusted to ignore the possibility of such a fatal flaw. Our very sense of enlightenment insists that anything that important could not escape our attention. Where could it hide? Parents would find it out. Doctors would see it. The courts would stop it. Victims would tell their psychiatrists. It would be obvious in psychological tests. Our best minds would know it. It is more reasonable to argue that young upstarts are making trouble. You can't trust kids. Untrained experts are creating a wave of hysteria. They ask leading questions. No family is safe from the invasion of the childsavers. It's time to get back to common sense (p. 51).

Summit and others argue that there is a natural tendency in our society to deny the extent of these types of social problems, which contributes to a public readiness to accept claims of an increase in false allegations.

Conclusion

Assessing the extent of false allegations is a matter of great importance, but there is currently a lack of adequate research studies that would allow us to reliably estimate the extent of the problem. Nonetheless, to claim that false allegations seldom happen is too simplistic. After all, it is certainly reasonable to conclude that a disturbed child may fabricate an incident of abuse, or an overzealous investigator may misdiagnose a case. That this may happen on rare occasions does not imply any fundamental flaw in the system. But if false allegations are as widespread as claimed, then a serious reevaluation of how child sexual abuse investigations are conducted in our society is warranted. While there are certainly improvements that can be made, the fundamental problem is that our society is still having difficulty believing children can be sexually abused in great numbers and that a well-funded child protective system is necessary to protect vulnerable children.

I believe the exaggerated claims about false allegations of child sexual abuse have had the effect of casting doubt on the ability of children to be effective witnesses to their own victimization. If these claims are accepted at face value, this will also call into question the ability of child protective service agencies to effectively handle these cases. While there certainly needs to be some attention paid to the prevention of false allegations, and staff members should have specialized skills before being allowed to investigate these reports, I believe our efforts should be focused on improving support services for the many children who are genuinely abused.

Rejoinder to Professor Pecora   MICHAEL ROBIN

My colleague is certainly correct when he states that many victims of child sexual abuse have difficulty disclosing their victimization. There are many studies that support the notion that much child sexual abuse is underrecognized and underreported. It is true that our society still seems to have a "blind spot" when it comes to acknowledging the sexual abuse of children. However, to say this does not take away from the problem of false allegations. It is not an either/or phenomenon. My belief is that children and their families are harmed when sexual abuse occurs or when they are victims of a false allegation.

If our professional responsibility is to "above all else do no harm," then professionals should do what they can to acknowledge the phenomenon of false allegations and take the necessary steps to prevent and/or ameliorate its negative consequences. Unfortunately, there are many in the child welfare field who have difficulty accepting the possibility that some alleged offenders are innocent, that some children give inaccurate accounts of abuse, or that faulty evaluations can lead, in some cases, to the misdiagnosis of abuse.

But the effective identification and treatment of both child sexual abuse and false allegations depends on the willingness of the professional community and the public to consider the feasibility of either situation. However, it seems that many professionals fear that to give any degree of attention to false allegations as a legitimate problem will undermine public support for abused children and the child protective system. Consequently, many of the concerns about false allegations have either been ignored or discounted. Many of those who have advocated for people they believed were the victims of false allegations, or who have raised the issue of false allegations in public forums, have found their own personal and professional integrity called into question. Those who raise these concerns are often presented as being part of a backlash against child protective services, rather than as people motivated, in most cases, by the desire to improve the quality of services offered to children and their families.

Many professionals minimize the extent and impact of false allegations by claiming they are "rare." They also claim that false allegations usually have typical characteristics that can be detected by experienced professionals. However, most child sexual abuse cases are enormously complex, and there are no simple means of differentiating true from false allegations. It is my conclusion that "to pose the issue of false allegations as a serious social problem is not to suggest that children should be disbelieved when they claim to be abused or that the child protection system needs to be rolled back. Child abuse and neglect still remains a serious problem that demands a social response, professional competencies and even greater public support than it now receives" (Robin, 1991, p. 29).

REFERENCES

Berliner, L. (1989). Resolved: Child sex abuse is overdiagnosed: Negative. *Journal of The American Academy of Child and Adolescent Psychiatry* (28)5, 792–793.

Bok, S. (1978). *Lying.* New York: Vintage Books.

Everson, M., & Boat, B. (1989). False allegations of sexual abuse by children and adolescents. *Journal of the American Academy of Child and Adolescent Psychiatry* 28(2), 230–235.

Faller, K. (1985). Unanticipated problems in the United States child protection system. *Child Abuse and Neglect* (9)1, 63–69.

Faller, K. (1984). Is the child victim of sexual abuse telling the truth? *Child Abuse and Neglect* 8, 473–481.

Jones, D., & McGraw, J. (1987). Reliable and fictitious accounts of sexual abuse to children. *Journal of Interpersonal Violence* 2, 27–45.

Pecora, P. J., Whittaker, J. K., Maluccio, A. N., Barth, R. P., & Plotnick, R. (Eds.) (1992). *The child welfare challenge: Policy, practice and research.* Hawthorne, NY: Aldine de Gruyter.

Robin, M. (1991). The social construction of child abuse and "false allegations." In Robin, M. (Ed.), *Assessing child maltreatment reports: The
problem of false allegations.* NY: The Haworth Press.

Sauzier, M. (1989a). Disclosure of sexual abuse. *Psychiatric Clinics of
North America,* 12(2), 455–469.

Sauzier, M. (1989b). Resolved: Child sex abuse is overdiagnosed: Negative.
*Journal of the American Academy of Child and Adolescent Psychia-
try* (28)5, 793–795.

Schetky, D. (1989). Resolved: Child sex abuse is overdiagnosed: Affirmative. *Journal of the American Academy of Child and Adolescent
Psychiatry* (28)5, 790–792.

Schuman, D. C. (1986). False allegations of physical and sexual abuse.
Bulletin of the American Academy of Psychiatry and the Law 14,
5–21.

Sgroi, S., Porter, F., & Blick, L. (1982). Validation of child sexual abuse. In
Sgroi, S. (Ed.), *Handbook of clinical intervention in child sexual
abuse.* Lexington, MA: Lexington Books.

Sorensen, T., & Snow, B. (1991). How children tell: The process of disclosure in child sexual abuse. *Child Welfare* 70(1), 3–15.

Summit, R. (1988). Hidden victims, hidden pain: Societal avoidance of
child sexual abuse. In Wyatt, G. E., & Powell, G. J. (Eds.), *Lasting
effects of child sexual abuse.* Newbury Park: Sage Publications.

Summit, R. (1983). The child sexual abuse accommodation syndrome.
Child Abuse and Neglect (7)2, 177–193.

Thoennes, N., & Tjaden, P. (1990). The extent, nature, and validity of
sexual abuse allegations in custody/visitation disputes. *Child Abuse
and Neglect* (14)2, 151–160.

Tyler, A., & Brassard, M. (1984). Abuse in the investigation and treatment
of intrafamilial child sexual abuse. *Child Abuse and Neglect* (8)2,
47–53.

Watson, R. (1984). A hidden epidemic. *Newsweek* (103)3, 30–36 (May 14).

White, S., & Quinn, K. (1987). *Problematic interview techniques in child
sexual abuse investigations.* Unpublished manuscript. Cleveland:
School of Medicine, Case Western Reserve University.

ANNOTATED BIBLIOGRAPHY

Faller, K. (1988). *Child sexual abuse.* New York: Columbia University
Press.

This book is an interdisciplinary approach that examines the critical
issues in the diagnosis, case management, and treatment of child
sexual abuse.

Hechler, D. (1988). *The battle and the backlash.* Lexington, MA: Lexington Books.

This is a lively discussion written by an experienced journalist who examines the controversies that have emerged in the child protection field. The book draws on the research literature, case studies, and in-depth interviews in an attempt to formulate a balanced and researched approach to the issues.

Robin, M. (Ed.) (1991). *Assessing child maltreatment reports: The problem of false allegations.* New York: The Haworth Press.

This is a collection of scholarly essays by leading researchers and practitioners in the child welfare field. The authors address the evolution of false allegations of sexual abuse as a social problem and provide practice guidelines for case assessment and management.

Is Community-Based Mental Health Care Destined to Fail?

EDITOR'S NOTE: Developments in the medical treatment of mental illness and successful lobbying against the incarceration of the mentally ill in psychiatric hospitals contributed to the gradual acceptance of a community-based philosophy of care in the 1960s. After decades of relying on large, custodial institutions to provide for the chronically mentally ill, mental health policy began to emphasize community-based treatment instead. Many mental institutions were closed, community-based mental health centers were established, and families became more involved in caring for their mentally ill members. Although these developments were favorably received, there is a recognition that deinstitutionalization has not been an unqualified success. Insufficient funding for community programs has resulted in inadequate services for the mentally ill, and many mentally ill people have become homeless. Some mental health experts now feel that community-based mental health programs are destined to fail. Others disagree, arguing that a greater commitment to community care through adequate funding and appropriate services can meet the needs of mentally ill people.

In this debate, John R. Belcher, Ph.D., argues, YES, community-based mental health care is destined to fail. Dr. Belcher is Associate Professor at the School of Social Work, University of Maryland at Baltimore. He has published numerous articles on mental health policy in scholarly journals and is the author is *Helping the Homeless* (1990), Lexington Books.

Kia J. Bentley, Ph.D., argues NO. Dr. Bentley is Assistant Professor at the School of Social Work, Virginia Commonwealth University. She has published widely on mental health issues in numerous social work and social policy journals.

YES

JOHN R. BELCHER

The Lack of Commitment

Is community-based mental health care destined to fail? In my opinion it is failing and will continue to fail. While we know what to do clinically, there has never been the commitment at any level of government to adequately fund community-based mental health care. In this era when state governments now determine mental health policy, some governments do a better job than others in adequately funding a community-based mental health care system. However, an adequately funded community-based mental health care system remains an illusion and a dream for the majority of the severely mentally ill.

The current fiscal dilemma confronting many Community Mental Health Centers (CMHCs) is not new. In fact, since the inception of CMHCs the lack of funding has been a significant problem. Insufficient funding highlights the fact that despite a great deal of political rhetoric, there has never been a commitment to develop a community-based mental health system. During the 1960s the federal government began a major effort to launch community-based mental health care. This effort, which was embodied in the Community Mental Health Centers Act, was destined to fail since the Act was based on smoke and mirrors as opposed to a commitment to adequately funded community-based care. President John F. Kennedy made the decision, like his predecessor President Franklin Pierce, to leave the funding of mental health care to the states. It is true that the federal government did provide seed money to pay for start-up costs of the CMHCs, but as this money expired most state governments were unwilling and often unable to pick up the tab. Consequently, over half the number of planned CMHCs were never built, and by the middle 1970s the majority of these CMHCs that were built were undergoing severe financial crises.

The CMHC Act was an illusion that begged the real issue of funding. What level of government would pay for community-based care? Many state officials in the 1960s never agreed to underwrite CMHCs. In fact, the decision-making process used to develop CMHCs often bypassed state officials. Politically, the CMHC Act was a masterful ploy of deception and the ultimate shifting of blame for inadequately funded community-based care. President Kennedy promised the development of community-based care, but only obligated the federal government to pay for five to seven years of start-up costs. At the end of these funding cycles, state officials were often blamed for not funding the CMHCs, and the federal government pretended to be the White Knight who chastised state officials. The General Accounting Office did issue a report in the 1970s which was highly critical of the federal government for not adequately funding the CMHCs, yet the federal government was able to largely escape responsibility.

The federal government's response to this crisis was to enact additional legislation, the Mental Health Systems Act. This act never came to fruition because President Reagan effectively abolished it with the passage of his Omnibus Budget Reconciliation Act (OBRA) of 1981. On the one hand, OBRA signaled a major shift in public policy by the federal government toward states becoming the major funders of community mental health. On the other hand, the federal government, despite its rhetoric to the contrary, has always shortchanged funding for community mental health and effectively placed fiscal responsibility for the care of the severely mentally ill on state governments.

Conservative State Governments

The vision of community mental health has often been a low priority among state legislators who owe their reelections to voters who demand lower taxes and noninterventionist state governments. Sensing that increased tax revenues are unlikely, some mental health policy strategists have advocated dismantling state hospitals and transferring these monies to the community. This clinically unsound approach offers little help for the chronically mentally ill who become indigent or who do not recover from their most recent acute episode in the number of days covered by Medicare/Medicaid. In addition, it makes the vision of community mental health less likely to come to fruition because it furthers the illusion that all severely mentally ill clients can be quickly treated in community hospitals.

The reality confronting those professionals concerned with guaranteeing a broader based community mental health system is that most state governments are unwilling to commit the tax dollars to adequately finance such a system, and the federal government has basically left the policy arena by providing no real support for the CMHCs. It is true that the National Institute of Mental Health (NIMH) funds demonstration projects that help to show mental health providers about services that do benefit the chronically mentally ill, but these projects are seldom adopted and funded by state governments committed to fiscal austerity.

The decision to place greater responsibility for the funding of community-based mental health care with state governments highlighted the states' rights controversy that has its roots in the Madisonian view of the division of government responsibility. James Madison, a wealthy landowner, argued that states were supposed to determine most public policy, and that the federal government was supposed to maintain an army and remain out of everything else. The Madisonian tradition is alive and well and has been active in both liberal and conservative federal administrations. President Kennedy shifted fiscal responsibility to the states, and President Reagan continued this approach.

Today, state legislators, with their historic tendency to be fiscally conservative, continue to slash funding for mental health programs. Instead of admitting that mental health care is underfunded, the severely mentally ill are often blamed for their plight.

Victim Blaming Instead of Adequate Funding

Examples abound that highlight the insurmountable fiscal problems confronting the community mental health system. In their haste to create community-based care, state legislators and commissioners of mental health have effectively emasculated state hospitals by overloading these facilities with the most difficult patients and not adequately funding the clinical care necessary to attend to the patients. When the patients are released from state hospitals into the community, they often are discharged to the street, to relatives who have rejected them in the past, or to addresses that prove upon further investigation to be places where the client is unlikely to remain. At this juncture, the client is labeled as noncompliant and is either cast out of the mental health system or may be lucky enough to become enrolled in one of the NIMH case management demonstration projects. The label of noncompliance is really an issue of inadequate funding. While the client may want to comply, a combination of premature or inappropriate discharge and a lack of mobile treatment teams exacerbate the client's illness and make him or her distrustful of treatment.

Research in Lieu of Adequate Funding

The process of blaming the victim is aided by the proliferation of mental health research that masks funding problems as clinical problems. NIMH spends millions of dollars on answering the question: Who are the mentally ill? Federal and state mental health planners are able to respond that they are diligently studying the problem. Meanwhile, system gaps that create hopelessness among the severely mentally ill continue to worsen. The next generation of NIMH research is apparently going to address the problem of developing services for the homeless mentally ill.

Few policy makers have stopped to ask the questions: What is homelessness? Isn't homelessness among the severely mentally ill a symptom of inadequate funding? Why is there a rise in the number of severely mentally ill who now reside, at least temporarily, in the nation's jails? These questions do not require millions of dollars of research money from the federal government. Instead, these questions cut to the core of the debate over the destiny of community-based care. Rather than provide adequate funding for community-based care, it is cheaper to fund researchers to study the problem and develop demonstration projects that, despite their merits, will most likely not be funded as part of the services system.

The real dilemma confronting advocates of community-based programs for the severely mentally ill is that the severely mentally ill are a dependent population that, despite the best efforts of committed clinicians from a variety of disciplines, will not recover sufficiently to begin lives of economic self-sufficiency. A minority of the severely mentally ill (SMI) will recover and move into the economic mainstream, but the majority will remain dependent upon state and/or federal subsidies. Henry Foley and Steve Sharfstein titled a book, *Madness and Government: Who Cares for the Mentally Ill?* They argue that this question boils down to a moral question.

A society can be judged on how well it cares for people unable to care for themselves. The severely mentally ill are often unable to care for themselves, but the United States as a nation has decided to inadequately fund programs that offer some hope of proper treatment. Clinicians know what kinds of treatment work. The effectiveness of community-based programs for the majority of the SMI have been proven to be effective. The dilemma is that many of these programs are as expensive, if not more expensive, than hospital-based care.

Rather than delude ourselves into believing that a silver bullet can be found to cure all severely mentally ill clients or that community-based care is always cheaper than hospital-based care, a more fruitful effort is to wrestle with ways to properly fund programs for the severely mentally ill that include both hospital- and community-based care. National health insurance offers one such hope, and it has proven to be cheaper to operate than the present health/mental health care system. The problem with national health insurance is that it changes the balance of power by capping the profits of health/mental health providers by forcing them to provide care to all citizens of the state on an equal basis. As long as the severely mentally ill receive their health care through a combination of Medicare/ Medicaid, it will be obvious that they are dependent. In a capitalist nation committed primarily to serving those who can pay market prices for services, consumers who are unable to pay market prices will continue to receive inferior care.

Is community-based mental health care destined to fail? In my opinion it is failing, has always failed, and there is nothing on the horizon that leads me to believe that the nation intends to begin adequately funding community-based care for the severely mentally ill.

Rejoinder to Professor Belcher   KIA J. BENTLEY

Dr. Belcher has made some interesting and even provocative points in his doom and gloom assessment of the future of community-based mental health care. He argues that the necessary financial commitment on any level is not, nor is it ever likely to be, adequate to accomplish the goals laid out since the 1960s. I have concurred that insufficient dollars is one of the significant restraining forces to moving the vision forward. I am fascinated, however, by the implication that planning in the early days of community mental health was really a "masterful ploy of deception" and was "designed" to make the system fail. If this is indeed true, perhaps we should all look forward to Oliver Stone's movie on this subject in the director's continuing exploration of the 1960s.

Indeed, Dr. Belcher's position might best be described as revisionist history. Rather than a conspiracy of self-centered capitalists, mental health policy leaders of the past forty years have been characterized by their excitement and optimism, as well as a commitment to what each thought was the "best interest" of consumers. Of course, economic, social, and professional factors are involved, as players try to create win–win solutions for the future. Henry Foley and Steven Sharfstein (1983), authors of a book that Dr. Belcher cites, write one of the most stirring descriptions of the early efforts in shaping policy in this area.

While Dr. Belcher portrays President Kennedy as a sort of "bad guy," most other policy analysts would recognize his leadership as a key and positive force in the movement toward community-based care. It was exactly thirty years ago that President Kennedy (1963) spoke to the nation about the urgent need for a revised system of mental health care, the first such presentation from a president. He proclaimed that "if our nation is to live up to its standards of compassion and dignity . . . then the tradition of neglect must be replaced by forceful and far reaching programs . . ." One wonders how long it will be before another president so boldly supports this vision.

One of the most titillating points made by Dr. Belcher is his suggestion that NIMH-sponsored research diverts attention and money from real problems and solutions. This is a gutsy and surprising stand since my colleague has been a benefactor of several NIMH grants. Nevertheless, one wonders if he would have us attempt to plan for meaningful change in the absence of meaningful data—a mistake that certainly recalls the days of old.

My own view is that it may be time to try a new strategy in staking a claim for the needs of persons with mental illness, and for reawakening the fire within today's mental health advocates. Perhaps it is time to focus on what we *have* done; to point to heartening and even dramatic advances in treatment, research, and policy; and to vigorously applaud and support the coalitions of families and consumers. It is also time that we genuinely listen to creative new ideas. It may be that our new legacy of negativity serves mainly to "discourage resource allocation, demoralize committed professionals, and perpetuate false stigma and hopelessness" (James, 1987, p. 448).

Maybe my force-field analysis is too complex for a problem that is really just a matter of money, as my colleague suggests. Maybe, it is really as simple as Dr. Belcher seeing the glass as half empty and my seeing it as half full.

NO

KIA J. BENTLEY

Numerous factors have been associated with the first rumblings and the eventual thundering of the deinstitutionalization movement in mental health. The most prominent factors cited are the advances in psychopharmacology beginning in the mid-1950s, landmark legal decisions, federal legislation, and a general shift in the philosophy of treatment. Specifically, a "community mental health philosophy" emerged in the 1960s and 1970s that said it is better to treat the mentally ill near their families, communities, and jobs, and in the least restrictive environment possible. Advances in psychosocial rehabilitation also contributed to the optimistic assumptions that community care would not only be better but also cheaper than institutional care.

However, as has been thoroughly discussed and debated in the literature, both the deinstitutionalization and community mental health movements, as they were implemented, have yielded disappointing, and some would say harmful, results. Policy makers, providers, consumers, and families can all point to the "transinstitutionalization" of patients to nursing or boarding homes, to jails, and to the streets. They can point to the fragmentation of services and responsibilities, and the huge numbers of unmet needs for both seriously emotionally disturbed children and severely mentally ill adults. These sad realities are undeniable. Yet there is an important question for the future: Can a community-based system of mental health care really ever become a reality, given the incredible legacy of economic, social, and political constraints? Are there forces out there that support a hopeful view for the future of community-based care? I certainly think so, as you will see below.

The Vision of Community-Based Care

Community-based care means simply that the community is, or should be, the major locus of care for a mentally ill child, adolescent, or adult. It also means that the community should have sole responsibility and authority for following an individual's care, no matter where he or she happens to be in the system. The goal of community-based care is to help establish and sustain a good quality of life for persons with mental illness by providing continuity of care through a continuum of services and supports. In the past few years, and in part due to federal initiatives such as P.L. 99-660, providers and consumers across the states have successfully worked together to articulate and build a consensus around a vision or model of community-based care, including its value bases and priorities. There is strong agreement that all services offered should be of the highest quality, flexible, tailored to the individual, well coordinated, easily accessible, and perhaps most importantly, consumer and family oriented.

We *are* moving toward realizing this vision. However, as in the past we are doing so slowly, unevenly, and imperfectly. That does not mean that we will not get there. The barriers to progress which contribute to the conservative nature of policy change can be identified, anticipated, and addressed. Likewise, forces that serve to facilitate movement toward the vision are gaining strength and acceptance. The results of this simple force-field analysis (see Figure 13.1) make me believe strongly that community-based mental health care is *not* destined to fail. Let me be more specific.

Figure 13.1   Force-Field Analysis of Community-Based Mental Health Care

Restraining Forces

low public opinion, discrimination, reimbursement incentives, inadequate funding, lack of a continuum of care, organizational and professional "turf" issues, mutual federal and state distrust, state hospital personnel employment security issues, and the long-term care concerns of families

Community-Based Mental Health Care

Facilitating Forces

clear vision and historical commitment, philosophical consensus among providers and consumers, research regarding effectiveness and efficiency, case law and the least restrictive alternative doctrine, and legislative mandates

Restraining Forces

Admittedly, there are powerful forces (some seemingly insurmountable) which stand in the way of achieving the vision of community-based care as defined earlier. There is low public opinion of the mentally ill (often based on myths) which serves to make the public afraid and therefore resistant to full community participation. There is outright discrimination in favorably reviewing mentally ill applicants for jobs, aid, and housing. This makes the creation of a network of supports much more difficult. There is also the well documented problem of reimbursement incentives which reward inpatient care over outpatient treatment or community supports. There is a lack of adequate funding that has been a pervasive drain on programs and personnel in the field. This contributes to an inadequate continuum of services in the community. Needed services and supports, including housing, job training, case management, and psychosocial rehabilitation, are often simply not there. Organizational and professional "turf" battles only serve to divert attention from the best interests of the consumer. Similarly, the states don't seem to trust the federal government and the federal government doesn't seem to trust the states. Everyone is suspicious of everyone else's motives. Even employees of inpatient facilities worry about their jobs and their role in the "brave new world" of community-based care. Families also worry that "the community" may not offer the same long-term security that "the asylum" has offered for centuries.

Yes, the restraining forces are formidable. But there are signs of change and reasons for hope. For example, the Americans with Disabilities Act (P.L. 101-336) will unquestionably reduce overt discrimination against persons with mental illness. The media will undoubtedly continue to be more sensitive to the treatment of the mentally ill in movies and on television. Advocacy organizations such as National Alliance for the Mentally Ill, the National Mental Health Association, and even our own National Association of Social Workers have active and growing campaigns to influence what we see in the media and thereby change the way the public views persons with mental illness. Many states have begun to seriously examine and implement ways to restructure the financing of both public and private mental health care away from institutionalization. These include incentive or single-stream financing, which rewards communities for decreased reliance on inpatient facilities. Numerous private insurers (including publicly based Medicaid) are covering nonmedical services such as case management and psychosocial rehabilitation. Regarding numerous "turf" battles, one can only hope that the increased attention on interdisciplinary, interagency, and provider–consumer collaboration (including academic–public liaisons at almost every level of service planning and delivery) are steps in the right direction. Regarding the concerns of state hospital employees, Goodrich (1990) describes how some states have creatively addressed their interests through a range of strategies including redeployment to the community, transfer, retraining, and early retirement. Likewise, some families who are able are paying more attention to long-term care issues such as estate planning, guardianship, and the like.

These brief examples of very complex forces and counterforces are not intended to dismiss the power of these very real barriers, or to imply a simple solution. They are offered only to point to glimmers (some large and some small) of hope and to make a case for the positive direction of change.

Facilitating Forces

One of the strongest forces that supports movement toward community-based care is the historical commitment to such a system on a number of government levels. At the federal level, an explicit commitment might be traced to the report of the Joint Commission on Mental Health and Mental Illness in the late 1950s, which proposed a national system of community mental health centers. In my own state of Virginia, there has been a parallel documentation of the state's explicit and unambiguous philosophical commitment to community-based care dating back to 1949 (Davidson, 1991). The unprecedented consensus (discussed earlier) among policy makers, providers, families, and consumers on the vision of community-based care is another powerful facilitating force. Three other forces are equally as important.

First, there is the research which consistently documents the cost effectiveness of community-based care versus inpatient care. Goldberg (1991) recently reviewed the large literature in this area and found once again that community care is generally cheaper and more cost effective, often offering superior results to hospital care.

Second, case law, especially the deeply ingrained legal principle of "least restrictive environment," continues to support community-based care. Indeed, the role of case law in influencing the structure of service delivery may be in its infancy. I am thinking specifically about the Protection and Advocacy Act (P.L. 101-509), which continues to widen its domain beyond the institutionalized patient toward all consumers of public mental health services. For example, in the reauthorization, the interpretation of "neglect" seems to have been expanded. It would be interesting to see what would happen if our failure to deliver adequate, tailored, flexible, accessible, consumer- and family-oriented services is eventually included somehow in the definition of "neglect."

Finally, there are numerous federal regulations that clearly support community-based care (Bentley, 1991). The two most important may be the mental health block grant portion of the Public Health Services Act, which explicitly specifies that money only be used for community services and activities, and P.L. 99-660, referred to earlier, which clearly mandates comprehensive planning by states toward a truly community-based system of mental health care *while* reducing hospitalization rates.

Conclusion

It is clear to me that even with powerful economic, social, and political constraints, community-based mental health care is not destined to fail. Like any complex effort, it will continue to evolve slowly but certainly toward a positive system that many can envision. Hopefully, we won't continue to have to close our eyes to see it in its fullest.

Rejoinder to Professor Bentley JOHN R. BELCHER

Dr. Bentley argues that as a society we are moving toward realizing the vision of community mental health, even though she admits we are doing so in a slow, uneven, and imperfect fashion. My reading of mental health policy over the last several decades, as well as an examination of the present state of the mental health system, leads me to argue that as a society we will fail to reach the goal of a community-based mental health system.

My pessimistic prediction is based on the unreality of the goal. Community-based care for all severely mentally ill clients is based on a clinically unsound and naive view of the disease process of severe mental illnesses, such as schizophrenia. People with severe mental health problems often need structured care, and community-based services are not able to adequately respond to their needs (Lamb, 1984; Belcher, 1988a). A more reasonable goal is to advocate for appropriate care for our clients, which for many should be community-based care. However, some will need continuing access to hospitals.

Arguing for community-based care for all mentally ill clients is similar to arguing for community-based care for all patients with cancer. What about cancer patients who need hospitalization? My contention is that community-based care has historically been a vehicle that fiscal conservatives have used to effectively divide mental health professionals and push forward an agenda that trades off hospital care for community-based care.

Whether I agree or disagree with the goal of community-based care for all mentally ill clients is irrelevant. It is more important that readers of this debate understand that the inability to reach the goal of community-based care for all mentally ill clients exists largely because the approach is clinically unsound. The fact cannot be ignored is that most state hospitals have become revolving doors for young severely mentally ill clients who cannot function in the community.

The rest of this debate will rebut some of Dr. Bentley's points. Dr. Bentley points out that there are powerful forces that may stand in the way of developing a community-based system. Among the forces she points to are "low public opinion of the mentally ill, . . . outright discrimination in jobs, aid, or housing, insufficient reimbursement incentives, and a lack of appropriate funding." I agree that these are powerful forces. However, Dr. Bentley fails to raise the important barrier of the nature of severe and persistent mental illness. A significant number of schizophrenic patients fail to continue their medication. Despite the best efforts of community mental health staff, many still require hospitalization, other severely ill patients do not respond to current medications and require structured care, and finally, many severely mentally ill individuals are not capable of working or even living on an ongoing basis in the community.

The restraining forces are "formidable," as Dr. Bentley appropriately points out. However, these forces are not as "formidable" as the disease process of severe mental illnesses, such as schizophrenia. It is true that many of these patients can live for a time in the community, but many will require periodic hospitalizations. Hospitalization should not be considered a failure or a sign that community systems are not functioning; instead, hospitalization is part of the normal process of life for many severely ill patients.

Dr. Bentley also points to " . . . the historical commitment to such a (community-based) system on a number of government levels." I read history much differently. The Joint Commission on Mental Health and Mental Illness did not chart a clear course for community-based care. The role and need of hospitals was also discussed, but ignored by Robert Felix and his colleagues at the National Institute of Mental Health. Many state governments did not welcome community mental health centers (CMHCs) with open arms, particularly since the seed money for the CMHCs would run out in five to seven years. Many states remain reluctant today to adequately fund CMHCs. Government at all levels has usually turned a blind eye toward adequately funding appropriate services for the mentally ill and exceptions, such as Governor Bill Celeste of Ohio, should be viewed as exceptions and not the norm.

Dr. Bentley cites Goldberg (1991), noting that community care is generally cheaper and more cost effective. In fact, good community care is sometimes as expensive and often more expensive than hospital care (Belcher, 1992; Borland, et al., 1989; and Franklin, 1988). Clients need different levels of care, and some clients only respond to a very intensive form of case management because of the severity of their illness.

The notion of the least restrictive alternative (LRA) is also cited as supporting community-based care. It is true that the LRA has been used by many advocates for community-based care. However, critics have questioned this point of view, noting that the original legal ruling that used the LRA did not issue an order stating that people should never be treated in the hospital (Belcher and Blank, 1989/90). Instead, the LRA was used to say that the treatment environment should be the least restrictive for that particular patient. For some patients the LRA may be the hospital. The LRA has also been questioned because of its clinical utility (Bachrach, 1980). Is the LRA always the best? Once again, it depends on the needs of the client. A client who is acutely psychotic and paranoid may need an LRA environment, such as a hospital, where he or she is left alone and given time to recompensate while adjusting to medication. Community living may exacerbate his or her condition and result in movement to a more restrictive environment. If we are zealots on a mission, then perhaps we should rally behind the LRA and demand community-based care for all mentally ill clients. If, on the other hand, we are mental health professionals, then we should consider the needs of the client and advocate for the LRA that best meets the needs of the client.

Dr. Bentley also notes that the Public Health Services Act "explicitly specifies" that money from the Act only be used for community-based care. This Act highlights the major reason why community-based care is destined to fail. It fuels the headlong rush to dismantle and close mental hospitals, yet it ignores the clinical realities of severe mental illness. Where will a person with schizophrenia who needs hospitalization go? The concept of "Never in the Hospital" is not in the best interest of clients, and more importantly, it increases decompensation in clients and results in many of them ending up in city jails where they become victimized (Belcher, 1988b).

It is interesting that the Public Health Services Act, which is grossly underfunded, mandates that states move toward community-based care. This same political tactic was attempted by President Kennedy, who mandated that CMHCs provide a wide array of services, but did not provide adequate federal funds to support the services. As it became evident that many CMHCs did not provide the appropriate services, the CMHCs and state governments were criticized for not complying with federal mandates. (Meanwhile, federal leaders avoided criticism.) The federal government is using a similar tactic today. States will be unable to comply with the federal mandates because of state politics. State leaders are generally elected on the promise of either reducing or limiting taxes (Bevilacqua & Noble, 1987), which makes it unlikely that state governments will adequately fund programs that do not directly benefit the middle class. The recent cutbacks and the elimination of welfare grants in many states highlight the tendency of state governments to move toward fiscal conservatism. History has shown that the federal government is the most likely level of government to develop and implement policies that support dependent populations (Belcher & DiBlasio, 1990). But, the Reagan revolution and the subsequent acquiescence of democratic lawmakers make increased federal support of programs for dependent populations unlikely.

Conclusion

Community-based care for *some* severely mentally ill people is a clinically sound approach, but it is unlikely to be adequately funded by any level of government during the next decade. Community-based care for *all* severely mentally ill clients is a clinically unsound approach that provides ammunition to fiscal conservatives at all levels of government who want to reduce services to this population. No services are inexpensive. Denied access to hospitals, many mentally ill people wander the streets in search of help. This fact is denied by many in the mental health field who argue that community-based care works for *all* clients and that the homeless mentally ill are an aberration or a "silver bullet." They argue that techniques such as case management will assist those unfortunate severely mentally ill clients who fall through the cracks of the system. The "silver bullet" has eluded this nation and will continue to elude it. Newly discovered drugs, such as Clozapine, have serious side effects and do not benefit some patients. Case management does work for most, but it can be prohibitively expensive.

As a society we face a moral dilemma. The way we care for our mentally ill is a disgrace. Instead of rhetoric driven by fiscal conservatism, it is important to move toward some sense of direction that is supported by clinical insight, services research, and sound judgment.

REFERENCES

Bachrach, L. L. (1980). Is the least restrictive alternative always the best? *Hospital and Community Psychiatry* (31)2, 99.

Belcher, J. R. (1992). Plan implementation and coordination: Clinical case management with the chronically mentally ill. In Vourlekis, B. S., & Greene, R. R. (Eds.), *Social Work Case Management.* New York: Aldine De Gruyter, 107–124.

Belcher, J. R. (1988a). The future role of state hospitals. *The Psychiatric Hospital* 19, 79–83.

Belcher, J. R. (1988b). Are jails replacing the mental health system for the homeless mentally ill? *Community Mental Health Journal* (24)3, 185–195.

Belcher, J. R., & Blank, H. (1989/90). Protecting the right to involuntary commitment. *Journal of Applied Social Sciences* (14)1, 74–88.

Belcher, J. R., & DiBlasio, F. A. (1990). *Helping the homeless: Where do we go from here?* New York: Macmillan.

Bentley, K. J. (1991). *Analysis of legislative mandates to support community-based care: A report to the Commissioner.* Richmond, VA: Department of Mental Health, Mental Retardation and Substance Abuse Services.

Bevilacqua, J. J., & Noble, H. H. (1987). Chronic mental illness: A problem in politics. In Menninger, W. W., & Hannah, G. (Eds.), *The chronic mental patient II.* Washington, D.C.: The American Psychiatric Press.

Borland, A., MacRae, J., & Lycan, C. (1989). Outcomes of five years of continuous intensive case management. *Hospital and Community Psychiatry* (40)4, 369–376.

Davidson, C. (1991). *Summary of the philosophical statements on community-based services: 1949 to present.* Richmond, VA: Department of Mental Health, Mental Retardation, and Substance Abuse Services.

Foley, H., & Sharfstein, S. (1983). *Madness and government: Who cares for the mentally ill.* Washington, D.C.: American Psychiatric Press.

Franklin, J. L. (1988). Case management: A dissenting view. *Hospital and Community Psychiatry* (39)9, 921.

Goldberg, D. (1991). Cost-effectiveness studies in the treatment of schizophrenia: A review. *Social Psychiatric Epidemiology* 26(3), 139–142.

Goodrich, D. (1990). *States' experiences in transferring financial and staff resources from inpatient to community mental health service systems.* Washington, D.C.: National Institute of Mental Health (Contract No. 278-87-0010 [ES]) Division of Applied Services Research.

James, J. F. (1963). Does the community mental health movement have the momentum to survive? *American Journal of Orthopsychiatry* (57)3, 447–451.

Kennedy, J. F. (1963). Message of the President of the United States relevant to mental illness and mental retardation. Speech to the 88th Congress and the Nation (Document #58). Washington, D.C., February.

Lamb, H. R. (1984). The need for continuing asylum and sanctuary. *Hospital and Community Psychiatry* (35)8, 798–802.

ANNOTATED BIBLIOGRAPHY

Brown, P. (1985) *The transfer of care: Deinstitutionalization and its aftermath.* Boston, MA: Routledge & Kegan Paul.

This book is a radical and engaging analysis of the evolution of mental health policy in the United States, with special focus on economic, social, and professional influences.

Foley, H., & Sharfstein, S. (1983). *Madness and government: Who cares for the mentally ill.* Washington, D.C.: American Psychiatric Press.

The authors, who were actual participants, tell a behind-the-scenes story of the development of federal mental health policy up to the Reagan years. Appendices include actual legislation and speeches by Kennedy and Carter.

Goodrich, D. (1990). *States' experiences in transferring financial and staff resources from inpatient to community mental health services sys-*

tems. Washington, D.C.: National Institute of Mental Health (Contract No. 278-87-0010 (ES)) Division of Applied Services Research.

This is one of several excellent, up-to-date reports by Goodrich, a consultant with the COSMOS Corporation. This report is on current innovations in mental health policy implementation around the country. Other reports, including families and consumers in planning, and restructuring financial incentives, are also available.

James, J. F. (1987). Does the community mental health movement have the momentum to survive? *American Journal of Orthopsychiatry* 57, 447–451.

This brief but refreshing article is one of a special series in this issue on public mental health policy. The article calls for an end to finger pointing and a "failure mentality." The author effectively highlights the needs for a strengths focus as a strategy for change.

Can Changing the Workplace Transform Child Welfare?

EDITOR'S NOTE: Child welfare services are currently under great strain. Inadequate funding, poorly trained personnel, heavy caseloads, and fragmented services have resulted in serious problems which have affected the quality of services. Many agree that something must be done. One suggestion is that the workplace setting in which child welfare services are provided needs to be overhauled. Bureaucratic programs, hierarchical organizational structures, and rigid procedures all contribute to the demoralization and ineffectiveness of staff. If a more flexible, humane, and responsive work environment were created, the quality of services would dramatically improve. While opponents of this idea agree that workplace changes would be helpful, they argue that such changes cannot solve the current crisis of the child welfare system. Major improvements in funding, proper training, new legislative mandates, and the professionalism of services are required. Opponents argue that while the work environment is a major determinant of staff commitment, it is naive to assume that such changes can solve the problem.

Examining these issues, Burton J. Cohen, Ph.D., argues YES, that workplace changes can change child welfare. Dr. Cohen is Adjunct Assistant Professor and Project Director of the Quality of Worklife Project at the School of Social Work, University of Pennsylvania. His research is concerned with redesigning work systems to improve the quality of work life in the human services. He has published on these issues in various social work and social administration journals.

Brenda G. McGowan, DSW, argues NO, that changing the workplace cannot change child welfare. Dr. McGowan is Professor of Social Work at the School of Social Work at Columbia University. She has published widely on child welfare issues and is the author of *Child Advocacy* (1973), U.S. Government Printing Office; *Why Punish the Child* (1978), National Council on Crime and Delinquency; *Children without Homes* (1978), Children's Defense Fund; and *Child Welfare: Current Dilemmas, Future Directions* (1983), Peacock.

YES

BURTON J. COHEN

Most observers would agree that the child welfare system in the United States needs to undergo a major transformation. The problems of the current system have been documented by many writers: rising caseloads, increases in the number of serious multiproblem families; fragmented services isolated from the communities; disillusioned and burned-out workers leaving the field; lack of resources; and an overly bureaucratized system that stifles innovation and is overly concerned with compliance and protection from legal liability. Critics also agree on many of the attributes that a transformed system should have. However, there is much less agreement about how to go about transforming the system.

The usual response is that transformation has to come from outside the system. The system itself is typically portrayed as powerless, overwhelmed, and suffering from a lack of resources and support. A recent national study (Kamerman & Kahn, 1989) found that family and children's services in most areas are barely coping and are forced to target their resources on only the most serious cases. The proposed solutions are broad-based changes in social policy, including a larger role for government, mandates for strong professional child protective services, more public funding, and more cross-system cooperation.

A second response is to add a new layer of programs, each aimed at filling a special need or gap in services. This, however, would not encourage a fundamental change in how services are organized or delivered. A third response is to view transformation as resulting from organized political action that could force a change through the intervention of the courts or by a higher level of government. The objective is to either replace those who are running the system or to force the allocation of more resources, or both.

The Need to Restructure the Child Welfare Workplace

Until recently, not much attention was focused on the need to redesign or restructure the work environment in which public child welfare services are provided. A conference sponsored in 1986 by NASW and the Administration on Children, Youth, and Families called for "an examination of agency working conditions around the country," and for "developing guidelines for enhancing the work environment" (University of Southern Maine, 1987). Some researchers have also begun to explore the relationship between bureaucratization and worker dissatisfaction and burnout (Arches, 1991). Others have made the connection between workplace conditions and the ability to recruit and retain social work staff (Ewalt, 1991).

It's time that we take a serious look at the need for restructuring the organizational settings and workplaces in which child welfare services are provided. Some have argued that a fundamental restructuring of the workplace is "both unlikely to be implemented and difficult to achieve." They have proposed "morale enhancers" (stress reduction classes, exercise, flextime, etc.) as the only way to improve the working environment (McNeely, 1988). Others have focused on the deficiencies of the workers and have proposed more training. A few critics have now challenged the tendency to focus on individuals. Esposito and Fine (1985), in their exploration of child welfare as a "world of work," concluded that workplace strategies targeted at individuals may only perpetuate the conditions that promote burnout, and that working conditions need to be addressed through structural changes, beginning with "the systematic disruption of the chain of command in child welfare." More recently, Arches (1991) criticized the lack of autonomy of workers and called for a new workplace that challenges the "assumptions about the efficiency of the bureaucratic organization."

But what do we mean by "changing the workplace"? The changes that are required are fundamental and substantive. The child welfare field needs to consider the same types of restructuring and work redesign that have occurred in other sectors of society during the past decade. For example, in many public school systems, "hierarchies of control and methodological prescriptions are giving way to more flexible, student outcome-oriented approaches" (Centron & Davies, 1989). These new approaches include downsizing schools, creating "schools-within-schools," and giving principals and teachers more responsibility and authority through school-based management and shared decision making. In comparing the response of the educational establishment to that in child welfare, Thomas (1990) concluded that "It is unclear, at the moment, whether the managers of the child welfare services system will exercise the courage and vision to promote a similar degree of experimentation to achieve reform, or whether they will opt instead to try to preserve the present top-down monolithic service structure."

Recommendations for Restructuring the Child Welfare Workplace

Changing the child welfare workplace means redesigning people's roles, the way the work itself is organized, and the manner in which decisions are made. In order to achieve this, four major changes are required:

1. *Promote continuous experimentation and learning in "sheltered settings" that represent a microcosm of the organization.* While it is often tempting to think that agency transformation can occur through the top-down promulgation of new policies or programs, experience in other settings has shown this to be a fallacy. More typically, successful organizational change starts at the periphery of the organization, is led by general managers of the smaller units, and then moves steadily back toward the organizational core (Beer, Eisenstadt, & Spector, 1990). In child welfare agencies, this means we should focus on parts of the organization as laboratories where new ideas can be nurtured and tested. These parts should be smaller than the whole organization, but large enough to contain a variety of roles and to be representative of the kinds of problems encountered in performing the work.

2. *Involve and empower child welfare staff.* Most child welfare workers feel that they have little say in decisions about how their work is to be performed. Empowerment means giving workers the authority and resources to make decisions and take initiative in ways that will improve services. It also implies the responsibility of management to support those decisions and stand by the workers if difficulties arise.

3. *Redesign work systems to "follow the clients" by breaking down barriers between staff functions.* Public bureaucracies are often designed more from the perspective of the managers than from that of the clients. They are often organized by functions (e.g., investigations, ongoing cases, adoptions), with each function forming a vertical division reporting up to a division head. This often results in a lack of communication and coordination across divisions. It also leaves it up to the clients to manage the transition from one division to the next on their own, a feat for which they are often ill equipped. Child welfare agencies should be redesigned so that the organizational structure follows the flow of work and supports clients in moving through the system. This will promote better continuity of service and will also improve work relationships within the agency by tearing down walls between divisions.

4. *Promote leadership on the part of middle-level general managers.* In order for selective parts of the organization to be used as laboratories, the managers of these parts have to see themselves as leaders and be willing to promote innovation, even if this involves taking risks. For many, this will be a new experience, since their job is often defined as one of quality control and ensuring compliance. Top management has to support those who take on this new role and reward those who succeed.

Examples of Workplace Restructuring

What might workplace restructuring look like in practice? Efforts to restructure the child welfare workplace are beginning in a small number of sites. The experience in one large public agency with which I've been working will serve as an illustration. This agency had been plagued for years with the problems of insufficient resources to deal with rising incidence of abuse and neglect, frequent media attacks, low staff morale, and infighting throughout the organization. Several studies and reports outlining the problems of the agency have had little impact. Training efforts aimed at upgrading the skills of individuals were of minimal use, since they ignored the systemic nature of many of the problems and the complex web of relationships that prevented individuals from being able to address the problems in isolation.

Finally, a new strategy evolved based on the principles stated previously. Rather than trying to change the whole agency at once, developmental efforts were focused on individual sections (each containing thirty staff) that were willing to view themselves as experimental. Opportunities for a high degree of worker involvement and participation in decision making were created. The role of the section administrator was redesigned from that of "quality control agent" to the leader of a work system that was responsible for finding ways to improve its performance and the job satisfaction of its workers.

The first experimental section was one of five sections in intake services. The second was one of ten sections that provide ongoing services. In each, a governance council was formed consisting of the administrator, each supervisor, and one worker selected from each unit. These councils met regularly to generate ideas and plan new initiatives. The remaining workers were involved in various committees. For example, each section had a committee that was responsible for planning professional development for the section. Each section also had a committee on workplace supports, as well as one on improving working relationships throughout the agency. Some of the ideas that were proposed could simply be implemented within the sections. Some required that formal proposals be written and submitted to top management for approval.

In the most significant initiative to date, the two experimental sections got together and proposed that they work on the same set of cases; that is, all cases entering the ongoing services section would come from the experimental intake section. This is different from the normal case flow in the agency in which cases move from intake to any one of ten identical sections. The one-year experiment was aimed at improving continuity and coordination and improving working relations between the two sections. It was approved by top management and has recently begun. Plans are now underway to expand this effort from two experimental sections to five, and to add three more next year. Some of the innovations have begun to spread informally to other sections in the agency, and serious attention is being given to how to manage the learning process, without mandating that certain changes will occur. In addition, thought has been given to ways of involving the unions so that they can be a partner in shaping the growth of the new approach.

While this effort is still evolving, it represents a model for transforming a child welfare agency. It seeks to change the workplace by empowering staff, emphasizing local initiative and experimentation, and redesigning the organization of the work itself.

Conclusion

Some will still say that only sweeping changes in national policies, new infusions of resources, and more government or court involvement will transform the system. However, these larger scale approaches have yet to produce the desired results, and the system continues to deteriorate, poorly serving both workers and clients. The alternative proposed here focuses on smaller scale initiatives designed and carried out in the workplace by those who are willing to look at what they have been doing and try something different. It's based on the idea that a series of "small wins" and the learning processes that they unleash can lead to fundamental change. Ultimately, involving workers in redesigning their workplace may prove to be a more viable way of transforming a system that clearly isn't working. At least it's worth a try.

Rejoinder to Professor Cohen   BRENDA G. MCGOWAN

I hate to be a spoilsport. Clearly, Professor Cohen is to be congratulated for the changes he has initiated in a large public child welfare office in Pennsylvania. The workplace reorganization he describes has undoubtedly led to better client service and higher staff morale. These are no small accomplishments in urban child welfare today!

But do these changes constitute a transformation of the child welfare system? Unfortunately, no. As Cohen himself states, the reorganized sections in this demonstration project are still experimental. And experimental projects can be eliminated as readily as they are introduced. Moreover, service demonstrations can seldom be repeated successfully because replication efforts tend to lack the financial support, administrative commitment, and professional leadership required to insure full implementation of the original concept. The history of social welfare provision in the United States is replete with examples of promising service initiatives that were abandoned because they conflicted with other interests, challenged traditional modes of practice, or simply failed to secure needed public support.

Thus, it is not difficult to think of a number of forces that could undermine the type of workplace changes that Cohen advocates. For example:

- A new welfare commissioner could be appointed who wants to maintain more control over the decision making of middle management.
- A union action could be initiated seeking reclassification of workers' jobs because the reorganization forces them to perform certain tasks that are out of title.
- A child abuse scandal in an experimental unit could be attributed in the press to the changed structure for decision making.
- The state budget office could rule that responsibility for certain ongoing cases must be contracted out to voluntary child welfare agencies in order to reduce the costs.

The other, perhaps more compelling reason for questioning my opponent's faith in organizational change strategies is that many of the problems now confronting the child welfare system derive from external forces. The most perfectly designed child welfare office imaginable cannot resolve the policy conflicts inherent in the current legal framework for service provision, eliminate the social problems leading to increased child abuse and out-of-home placement, or create the new resources required to meet the needs of the expanding population of children entering the child welfare system.

It is true, as Cohen notes, that large-scale approaches to changing the child welfare field have yet to produce the desired results. But that does not indicate such efforts are unnecessary. It only means that if a true transformation of the child welfare system is to be achieved, such initiatives must be better designed, more comprehensive, and more carefully implemented. Workplace changes are likely to be a critical component of any meaningful reform effort. But alone, such initiatives will produce little lasting change.

NO

BRENDA G. MCGOWAN

As a professor of social work practice who has spent many years teaching organizational change strategies to clinicians eager to improve the quality of agency practice, it would be gratifying to answer this question affirmatively. However, I have spent much of my professional career advocating for change in the child welfare field, and based on these efforts, I must conclude that changing the workplace cannot transform this field of practice in any significant way. Although workplace initiatives are clearly a *necessary* component of reform — and may actually result in better services for some clients — such efforts alone will never be *sufficient* to produce the systemic changes required in the child welfare system.

Ironically, when the first major critiques of the child welfare system were issued a generation ago, it might well have been possible to effect major reform through workplace changes alone. However, child welfare agencies ignored this opportunity to make needed changes in their policies and practice, and the context for delivery of child welfare services has changed so radically during the past twenty years that it is simply not realistic now to think that workplace changes can be made in isolation from the larger forces shaping service provision in this field.

There are five traditional determinants of child welfare policy: federal and state laws; governmental administrative regulations and guidelines; court decisions; funding allocations; and program decisions. In earlier years, program or workplace decisions in child welfare tended to be important because of the relative absence of action in the other potential spheres of influence. But due to significant shifts in the context for delivery of services, those hoping to reform the child welfare system must now employ a broader range of change strategies.

Four of the recent trends in child welfare that minimize the impact of program decisions on policy and practice will be reviewed below. As this discussion will demonstrate, workplace initiatives alone cannot produce the structural transformation required in child welfare.

Child Welfare Has Become a Major Public Policy Issue

The child welfare system, like any public service bureaucracy, must respond to a number of different audiences and interest groups. In addition to its actual and potential client population, these include the legislature, the courts, the press, state administrative agencies, private funding sources, local politicians, other service bureaucracies, church groups, unions, professional associations, building and resource suppliers, community groups and organizations, and the public at large. But traditionally, few of these potential audiences had any real interest in child welfare. Thus, until the 1960s the field operated as a small, rather self-contained service system with limited staff and resources, and it maintained rigid service boundaries. Relatively free from public preview, it was able to delegate most policy decisions to the professional program staff.

Now that child welfare has become "big business" and problems of child abuse and foster care have started to occupy a prominent place on the public agenda, the policies and operations of the child welfare system are subject to extensive scrutiny by various interest groups and are debated widely in the press. As a consequence, it is almost impossible today for an agency administrator or practitioner to introduce a new program, policy, or procedure without subjecting the proposal to review by all of the interested parties. The benefit of this shift, of course, is that it insures greater equity and public accountability in the delivery of services. The major disadvantages are that it restricts professional innovation and mediates against individualization of client need, thus limiting the potential impact of any workplace initiated reforms.

New Legislative Mandates

The mandates of the Child Abuse Prevention and Treatment Act of 1974 (P.L. 93-457) and the Adoption Assistance and Child Welfare Act of 1980 (P.L. 96-272) place new and conflicting demands on the child welfare system. Child welfare services in the United States are now defined almost entirely by the provisions of these two federal laws. Although both were fashioned to address obvious deficiencies in the system, they were passed independently and reflect different value assumptions about the appropri-

the gaps in the mental health, developmental disabilities, education, and juvenile justice systems that contribute to the current crisis in child welfare.

Conclusion

Unfortunately, space constraints do not permit an analysis of the specific forces now contributing to the institutionalization of change initiatives in the child welfare system. But readers familiar with the history of such recent developments as permanency planning, intensive family preservation services, or kinship foster care can identify the range of fiscal, legislative, political, and judicial forces leading to the successful implementation of these concepts.

The impetus for creative service initiatives often arises from the insights — or frustrations — of local practitioners and program administrators, but many valuable change ideas are also blocked at this point. Some are successfully implemented in one location, but never replicated. Other workplace initiatives never move beyond the experimental or demonstration stage. Few local reform efforts lead to significant systemic change.

Social workers should certainly applaud every effort to improve child welfare services at the workplace. But it would be naive to expect that decisions regarding replication and institutionalization of such initiatives will be based solely on professional leadership and the assessment of the potential cost-benefits. Service innovations tend to flourish or die because of their fit with the many competing interests that shape the delivery of child welfare services, not simply because of their impact on clients. Real transformation of the child welfare system will require public support and clarification of the objectives of child welfare policy as well as a major restructuring and the investment of new funds.

Rejoinder to Professor McGowan
BURTON J. COHEN

Professor McGowan has provided us with ample evidence that broad-based change strategies (e.g. new legislation, government regulations and guidelines, and promises of fiscal reform) can have an impact on the child welfare system. In fact, as her examples so clearly illustrate, it is these very interventions that are largely responsible for the paralysis and stalemate that is so pervasive today in service delivery. Dedicated child welfare workers are constantly frustrated by the contradictory mandates and excessive reporting requirements that are the result of some well-intentioned social reforms. Furthermore, she gives us little reason to believe that a new dose of this same medicine offers any more hope of "real reform" than the last dose.

Dr. McGowan's analysis of the trends that minimize the impact of program decisions seem to boil down to two issues. The first is that managers and workers in the child welfare system are too constrained (by public scrutiny, and legislative and judicial mandates) and have too little discretion. I would tend to agree with this. But the solution isn't to impose more regulations and guidelines; instead, it is to free up those who are most in touch with the clients of the system. Many of the constraints to innovation are self-imposed through an overly bureaucratic and monolithic service structure. We haven't really given managers and workers the opportunities and motivation to be creative at the service delivery level. The public education system is also highly regulated and has come under even more attack for not producing positive results for child welfare. The response has been to give more discretion to principals and teachers who have the imagination and courage to be innovative. School-based management and shared decision making are spreading, along with innovations in instruction such as "cooperative learning" and "team teaching." We should expect the managers of the child welfare system to exercise the same degree of imagination and courage in order to achieve reform.

Dr. McGowan's second argument is that the problems facing child welfare are just too large and complex to be addressed at the service delivery level. Well, I don't think we can afford to wait until the "deficiencies in social and economic policies" are resolved at the national level. In describing the significance of "small wins," Weick (1984) reminds us that "it seems useful to consider the possibility that social problems seldom get solved, because people define these problems in ways that overwhelm their ability to do anything about them." The seeds of reform have to be sown somewhere. Intensive family preservation services didn't start out as a national policy, but as an innovative program in one locality. Workers and managers need to be empowered to sow more of these seeds.

I do agree with Professor McGowan that workplace initiatives alone cannot transform child welfare. The task of spreading innovations and moving from experiment to policy should be supported by broader, systemic changes. But these changes should promote continuous experimentation, learning, and improvement in the child welfare workplace, not a new set of constraints.

REFERENCES

Arches, J. (1991). Social structure, burnout, and job satisfaction. *Social Work* (36)3, 202–206.

Beer, M., Eisenstadt, R., & Spector, B. (1990). Why change programs don't produce change. *Harvard Business Review* (Nov/Dec), 8–16.

Centron, M., & Davies, O. (1989). *American renaissance.* New York: St. Martin's Press.

Esposito, G., & Fine, M. (1985). The field of child welfare as a world of work. In Laird, J., & Hartman, A. (Eds.), *A handbook of child welfare.* New York: The Free Press.

Ewalt, P. (1991). Trends affecting the recruitment and retention of social work staff in human services agencies. *Social Work* (36)3, 214–217.

Gershenson, C. (1991). Dynamics of the flow of children into foster care. Paper presented at the American Enterprise Institute, Conference on Child Welfare Reform Experiments, February 20–21.

Jiminez, M. A. (1990). Permanency planning and the Child Abuse Prevention and Treatment Act: The paradox of child welfare policy. *Journal of Sociology and Social Welfare* 17(Sept), 55–72.

Kamerman, S. B., & Kahn, A. J. (1989). *Social services for children, youth and families in the United States.* New York: The Annie Casey Foundation.

Lipsky, M. (1987). *Street-level bureaucracy.* New York: Russell Sage.

McGowan, B. G. (1991). Child welfare: The context for reform. In *Child welfare reform.* New York: National Center for Children in Poverty.

McNeely, R. (1988). Five morale enhancing innovations for human services settings. *Social Casework* (April), 78–87.

National Commission on Child Welfare and Family Preservation (1990). *A commitment to change.* Washington, D.C.: American Public Welfare Association.

Tatara, T. (1991). Substitute care flow data for FY 1990 and child substitute care population trends since FY 1986 (Revised Estimates). *VCIS Research Notes* (May 3), 18–23.

Thomas, G. (1990). 'Bottomed out' in a 'bottom up' society: Social work education and the default and recapture of professional leadership in child welfare. Paper presented at the Council of Social Work Education Annual Program Meeting, Reno, Nevada.

University of Southern Maine. (1987). *Professional social work practice in public child welfare: an agenda for action.* Portland, ME: National Child Welfare Resource Center for Management and Administration.

Weick, K. (1984). Small wins: Redefining the scale of social problems. *American Psychologist* (January), 23–46.

ANNOTATED BIBLIOGRAPHY

Kamerman, S.B., & Kahn, A.J. (1989). *Social services for children, youth and families in the United States.* New York: The Annie E. Casey Foundation.

This report of a major national study documents the policy and programming issues and resource deficits confronting current child welfare administrators.

Lipsky, M. (1987). *Street-level bureaucracy.* New York: Russell Sage.

This book presents a stunning analysis of the political and structural forces that inevitably prevent "street-level bureaucrats," such as child welfare workers, from attaining their alleged public policy objectives.

McGowan, B. G. (1991). Child welfare: The context for reform. In *Child welfare reform.* New York: National Center for Children in Poverty.

This is a concise summary of current issues in child welfare and their historical evolution. This chapter was prepared as part of a briefing for federal legislative staff.

National Commission on Child Welfare and Family Preservation (1990). *A commitment to change.* Washington, D.C.: American Public Welfare Association.

This monograph presents the recommendations of a task force composed of some of the major leaders in the field of child welfare, regarding the changes required to effect real transformation of the child welfare system.

Are Single-Issue Advocacy Organizations Good for the American Welfare State?

EDITOR'S NOTE: Today, advocacy groups play a vital role in shaping social policy and securing services for those in need. Organizations that represent particular groups of needy people have become especially active, lobbying to maintain services and programs for their members. Although these organizations make an important contribution, their role is controversial. It has been argued that single-interest groups are too narrowly concerned with the needs of their members and that they ignore the welfare of those who are not as well organized. Opponents of single-issue advocacy organizations contend that cooperative effort on behalf of all needy people, rather than sectional interests, is required. This view has been countered by those who argue that cuts in social service budgets require highly organized and focused efforts on behalf of particular groups. They argue that political action on behalf of generalized welfare goals is likely to be ineffectual.

Karen S. Haynes, Ph.D., supports the claim that single-interest advocacy organizations make a positive contribution to the American welfare state. She is Professor of Social Work and Dean of the Graduate School of Social Work at the University of Houston. Dr. Haynes has a strong interest in advocacy, and has published extensively on this issue. Her books include *Access to Human Services: International Perspectives* (1984), Sage (with Risha Levinson); *Affecting Change: Social Workers in the Political Arena* (1986) Longman (with James Mickelson); and *Women Managers in Human Services* (1989) Springer.

Robert Fisher Ph.D., contends that single-issue organizations do not make a positive contribution to the welfare state. He is Associate Professor of Social Work at the Graduate School of Social Work, University of Houston. His major research interests are in community organization, social movements, and urban studies. He is the author of *Let the People Decide: Neighborhood Organizing in America* (1984), Twayne; and co-editor with Peter Romanofsky of *Community Organization for Urban Social Change* (1981) Greenwood.

YES

KAREN S. HAYNES

Advocacy has been a central component of social work practice since social work's formal initiation in the United States before the turn of this century. Moreover, according to the NASW Code of Ethics, advocacy is a basic professional obligation. Not surprisingly, then, formalized advocacy efforts are also an historical part of social work practice. The primary purpose of advocacy is to speak on behalf of individuals who are ineffective at or unable to do so on their own behalf. While the demarcation between single-issue and coalitional advocacy efforts may be debated on its own merit, for the purposes of this debate, single-issue advocacy efforts will be defined within a narrow context.

The Importance of Single-Issue Advocacy Groups for Social Policy

Many social work clients in the past, and well into the future, will lack the ability to forcefully present their needs due to their age (young children and the very old); their disability (the severely mentally ill or the catastrophically ill); or because of society's status or power differentials (racial and ethnic groups, women). Consequently, many of these groups need an advocate to speak forcefully on their behalf *and only on their behalf*. It is likely that from a healthy self-interest, many of these unempowered and disenfranchised individuals view any attempt at coalition building with other groups (whose issue and/or demographics are different) as either "selling out" or "watering down" their own goals.

Successful advocacy requires advocates to identify problems or issues and to articulate specific solutions. It also requires advocates to utilize a variety of strategies; to work within as well as outside of the system; and to empower their clients in the process. Successful advocacy must "make a difference." In order to accomplish this, it needs to maintain a centrality of mission and the emotionality of an issue, at least until success is achieved.

Although some single-issue advocacy efforts may be more short term and goal focused than coalitional efforts, this is probably a false dichotomy. Most advocacy endeavors need persistent and continuous effort, either because the issue — such as accessible and affordable prenatal care for low-income and high-risk women — does not get rectified in a short period of time or because the issue may become redefined due to new knowledge, improved technology, and/or changing values. For example, the March of Dimes was initiated to reduce birth defects. Not only did this single-issue advocacy organization achieve moderate success, but in so doing, it came to realize that the root problem was not the absence of medical technology and expertise, but the lack of early prenatal care. Nevertheless, due to the relatively narrow focus and the emotionality of its identified goal, the March of Dimes has managed to sustain its advocacy efforts over a long period of time.

The Components of Successful Advocacy

In supporting the effectiveness of single-interest advocacy efforts above coalitional efforts, it is necessary to talk about the important ingredients. In order to provide an effective voice for otherwise powerless and ineffectual populations, successful advocacy requires a power base, high visibility, defined and measurable goals, and an arsenal of acceptable strategies and achievable intermediate successes.

Power may be derived from several sources: (1) an economic base; (2) large numbers of people; (3) information or expertise; (4) position; or (5) status. Although overly simplified, single-interest advocacy groups can usually achieve more power, and in more diversified forms, than coalitions.

While adequate funds are not the only requirement for success in advocacy, it certainly is an important ingredient. Despite the initiation of coordinated fundraising for social services — often aimed at reducing unhealthy competition and increasing the total amount raised — some single-issue advocacy organizations have opted out of joining this "united fund." They have done so because they understand the strategic pull of a single cause. Perhaps some of the general success of single-issue advocacy fundraising can be attributed to donors feeling more in control of where their contributions go, or because they have a personal and emotional attachment to one cause.

It is not necessarily true that if power is derived from large numbers of members, a single-issue advocacy organization may neither represent as large a client group nor have as large a membership as a coalitional effort. Unlike many coalitional efforts — which may be locality based or have loosely affiliated members — single-issue advocacy efforts are often national in breadth and have stable long-term members. Furthermore, what a single-issue advocacy group may lack in size, it may more than make up for in its ability to attract wealthy and/or well-positioned individuals to lend their names, positions, or funds to an effort. In some cases they may be the "front" person for the issue, such as Jerry Lewis for Muscular Dystrophy and Magic Johnson for AIDS.

Power derived from information can take the form of using members of the affected client group in the advocacy effort as well as "experts." These efforts can utilize life stories which are passionate yet combined with data—powerful tools for any advocacy effort. By contrast, coalitions often dilute their ability to be poignant because of the breadth and diversity of their targeted efforts.

Visibility may be closely aligned with the elements of power. Specifically, large numbers of affected people may make the issue more visible. Or, high status individuals speaking on behalf of a usually "invisible" group may provide the necessary visibility. Certainly not all single-issue advocacy efforts provide for high visibility or easy media coverage. But the broader the coalitional effort, the harder it will usually be to depict the issue in layperson's language, in short news stories, or in printed materials. Advocacy organizations like the Multiple Sclerosis Society, the March of Dimes, and the Muscular Dystrophy Association have learned the very effective and powerful use of a single picture to heighten the visibility of the need. A picture of a disabled or abused child quickly presents the problem to the public. The "Coalition for a Better Houston," for example, cannot be captured as cogently. Similarly, having money and information about an issue will promote avenues of media access otherwise unavailable (i.e., paid nationwide Public Service Announcements as opposed to free 10-second sound bites on a local news broadcast).

Why Single-Issue Advocacy Groups Are Important

It is almost axiomatic that a single-issue advocacy organization can more effectively identify an understandable and measurable goal than can coalitions. While the potential for disagreement about outcomes, strategy, or even purpose exists in any group, single-issue advocacy organizations can significantly reduce the time, effort, and energies needed to resolve these problems. The larger and more diverse an organization's membership is, the greater is the likelihood that its goals will be multiple, abstract, and consequently, less measurable and attainable. To the extent that a coalition must provide "win/win" strategies for its diverse membership, clients' goals may be lost.

Success in an advocacy struggle is critical in sustaining the effort of an organization. While a goal such as "reducing infant mortality" is not easily attainable, I would argue that it is much more easily measured than "improving the quality of life in neighborhood *X*." Even small victories in single-issue advocacy efforts can be celebrated. Although unfortunate, it is true that people invest time and money to support "winnable" issues.

Advocacy strategies may range from an informational campaign to a protest march, to the submission of policy positions (e.g., proposals for federal legislation, state statutes, administrative regulation, etc.), and even to a boycott. The array of strategies is vast. Moreover, the choices depend on a number of variables such as the nature of the problem, the political climate, the societal attitudes, and the composition of the advocacy organization's membership. Once again, the narrower the issue is, the quicker the decision on a strategy is likely to be.

Time can also be used more effectively by single-issue advocacy groups to refine or evaluate strategies, to increase visibility, to further fundraising efforts, and/or to collect and disseminate additional information. On the other hand, coalitions expend much time to develop internal win/win solutions, to prioritize issues, or to find compromise positions. While the breadth of coalitions is impressive, it is often also oppressive.

Advocacy efforts on behalf of others are always suspect, at least to some people. However, advocacy which includes the clients, the family, or others significantly impacted on by the problem are more likely to be given credibility and even sympathy. "Self-serving and self-interested" are not supportable criticisms of a group of wheelchair-bound individuals pushing for "barrier-free living." On the other hand, coalitions formed from many groups may raise the specter of "any means justifies the end."

Some pundits argue that single-issue advocacy efforts pit one deserving group against another (e.g., the child advocates versus the advocates for the elderly). However, that argument only holds if we believe that winning is a zero sum game. Increasing children's rights does mean taking rights away from the elderly. Increasing funds for prenatal care does not necessarily lead to reducing funds for cancer research.

At a time when human service decisions are increasingly being made in the legislative and judicial arenas, single-issue advocacy efforts are more easily understood, measured, and successful. Conversely, the compromises entailed in coalitions are too costly for our clients of today.

Rejoinder to Professor Haynes   ROBERT FISHER

Karen Haynes's essay is a well argued, clear, and practical defense of single-issue advocacy organizations. Its tone is pragmatic, seeking to recognize the opportunities and limits in the current American context, and to make the most of them. I admire her realism and recognize her impressive knowledge of the advocacy scene. I acknowledge that our essays are different not only because we have chosen different sides but also because of our different approaches to the question. I also know that Karen Haynes has limited her views to meet the constraints of this debate. And I certainly do not disagree with her points about the need for advocacy organizations, the "pull of a single cause," and the various difficulties inherent in coalition formation.

Nevertheless, the argument in favor of single-issue advocacy organizations validates all of my concerns. While there is no doubt about the ability of advocacy organizations to affect social problems, their impact remains inherently constrained within the parameters of the current political economy, that is, within the privatization and dismantling of the welfare state. Our contemporary context demands more than single-issue advocacy efforts. Of course, organizations must be built at the grassroots; we need persistent and continuous efforts, as Haynes writes. But we cannot stop there; we cannot stop with advocacy grassroots efforts which, Haynes notes, speak "only on their behalf." The argument why we must expand our efforts into coalitions, alliances, networks, and political parties is discussed in my essay. But some examples from Haynes's essay in support of single-issue advocacy efforts as a positive contribution to the welfare state illustrate well the dilemmas in such a position.

Take the argument about the ability of the March of Dimes to reduce birth defects and promote early access to prenatal care. What about the continued persistence of high infant mortality rates in the United States? This persists, in part, because of limits in the welfare state (other nations have national health insurance) and because of, unintentional or not, organizations like the March of Dimes, which as private, voluntary, charitable, single-issue advocacy efforts not only are unable to meet the larger needs and demands but also serve as an alternative — private charity — for reactionary forces interested in limiting the welfare state and continuing to promote privatized, voluntary, charitable social services and solutions to social problems. It is not by accident that Haynes is forced in her response to summon the wealthy and well-positioned individuals (Jerry Lewis and Magic Johnson) and charitable efforts like Multiple Sclerosis, Muscular Dystrophy, etc. There is no doubt, of course, as to the good these kinds of efforts do in targeting a problem; there is certainly a place for grassroots advocacy and empowerment efforts — we must act locally. But these efforts fail to address widespread health problems; they oppose, by their very existence, the expansion of the welfare state to be able to address the health concerns of *all* Americans, not just those judged deserving; and they depend on the "noblesse oblige" of the rich and famous. To this extent, such efforts both do damage and are insufficient.

As the author of books and articles on the importance of community organization, I certainly appreciate and support single-issue advocacy efforts. But current social problems demand a larger vision and impact than single-issue advocacy organizations offer. They might be "more easily argued, measured, and understood," but voluntary grassroots organizations cannot alone affect needed social changes. And to the extent that they become the primary form of social change, they undermine the very existence of the welfare state programs which only a generation ago were seen by many as *the* major social victories of the twentieth century.

NO

ROBERT FISHER

Unlike other topics offered in this text, the question posed here does not yield a clear "yes" or "no" answer. Moreover, my subsequent argument is not meant to imply that single-interest advocacy organizations do not make important contributions to the American welfare state or to the policy-making process. Social policy is a dynamic process. As such, the American welfare state is shaped and reshaped. This reshaping occurs not only from the "top down" by "policy makers," but also by activists, constituents, and organizations at the grassroots level. Single-issue advocacy organizations are key elements in this social policy process.

The Limitations of Single-Issue Advocacy Groups

Despite their virtues, grassroots organizations are simply not enough. The reasons are twofold. First, voluntary efforts are not of sufficient size or clout to effectively challenge the massive social problems we face. Activist Heather Booth noted recently at a Bertha Capen Reynolds Society conference that "We live in a society that is like a house on fire, and it's arson." Our cities and social problems have been intentionally ignored for more than a decade. Second, voluntary efforts fit too neatly into larger restructuring efforts that diffuse power and enable the owners of capital to maintain and increase their share of it. We do not need more single-issue advocacy organizations. In our postindustrial world, resistance and advocacy have already become too fragmented and too privatized. Think about it. At this very moment, thousands of voluntary grassroots organizations have emerged around issues of race, gender, sexuality, ethnicity, age, disabilities, and so forth. While these organizations promise to provide people with more control over their lives, their level of power to affect policy and their access to resources have actually diminished.

Accordingly, I argue that we must go beyond single-interest advocacy efforts to include larger scale mobilizations—coalitions, alliances, international networks, and progressive political parties. We need more than single-issue advocacy efforts because their very existence reinforces both anti-statist ideology and the decline of the state, which in turn, forces more voluntarist efforts to come into existence. And the more fragmented the efforts become, the less likelihood there is for progressive activists to develop a *unified* vision, a unified problem analysis, and a comprehensive policy solution. Without broad efforts like alliances, and without a unified understanding of the need to struggle for state power, voluntary, single-issue advocacy efforts may do valuable local work in empowering constituents, building community capacity, and meeting the needs of clients, but they will remain unable to effectively challenge the very system whose policies oppress them.

The underlying thesis presented here is that the current service/postindustrial economy requires a different form of organization than the earlier industrial economy. The old structural bases of mobilization—organized around class and labor issues—are giving way to a new conception. As such, the reality which spawned the older forms of organizing is being replaced by a new economy—global, hi-tech, decentralized, and fragmented. This new economy shifts political demands and the social struggle away from being mainly class-based to being citizen-based, identity-based, and issue-based. Whereas the old industrial society revolved around the factory and concerns of the American welfare state revolved around issues related to the working class and poor, the new service/postindustrial economy muddies class identity. As the speed of international capital and new technologies destabilizes and fragments cities and communities, people's political identities also fragment. As such, people experience their grievances as African Americans; Hispanics; women; homosexuals; community residents; or victims of domestic violence, AIDS, and so forth. These communities of geography and identity become the sites of grievances which initiate social action. The extraordinary expansion of single-interest advocacy efforts in the United States reflects the extent of both grievances and political fragmentation.

This thesis assumes that the proliferation of grassroots efforts is a logical development. As economic changes force people to resist, as global capitalism destroys communities, and as "privatization" strategies undermine social service delivery, the proliferation of oppositional efforts, situated in communities and organized around the interests of diverse constituencies, gives voice to groups who were previously silent. These grassroots organizations have become the dominant form of mobilization and resistance. They also form the bulwark for implementing potential policy changes in the United States and throughout the world. Their proliferation is the first line of resistance against conditions which are worsening worldwide for the poor and much of the middle class.

While we must not underestimate the advantages of diversity, we need to remember that this grassroots diversity is both the product of and a challenge to the economic restructuring of global capital. It represents not only a creative and positive reaction to persistent domination, but also reflects the organizational form and the public discourse in the new global economy. It should therefore come as no surprise that political conservatives in the United States applaud the proliferation of voluntary efforts as "a thousand points of light," which supposedly fill the vacuum left by a retreating public sector. For those seriously interested in ameliorating social conditions, grassroots organizations have become not only part of the solution but also part of the problem.

Because they are so highly fragmented and highly privatized, single-issue advocacy organizations must form larger, more powerful social change units. We need to forge broad coalitions and alliances large enough to challenge the enormous power of corporate capital and conservative centralized government. The problems people now face almost always originate beyond community borders. Therefore, the ability to effect significant change depends in large measure on building or rebuilding coalitions, alliances, networks, and political parties. Of course, this is no small feat. Coalition work is one of the most difficult types of organizing. Groups are reluctant to join efforts that will further siphon already scarce resources, and most groups seek to get more out of a coalition or an alliance than they are willing to put into it. Nevertheless, the fact remains that the fragmentation of social change and social service organizations must be countered. Jesse Jackson's idea of a Rainbow Coalition reflected this realization. So, too, does Citizen Action in the United States, the Green parties in Western Europe, Solidarity in Poland, and the host of allied "new social movements" throughout the world.

Moreover, grassroots advocacy organizations are limited because community organizations often do not understand the critical role of the welfare state. The current anti-statist critique of those in power—from Washington D.C. to Moscow—argues that the state is the source of social troubles. This view is widespread not only among "privatizers," but also among community practitioners who see the centralized state as a reactionary force. As the public sector increasingly becomes synonymous with bureaucratic inefficiency and the encroachment on political liberties, and as the local, private "marketplace" of individual competition, consumption, and charity is exalted by those in power, the public sector is increasingly delegitimized as a source of solutions or a site for struggle. In such a context, the very existence of widespread, single-issue, voluntary efforts contributes, intentionally and unintentionally, to the delegitimization of the state. It also offers evidence that an activist state is not needed in a new decentralized social change milieu.

The localist view inherent in many single-issue advocacy efforts does not recognize the critical role played by the state in progressive social change and social policy. Many do not understand the importance of the welfare state. Specifically, they do not understand how it is the product of grassroots demands as well as elite initiatives, and how it alone, when pushed, incurs public responsibility and a degree of public responsiveness to its constituents. If they understood the welfare state better, they would understand the need to go beyond single-issue advocacy efforts to form organizations and frameworks with a unified view of the potential for a progressive state. This is especially true in our electronic global economy where capital moves invisibly, at high velocity, and where the private sector is a swift and faint target.

In the absence of an organized movement to confront the policies of corporate sector coalitions, our best bet for now in fulfilling the mission of the welfare state is to develop networks and political parties that will challenge the public sector. Without an expanded public sector, public life cannot even begin to be restored. Without an active public sector, voluntary advocacy efforts devolve into self-help strategies that increase fragmentation and perpetuate the use of private, voluntary solutions to massive public problems. To assume that single-issue organizations can replace the state is a misleading notion. To assume that a unified vision of social problems will evolve from increasingly fragmented, single-issue grassroots efforts, is equally misleading.

However, "bringing the state back in" is not in itself sufficient to further the cause of progressive social policy. Wolch (1990) argues that it never left. She fears that the current hegemony of the neoconservative and privatization strategies will result in the creation of a "shadow state." In this scenario, the voluntary sector becomes more and more dependent on very limited state funding and conservative policies, while at the same time, the state assumes less and less public responsibility for such services. What occurs, then, is not a retreat of state intervention like in the 1980s and 1990s, but rather, "an extended and increasingly diversified pattern of state intervention via voluntary groups" (Wolch, 1990, p. 218) into the lives of people. Wolch argues that what looks like greater freedom and diversity in the countless single-issue organizations may in fact represent just the opposite.

Conclusion

The coalitions, alliances, international networks, and political party formations that I argue for in this essay will require a struggle to win and hold state power. They must fight for the expansion of progressive social policies and the implementation of new, more comprehensive ones to meet the nation's social needs. This is not to propose some simple-minded, state-dominated, social utopia. A new state must be grounded in diverse, community-based, democratic resistance. But that resistance must also have an analysis and vision that transcend the grassroots. As Flacks (1990) notes, we need to simultaneously reconceptualize the welfare state, not as the source of control or the single solution to problems, but "principally as the potential source of capital and law that would enable people to solve their problems at the level of the community" (pp. 48-49). We must build coalitions, alliances, networks, and parties based on grassroots efforts in order to take control of the state. Only in this way can we democratize the process of social policy and social service delivery. The task ahead is to tie grievances and problems to a unified analysis of political economy and social policy which builds upon current grassroots efforts, takes them beyond a myopic localist perspective, and returns resources and power to the decentralized communities and constituencies with which most activists and clients identify. If grassroots efforts are not tied into this larger project, these organizations will remain an ambiguous development for the American welfare state.

Rejoinder to Professor Fisher   Karen S. Haynes

While I applaud the lofty idealism embodied in the position taken by my esteemed colleague, Bob Fisher, I caution the readers that large scale coalitions, per se, are neither structured nor oriented to reduce corporate power or centralized government. Furthermore, I certainly do not disagree with the premise that social services have become too privatized and that we need a unified vision. However, it is also somewhat naive and simplistic to suggest that single-issue advocacy efforts buy into and support "privatization" and the "charity" model. Fisher's presumption that single-issue advocacy efforts do not challenge the status quo, do not advocate for increased public efforts, and do not support the need for an expanded welfare state, is incorrect.

Fisher's contention that "the problems people face almost always originate beyond community borders" is submitted, I suspect, to support his position for coalitional efforts. Without getting involved in yet another debate about the definition of community, I argue that this is not uniformly true. Further, even when problems originate beyond community borders, the implicit extension of this argument is that solutions, therefore, are achievable only beyond those community borders. Certainly a national health plan would be more comprehensive in coverage, more equitable in cost, and better able to address these issues. However, access to health care is a crucial issue and one defined within "community borders." It is also an issue which may be more effectively addressed by a local, single-issue advocacy effort directed at locating a public health clinic in a specific geographic area of a community.

While pragmatism may be part of the basis for my argument, the populist notion of restructuring government through coalitional efforts seems farfetched. I have not argued that single-issue advocacy efforts should always result in privatized solutions nor that the public sector should not be the target for these efforts. However, Fisher seems to argue that the large-scale goals of coalitions "must [be to] struggle to win and hold state power." Will this not supplant the old form of dominance with a new form of dominance?

I have no doubt that despite our seemingly opposite views, Fisher and I agree that many of the central issues for the American people are not addressed by the current public sector. They are also not addressed by the present welfare state. The disagreement is that Fisher argues that single-issue advocacy efforts "undermine the very existence of the welfare state programs," while I, on the other hand, argue that their very existence provides the essential underpinnings for reform.

REFERENCES

Flacks, D. (1990). The revolution of citizenship. *Social Policy* (21)2, 37–50.
Wolch, J. (1990). *The shadow state: The government and voluntary sector in transition.* New York: The Foundation Center.

ANNOTATED BIBLIOGRAPHY

Epstein, B. (1991). *Political protest and cultural revolution: Nonviolent direct action in the 1970s and 1980s.* Berkeley: University of California Press.

Epstein discusses both the limits and the potentials of grassroots movements, emphasizing that if these efforts are to truly alter the relations of power, they must go beyond their own limited cultural and community universe.

Wolch, J. (1990). *The shadow state: The government and voluntary sector in transition.* New York: The Foundation Center.

This is a superb analysis of the dialectical interaction between voluntary efforts and the state. Wolch sees the recent growth of grassroots voluntarism as one component of a global restructuring which curiously ends up delegitimizing the state at the same time that it increases its control over voluntary efforts.

Is There a Feminization of Poverty?

EDITOR'S NOTE: Research into the incidence of poverty has found that women are disproportionately represented among the poor. Studies have also shown that the proportion of poor women is increasing. These findings have led social scientists to formulate the concept of the feminization of poverty, which suggests that poverty is essentially a function of women's position in society. Policies designed to deal with the problem of poverty must, therefore, deal with the wider issue of patriarchy. While patriarchal values and institutions dominate society, women will continue to comprise the majority of poor people. Critics of this position disagree, claiming that the data exaggerate the problem. Although women may be statistically overrepresented among the poor, this is not a function of patriarchy, but of other social, demographic, and economic factors. In addition, the idea of the feminization of poverty compartmentalizes the issue and detracts from the need for policies that address the poverty problem in its totality and not just for one section of society.

Mary Ann Reitmeir argues that there is a feminization of poverty. She is Associate Professor and Coordinator of the Social Work program at Bemidji State University in Minnesota. Her major research interests are in women's issues, social policy, and social work.

Kit R. Christensen, Ph.D., disagrees, and argues against the notion of the feminization of poverty. Dr. Christensen is Professor of Philosophy and Chair of the Department of Philosophy at Bemidji State University. His major research interests are in political and moral philosophy, and he has published on these issues in various scholarly journals.

YES

MARY ANN REITMEIR

That women and children are poor, that they are disproportionately represented in social work "caseloads," and that they are often "dependent" in that they are in need of financial support, is old news. Although the notion of the feminization of poverty which was articulated by Diana Pearce in 1978 is a relatively recent one, it describes a phenomenon that has characterized women's position in society for a very long time. For centuries, women have found themselves in conditions of poverty and deprivation.

The association of poverty with women is not particular to the United States, to a capitalist economy, or to industrialization. Women's impoverishment is global, and regardless of race, class, or association with a male partner, women throughout the world find themselves in a disadvantaged position relative to men. It is the inequality between women and men that lies at the core of the feminization of poverty. As Sivard (1985) notes, "what women have found to bond them together is a single thread that winds all cultures. They share a sense of inequality of opportunity, the injustice of a traditionally imposed second place whether in the family, social, economic or political setting" (p. 7).

The Existence of the Feminization of Poverty

The concept of the feminization of poverty relates to those women and children whose household income falls at or below established minimum standards for subsistence living (Goldberg & Kremen, 1991). However, the feminization of poverty is relative to what constitutes the poverty standard of adequate material goods for subsistence living within a particular society. Children are included because the assumption of who is responsible for children, and thus for acquiring the material supports necessary for their subsistence, is most often tied to women. Within this conceptualization, what is poverty, who is poor, and how many are poor, varies greatly. What is defined as subsistence in one society might constitute affluence in another. Nevertheless, data on the incidence of poverty in all societies indicates clearly that there are a disproportionate number of women (and their children) among the destitute and poor throughout the world.

The statistics show that women worldwide are increasingly the sole means of support for almost one-third of all families. In the developing countries, two-thirds of the women over age twenty-five have never been to school, and boys continue to be enrolled in primary and secondary schools at substantially higher rates than girls (Sivard, 1985). Employment is difficult to secure because of physical, cultural, and social constraints, and even if they are employed, women are usually confined in segregated, gender-related jobs. Families are increasingly separated as a result of the out-migration of men to urban areas in search of paid labor, leaving their female partners to provide for the household, care for children, and support frail family members. Rural women's work averages eighteen hours a day and includes "household, labor and reproductive roles" (Sivard, 1985, p. 11).

In the industrial countries, women increasingly serve as heads of households and sole or primary wage earners for their families. In the United States, approximately 60 percent of families in poverty are female headed (U.S. Bureau of the Census, 1989, p.11). This statistic would increase dramatically if male support were removed. It is estimated that two-thirds to three-quarters of working age women in the United States would be impoverished if their association with a supporting male came to an end (Scott, 1986). Contrary to the popular image of the middle-class housewife who spends her time entertaining guests and attending social functions, most women in the industrialized countries carry a heavy burden. In addition to having full-time jobs, many are responsible for household management, the care of children, and the support of frail relatives (Scott, 1984).

However, it is important to recognize that the feminization of poverty is not only attributable to low paying jobs, women's separation from male breadwinners, or their increasing assumption of heavy household responsibilities. Women's poverty is rooted in a patriarchal ideology which defines social citizenship, and the rights and benefits that are attached to citizenship. This ideology not only intersects with the economic system, but is the foundation of that system and all institutional structures that shape citizens' lives. Patriarchal ideology creates a material base to men's control over women's lives through social institutions. It informs social structures and practices that determine gendered roles, citizenship status, and rights and benefits.

The ideology of patriarchy is sanctioned and supported by the state. The state defines the status of women and their contributions in state operations. As Walby (1990) notes, the dominance, exploitation, and oppression of women has been inherent in the formation of state societies. According to Eisenstein (1980, pp. 330–331), the state represents and defines the separation of public and private life in terms of the differentiation of woman from man. Patriarchy transforms biological attributes into a politicized gender which gives men priority while making women unequal. It also creates the sexual division of labor and the distinctions of the family and market. Although the specific historical source of patriarchal control has shifted from the father or husband to the state, the process of hierarchically differentiating woman from man ensures the continuity of patriarchy.

Women play a vital role in the maintenance of modern societies. It is their prescribed gender role as domestic caregivers that insures the reproduction of labor power and the provision of physical, social, and psychological nurturance which prepares family members for work on a daily basis. Domestic caregivers are also charged with socializing the next generation of workers and reproducing the relations of production. This caregiving role is multifaceted and complex, and it is influenced by historic cultural, social, and economic factors. It involves not only the many detailed tasks and activities of caring, but also the identity of the caregiver and the relationship with those receiving the care (Land, 1991).

Paradoxically, the vital role that women play in society is neither recognized nor rewarded. While domestic caregiving serves the state, women's work is invisible and devalued. Hilda Scott (1984) notes that women's unpaid work underpins the world's economy, yet it is peripheral to the world's economy as men define it. Despite the fact that over 90 percent of unpaid labor is performed by women for a value of "$4,000,000,000,000 to the world's economic product (Sivard, 1985), women are regarded as a category of persons who are economically invisible, whose work is nonwork, who have no experience or skills, who do not need a regular income because their husbands supports them" (Scott, 1984, p. 8).

The assumptions about women's role as caregivers, mothers, and wives inherent in the notion of women's citizenship ensure the imbalance of women's power and the devaluation of their labor. Definitions of citizenship and societal institutions are gendered in a way that assumes male as the norm and female as different and thus unequal. As primary workers, men hold a favored relationship to the state based on individual performance and contract. Women's relationship on the other hand is devalued and relegated so that the feminization of poverty becomes an inevitable consequence of the way gender biases are institutionalized in the social structure.

Exacerbating the Feminization of Poverty

The feminization of poverty is exacerbated through the way the social welfare system defines women's roles in many industrial countries (Fraser, 1987, Jones, 1990). In the United States, the social welfare system defines claims as well as the arrangements for making claims, either in terms of "rights" or based on a means test. Fraser (1987) has identified two separate and unequal tiers for obtaining benefits. In the first tier, the "masculine" social insurance schemes, claimants are "rights-bearers." The benefits they receive are paid for as a result of having sold their labor power to an employer for a wage and thus for social security credits. As rights-bearers, it is understood that they deserve benefits and are not stigmatized as claimants. Fraser (1987) notes:

> Proprietors of their own persons who have freely contracted to sell their labor-power, they have become participants in social insurance schemes and, hence, paying consumers of human services. They therefore qualify as social citizens in virtually the fullest sense that the term can acquire within the framework of male-dominated capitalist society (p.11).

The second tier, which Fraser describes as the "feminine sector," consists of a "set of programs oriented to the household" (Fraser, 1987, p.108). These programs are designed to compensate for the absence of a waged income usually provided by a male breadwinner. Benefits of these programs are not associated with an individual, but with a household and family, and the failure of the family in most cases to meet the ideal of what is normative (male breadwinner, female homemaker). Claimants of programs in this tier—AFDC, Medicaid, Food Stamps, and public housing assistance—are welfare recipients. Consequently, they are stigmatized and punitively treated. Financed out of the general budget and administered by the states, benefits vary greatly and are distributed only after the prospective claimant is determined to be genuinely in need through a degrading means test.

As individuals, women have relatively little access to the masculine welfare system. Often their claim for these benefits rests on their relationship to a male (husband or father) and benefits are often paid at differential rates (Fraser, 1987; Nelson, 1984).

Conclusion

Patriarchal ideology creates and promotes a sexist bias that forms the essence of a state's systems, structures, and institutions. This bias not only prescribes women's role and subsequent work in society, but it also devalues and ignores the contributions of this work—the caring and sustenance of citizens. Patriarchal ideology intersects with all economic systems; it is the essence of systems that identify and define citizenship and the accompanying rights and benefits based on male norms. Patriarchal ideology relegates women to the position of second class citizens and ensures their economic marginality in domestic, social, and economic institutions (Keller, 1988). It is little wonder that women are disproportionately represented among the destitute. A conceptualization of citizenship that displaces women, devalues their work, and diminishes their contribution is bound to generate inequality, deprivation, and poverty. While women continue to be regarded as second class citizens, the feminization of poverty will continue apace.

Rejoinder to Professor Reitmeir KIT R. CHRISTENSON

Professor Reitmeir's essay makes apparent the general agreement we have regarding the problem of poverty among women in modern society, but also our fundamental difference in theoretical approach when it comes to explaining this phenomenon within the larger context of economic, cultural, and political life. I believe that poverty among women (and all other groups in society) is attributable not to specific gender-related events, but to the class nature of capitalist society. This explanation is fundamental to the historical materialist approach to which I subscribe. Historical materialism posits that the economic base of capitalist society determines all cultural institutions including religion, marriage, and formal education, and all ideological products such as theological or political doctrines, ethics, art, mass media, and representations of family life. While Professor Reitmeir believes that patriarchy is closely related to gender differences and that it alone determines women's oppression, I have argued that patriarchy as an ideology is just another manifestation of capitalism and its exploitation of both women and men.

Professor Reitmeir makes it clear that she rejects the historical materialistic account of the dynamics of poverty. Her position that patriarchal ideology is responsible for poverty among women, her attempt to define class in noneconomic terms, and her view of the social division of labor in terms of citizenship roles all demonstrate her fundamental disagreement with my analysis. In taking this approach, she reveals her commitment to another, longstanding theoretical tradition in western social science, that of liberal democracy, whose proponents have for well over two hundred years presupposed the causal primacy of belief systems over economic relations in their own attempts to explain and morally assess hierarchical social organization and institutionalized power.

The liberal democratic vision of society is an ideologically distorted and superficial one which fails to account satisfactorily for poverty and deprivation in society. To use it to explain the nature and scope of poverty among women is to guarantee that a distorted version of this human problem will emerge.

NO

Kɪᴛ R. Cʜʀɪsᴛᴇɴsᴇɴ

It is very difficult to answer the question of whether or not there exists in the world today a "feminization of poverty" for the simple reason that nobody has yet defined this concept satisfactorily. Sometimes the concept is used to refer in a factual manner to a specific, distinct phenomenon and at other times it is used in a highly abstract, theoretical way. However, no matter how it is used, there is little value in a concept that cannot be defined precisely and in ways that permit its operationalization for purposes of research. Although it is true that the failure to have a clear and adequate definition of concepts is not always regarded as an impediment by social scientists (much to the exasperation of their readers), in the present case the definitional issue is crucial, especially if the phenomenon of the feminization of poverty is to be usefully applied in research. The failure to define the feminization of poverty must therefore engender a great deal of skepticism about its existence as a phenomenon and its value in both academic settings and organized attempts to foster progressive change.

Problems in the Concept of the Feminization of Poverty

Nevertheless, for the purposes of this debate, some common ideas do appear to run through the different definitions which have been offered of this problematic concept. These include the idea that the feminization of poverty is an objective tendency for women to be the victims of material deprivation to a greater degree and with greater frequency than men. Another common notion is that the feminization of poverty is an international phenomenon even though the severity and proportionality of the impoverishment experienced by women relative to the male population in any given society varies widely. Another shared idea is that the feminization of poverty is not confined to the present time but that it has existed in the past and is likely to affect more women in the foreseeable future.

Used in this general way, there may be some empirical evidence to support the notion of the feminization of poverty. There is evidence to show that more women than men are impoverished worldwide and that the incidence of poverty among women is increasing. But this evidence is of a very general kind and does not stand up to rigorous analysis. For example, what counts as "poverty" or "material deprivation" is not always clear, given the cultural, geographical, and historical relativity of such concepts particularly if basic biological needs (for adequate food and shelter) are met. In contemporary cultures where social relations are organized more atomistically, and where the nuclear family consisting of husband, wife, and children is a primary economic unit, poverty is often defined as the lack of "life-chances" for personal self-sufficiency, comfort, and independence. On the other hand, in cultures organized along more organicist lines, especially where an extended family or clan is the primary source of care-giving, poverty may be defined very differently. The tendency for Western researchers to define poverty in these societies in terms of their own assumptions often produces ethnocentric distortions which invalidate the use of concepts such as the feminization of poverty.

Another problem with the idea of the feminization of poverty has to do with the inclusion of males within the concept. This is reflected in the general agreement that children form an integral part of the feminization of poverty. Although children are probably included because women typically have primary responsibility for child care, what remains unclear is how this use of the language accounts for the obvious fact that children themselves are both female and male. In a similar vein, one also must ask if the notion of feminization can account for the heightened susceptibility of the elderly (both male and female) to the debilitating effects of material impoverishment. Statistical evidence from many societies clearly shows that elderly persons of both genders are increasingly falling into poverty.

Another problem is how to make sense out of the idea of victimization which forms an integral component of the notion of the feminization of poverty. There are many different ways that people can become victims in an environment of material deprivation and this again has affected both men and women. An extreme form of victimization arising from deprivation includes death from malnutrition and the consumption of unsafe drinking water which is suffered disproportionately worldwide by children and the elderly of both genders. Another form of victimization arising from poverty is death through armed conflict which is disproportionately suffered by poor men worldwide. Men from poor families are coerced or duped into military service on behalf of the dominant interests of society and are used to maintain the deprivation of the many for the benefit of the few. In this regard, they are both the perpetrators and the victims of oppressive social systems.

Conceptual Problems with the Feminization of Poverty

If the discussion is taken beyond the empirical realm to the level of theoretical explanation, the concept of the feminization of poverty becomes even more problematic. The argument that women are the primary victims of inequality, poverty, and deprivation ignores the substantial body of theoretical work which, since the time of Marx, has shown that poverty is a function of class societies. Habitual differences between poverty and wealth within an identifiable social formation such as capitalism reflect the class nature of capitalist society and the social relations which are determined by capitalism. Differences in poverty and wealth associated with gender (and other factors) are a product of this structure and are not generated by gender differences themselves. The ownership and control of the means of production by the few gives rise to differences in material wealth and poverty, the level of power which people enjoy, and their degrees of social vulnerability. Poverty is a function of class and not of the fact that people are differentiated by being male and female.

The only plausible way to counter this argument is to argue, as Shulamith Firestone (1970) and some others have done, that the two biological sexes are separate and antagonistic classes evolving from a more primeval human division of labor. Even if plausible, this theoretical possibility would not negate the historical materialist, class-based account of the nature of the various types of maltreatment some human beings experience as a result of the actions of others. Some feminist writers such as Angela Davis (1984) do recognize the importance of a historical materialist explanation of gender oppression. In her foreword to the English language translation of Clara Zetkin's writings, she pointed out that working class and racially oppressed women confront sexist oppression in ways that reflect complex interconnections between class exploitation, racism, and male supremacy. While white middle-class women experience sexism in an isolated form, the experiences of working-class women place sexism in the content of class exploitation. Similarly, Black women's experiences incorporate the additional feature of racism. It is important to recognize, as Davis (1984, p. 15) contends, that: "These are by no means subjective experiences; rather there is an objective interrelationship between racism and sexism in that the general context of both forms of oppression in our time is the class struggle unfolding between monopoly capitalism and the working class."

In a class society, there evolves a dominant ideology which serves to legitimize the interests of the ruling class. What is designated as patriarchal ideology, legitimizing the subordination and exploitation of women by men, apparently has existed in some version or another in all forms of class society, but the empirical connection between the patriarchal oppression of women and their distinctive susceptibility to poverty only becomes real after class divisions determining the ownership and control of the means of production have emerged. From a historical materialist perspective then, the ideological justification of the relegation of women to positions of greater vulnerability to impoverishment have emerged as a means of reinforcing the economic dominance of the ruling class. What this also implies is that patriarchal ideology, however real, does not exist in a vacuum, but that it is determined by the social relations of capitalism.

Conclusion

It seems as though contemporary talk of the feminization of poverty is really a way of focusing on only one dimension of a larger problem. Within the context of global capitalism, women worldwide do seem to be economically vulnerable, but this vulnerability must be understood within the broader context of capitalist exploitation and not as a phenomenon on its own. Although class divisions are not the sole cause of sexist oppression and exploitation, it is obvious that class society provides the fertile ground in which patriarchy thrives. Thus, overcoming capitalism is the necessary prerequisite for the liberation of women from their susceptibility to the material impoverishment which is imposed on them by class society.

Rejoinder to Professor Christensen

MARY ANN REITMEIR

My colleague seems to agree the feminization of poverty exists, although he maintains that the definition and operationalization of this definition pose problems in terms of including children, accounting for the elderly's susceptibility to poverty, and considering issues around socioeconomic class, given that some males also experience material deprivation. He also expresses concern about the possible ethnocentrism involved in universalizing the definition to account for what is material deprivation in the non-Western, developing world. He seems to ignore my qualifications in developing a definition and also my point in creating a universal thread out of women's experiences as wives, mothers, domestic caregivers, and other experiences that determine their citizenship within a state, thus placing them in a vulnerable economic position.

What disturbs Professor Christensen most is the seeming subtle difference in focus between our respective arguments and particularly the question of whether gender or class are the determinants of women's impoverishment. His reading of Firestone (1970), I believe, is incorrect. Firestone in fact developed a historical materialist explanation based on her concept of sex-class and the premise that sex-class rather than economic-class is central to understanding women's oppression and, for our purposes, women's impoverishment.

I agree that the interweaving of class (and race) with sex is important, and particularly that the intersection of patriarchal ideology with capitalism is significant in understanding women's oppression. However, I maintain that whether women can, choose to, or are interested in "fulfilling" their reproductive role, it is this role that defines and establishes the parameters of women's citizenship and thus their claims to rights and benefits as citizens. This is equally true of their access to welfare benefits. As Abramovitz (1988) points out, the family ethic (the ideology of women's roles) permeates the structure of the welfare state and, of course, the rules for participation in social welfare programs. At the same time it informs theoretical perspectives on normal, functional, and appropriate behaviors. The family ethic assures women's economic dependence, vulnerability, and subordination to men and to the welfare state.

If we believe in the importance of nurturing and shaping the lives of tomorrow's citizens, and if we believe in caring for those citizens who have already made their contributions, domestic caregiving is vital to the functioning and operations of society. Social work's challenge is to confront the ideology that renders this work secondary, and the workers second class citizens, and structurally ensures their vulnerability to poverty.

REFERENCES

Abramovitz, M. (1988). *Regulating the lives of women.* Boston, MA: South End Press.

Davis, A. (1984). *Foreword.* In Foner, P. S., (Ed.), *Clara Zetkin: Selected Writings.* New York: International Publishers.

Eisenstein, Z. (1984). The patriarchal relations of the Reagan state. *Signs* 10(2), 329–337.

Firestone, S. (1970). *The dialectic of sex.* New York: Bantam Books.

Fraser, N. (1987). Women, welfare and the politics of need interpretation. *Hypatia* 1(1), 103–121.

Goldberg, G. S., & Kremen, E. (1991). *The feminization of poverty: Only in America?* New York: Praeger.

Jones, K. B. (1990). Citizenship in a woman-friendly polity. *Signs* 15(4), 781–812.

Keller, E. F. (1988). Feminist perspectives on social studies. Bernard Occasional Papers on Women's Issues, 3, 10–36.

Land, H. (1991). Time to care. In Maclean, M., & Groves, D. (Eds.), *Women's issues in social policy.* London: Routledge, 7–19.

Nelson, B. (1984). Women's poverty and women's citizenship: Some political consequences of economic marginality. *Signs* 10(2), 209–231.

Scott, H. (1986). *Women and the future of work.* Unpublished paper, Cambridge, MA.

Scott, H. (1984). *Working your way to the bottom.* London: Pandora Press.

Sivard, R. (1985). *Women: A world survey.* Washington, D.C.: World Priorities.

U.S. Bureau of the Census (1989). *Poverty in the United States: 1987,* Current Population Reports, series P-60, No. 163. Washington, D.C.: U.S. Government Printing Office.

Walby, S. (1990). *Theorizing patriarchy.* Cambridge, MA.: Basil Blackwell.

ANNOTATED BIBLIOGRAPHY

Fraser, N. (1987). Women, welfare and the politics of need interpretation. *Hypatia* 1(1), 103–121.

This article provides an excellent examination of the gendered philosophy and values underlying the United States welfare state and public welfare programs.

Goldberg, G. S., & Kremen, E. (1991). *The feminization of poverty: Only in America?* New York: Praeger.

This book offers a sound examination of the concept and phenomenon of the feminization of poverty in four capitalist and two socialist countries.

Land, H. (1991). Time to care. In Maclean, M., & Groves, D. (Eds.), *Women's issues in social policy.* London: Routledge, 7–19.

This is an excellent discussion of the contribution and value of women as caregivers in Britain. The chapter discusses the dimensions of caring, the necessity and value of caring to the state, and the assignment of women as caregivers.

Nelson, B. (1984). Women's poverty and women's citizenship: Some political consequences of economic marginality. *Signs* 10(2), 209–231.

This is a good analysis of women's and men's state membership as citizens and the claims to rights and benefits associated with gendered notions of citizenship.

Should We Expect to Change Clients' Behavior in Exchange for Aid?

EDITOR'S NOTE: Recent debates about welfare have focused on the behavior of clients. Underlying these discussions is the assumption that most recipients of welfare engage in socially unacceptable behavior. Substance abuse, truancy, indolence, crime, promiscuity, and other reprehensible behaviors characterize the lifestyles of the poor. Since the costs of welfare benefits are met by decent, hard-working taxpayers, it is appropriate that recipients should change their behavior and become responsible and self-supporting citizens. Critics of this position claim that most welfare recipients are hard-working, respectable individuals who are in temporary distress and who require short-term assistance. It is wrong to accuse them of engaging in unacceptable behavior. In addition, they argue that the obsession with the behavior of the poor deflects attention from the root causes of poverty which are to be found in broader social and economic conditions in society. Changing individual behavior, they contend, will not magically solve the poverty problem.

This issue is examined by Mark Lusk, Ed.D., who argues YES, that clients should be expected to change their behavior in exchange for aid. Dr. Lusk is Professor of Social Work and Chair of the Department of Social Work at the University of Wyoming. Dr. Lusk has undertaken research into rural development, social policy and international development. He is the author of *Farmer Participation and Irrigation Organization* (1991), Westview Press, as well as numerous articles in leading social work and social policy journals.

Diana M. DiNitto, Ph.D., takes the opposite side in this debate. She is Professor of Social Work at the School of Social Work, University of Texas at Austin. She is the author of *Social Welfare: Politics and Public Policy* (1991), Prentice Hall; and *Social Work: Issues and Opportunities in a Challenging Profession* (1990), Prentice Hall (with C. Aaron McNeece).

YES

Mark Lusk

Early efforts to remediate poverty in Western industrial societies were often paternalistic and condescending. Home visitors and charity workers saw poverty as a product of idleness or sloth and rarely looked to what are now commonly recognized as the structural bases of poverty. With the emergence of modern social science, social workers and policy makers began to recognize that poverty is a highly complex phenomenon, growing in part out of the dislocations associated with industrial society. In an effort to reduce the stigma associated with poverty and poverty relief, social policy now stresses a value-neutral stance. In order to stop "blaming the victims" of poverty for their own plight, welfare benefits have been disassociated from any requirement to behave in any particular way in exchange for aid. While commendable in its desire to free clients from stigma and blame, the move to disassociate benefits from client behavior has gone too far.

No economic transaction is strictly unilateral. Such is the nature of exchange relations. Services and goods have value and costs. The policy decision to give aid in the form of money, services, or goods is to transfer wealth produced and accumulated by one group to another. No such exchange can be value-neutral. While we may examine and challenge the motive for such a transfer, we must concede that it is an exchange of real assets. Whether one transfers wealth out of compassion or to "buy the peace," income transfers or aid are never "free."

The challenge to social policy is not to make welfare benefits free or without value, but to make explicit the terms of the exchange. By continuing to deny that welfare should be contingent on any behavior change, it is impossible to openly and fairly define the terms of the exchange in the interests of both the client and society. However, once this is recognized it becomes possible to place legitimate demands on recipients which are neither stigmatizing nor paternalistic. As long as welfare is freely given, it will be freely taken. Is this what we really want?

Social Work and Social Values

Social work is also not value free. Curiously, when it is convenient to do so, social workers will argue that the profession assumes a culturally relative and value-neutral stance with respect to clients, but at the same time they

Rejoinder to Professor Lusk
DIANA M. DINITTO

As so often occurs in a debate, my opponent and I agree on many points, but not necessarily for the same reasons. Professor Lusk is correct in his recognition of the structural causes of poverty and other social problems; indeed, we should stop "blaming victims" for circumstances beyond their control. He is also correct in stating that aid is never free, but he has missed an important point in stating why these benefits are not free. They are not free because many recipients have worked or will work to insure that these public assistance benefits will be available if needed, not only for themselves, but also for others in need. Social Security retirement and disability benefits are not regarded as welfare benefits (even though they are more similar to most public assistance benefits than some people realize[1]) because employees contribute some of the taxes used to pay for these retirement and disability benefits. Public assistance benefits are regarded as welfare because there is no earmarked tax that pays for them. But as we know, there are income taxes that go into a general revenue fund that pay for these so-called "welfare" benefits.

Many public assistance recipients have worked or will work and have contributed or will contribute to the general revenue fund. Given this point, most welfare recipients have or will embrace the behaviors of the work ethic that unknowing members of the public accuse them of not embracing or even disdaining. The work requirements of social welfare programs and the demands for verification of income and assets are often based on the incorrect assumptions that the values of social welfare recipients are different from the values of nonrecipients.

As my colleague notes, few deplore dependency more than welfare clients themselves. It is available opportunities that frequently distinguish recipients from others; being a "have" or a "have not" is often a matter of timing. An individual works but becomes ill, receives benefits temporarily, and then returns to work. Another individual divorces, receives assistance to raise her or his children, and when these children are older, is able to enter or reenter the workforce. Each of us gives and takes at different times, or does so simultaneously with a combination of work and assistance. Very few of us will spend our entire lives in one or the other of these positions. We will contribute to the Social Security retirement fund and take our benefits when the time comes; we will contribute to the general revenue fund and accept Medicaid, food stamps, a student loan, or a government-backed mortgage when needed. Most individuals who receive government benefits without any work or monetary contribution are those with especially serious mental and physical disabilities, and no one is arguing that they should not receive publicly supported services.

Professor Lusk is also correct that social work is a value-laden profession. Social workers embrace many values such as the dignity of the individual and client self-determination. It is values such as these that social workers, clients, and hopefully most other members of society wish to preserve through a social welfare system that is just, one that does not impose on clients expectations that are rarely possible to achieve, such as obtaining a job when access to good education and training and to decent jobs is limited. Expectations for behavioral changes on which all of us agree are only legitimate to the extent that they can reasonably be achieved.

I am delighted to have engaged Professor Lusk in this debate and recognize that in this process he and I have come full circle. We have recognized that most of us — whether we are "haves" or "have nots" at this moment — want to be self-sufficient and to work. It is also clear that until structural changes occur, it will remain difficult for many to act in ways that are totally consonant with their values.

NOTE

1. It should also be remembered that employers pay amounts equal to employees. Social Security retirement and disability benefits are not so different from public assistance, because many current retirees receive payments that might be considered generous in comparison to their contributions. In addition, current workers are paying in at higher rates than ever before to insure that retirees receive these payments.

NO

DIANA M. DINITTO

In considering the topic of this debate, the first image that comes to mind is the workhouses of the Elizabethan period where those individuals labeled the "non-deserving poor" were forced to do menial labor in return for only the barest of life's necessities. Virtually every student of social welfare is aware of the expectations that the overseers of these institutions placed on the recipients in their charge. Every astute student of social welfare is also aware that during each period of social welfare in the United States, some form of these same Elizabethan attitudes toward the recipients of aid have prevailed. In this century, perhaps nowhere have these attitudes been more apparent than in the Aid to Families with Dependent Children (AFDC) Program.

Mothers receiving AFDC were subjected to "midnight raids" to make sure that they were not consorting with men who might benefit from their public assistance check. More recently, workfare provisions of the AFDC program have escalated as a result of the Family Support Act of 1988, even in light of information that such requirements (1) rarely improve the job skills of participants, (2) generally do not reduce welfare costs, and (3) do not discourage malingering, because recipients already prefer decent jobs to welfare (Goodwin, 1981). In fact, recipients are now not only responsible for their own behavior, but they can be held hostage for the behavior of others. Young children may be denied part of their families' AFDC benefits if their teenage parents do not attend school. Under Wisconsin's Learnfare program, an AFDC family can have its payments reduced if a teenage child drops out of school, which is defined as "missing three days of school in a month without a valid excuse" (Budget of the United States Government, 1990, p. 176). Families in public housing may be evicted if one member is involved in illegal drug activities.

Over-Scrutinizing the Poor

On the surface, the position that clients can or should be expected to change their behavior is beguiling. For example, defenders of this position might couch their argument in such a way that exchange theory (Blau, 1964; Hasenfeld, 1983) is used to justify the notion that with every action (in this case, the giving of aid) comes the expectation for a reciprocal action (in this case, change in recipients' behavior). But in the case of social welfare, this expectation of change is often based on the assumption that the behaviors of the receivers of cash and services are inappropriate if not sometimes immoral.

Expectations of the behavior of welfare recipients are not always consistent with the expectations of the behavior of other citizens. The Food Stamp program is a case in point. A citizen complains that in his or her eyes a recipient made a purchase that is unjustifiable (an expensive item or non-nutritious foods); yet these concerned citizens make no such pretensions about scrutinizing the shopping baskets of those who are not using food stamps, regardless of the expense in relation to the purchaser's income or the nutritional value of the purchases. And they offer no evidence to support the contention that food stamp shoppers need more guidance in selecting foods than other shoppers.

The printing, distribution, and collection of food stamps costs millions of dollars each year. Substantial savings could accrue through "cashing out"[1] food stamps, but this cost-saving measure has been rejected because concerns about controlling recipients' behaviors by insuring that they purchase food is viewed as the greater public good. Continuing paternalistic and maternalistic attitudes about public assistance reinforce the perception that those who receive aid are not poor because they have no money[2] (and therefore lack access to education and employment), but because their own personal shortcomings prevent them from using assistance wisely.

The Inadequacy of Social Aid

When aid is given, it is generally at levels far too low to help recipients (*beneficiaries* may be too euphemistic a term) make the changes they desire, let alone justify many of the expectations for behavioral changes imposed by others. Even with the addition of Food Stamps and Medicaid (and in some cases, housing benefits), AFDC parents are lucky to make ends meet. Clients have a full agenda complying with the requirements of each of these programs, taking care of their children, preparing meals (which takes longer on a food stamp budget), caring for their dwellings, and so forth. The additional work requirements of these programs are often unrealistic, because adequate training and education, jobs, and child care are frequently unavailable. Benefits are rarely provided at a level that would allow individuals and families to cross the threshold into nonpoverty status. In the effort to control clients' behavior and get them into the mainstream, social welfare programs are fraught with restrictions that often make it difficult, if not impossible, for many clients to achieve the independence that they, policy makers, and the larger society want. In our "upside-down welfare state," far fewer demands are placed on the recipients of many other government benefits such as business loans and tax breaks (Walz & Askerooth, 1973).

In addition, clients are asked to make *individual* behavioral changes in order to rectify the problems they face which are usually *structural* in nature. Social work students are taught to assess client problems and to identify an intervention at the *appropriate* level (individual, family, school, community, and so forth). Clients, however, are expected to make micro-level, individual behavioral changes to rectify macro-level structural problems that require interventions in broader levels of society. They are being asked to take care of social problems that local, state, and federal policy makers and officials have failed to ameliorate.

Conclusion

The lack of knowledge of the human condition (of the causes of poverty and other social problems), the inabilities of professionals and policy makers to design effective strategies to improve peoples' lives, and the persistent discrimination suffered by many segments of society should be sufficient to temper views about how much change in people's behavior can be expected in exchange for assistance. Women, Native Americans, African Americans, Hispanic Americans, and other groups continue to have a more difficult time obtaining employment, and they earn less than males and whites even after overcoming structural barriers and obtaining the same education. And everyone deserves humane treatment — a clean bed, a hot meal — regardless of the problems from which they suffer. Jailing alcoholics and addicts for their chemical dependency or limiting the number of times these individuals can enter a treatment program suggests that we know the causes of alcoholism and other drug addiction and that it is the individual's lack of motivation to change, not professionals' lack of knowledge of how to effectively treat such problems, that prevent rehabilitation and recovery.

NOTE

1. "Cashing out" refers to giving cash benefits instead of "in kind" benefits in the form of the stamps or coupons that are currently used. Food stamps or coupons can only be used to purchase food, not other goods like paper and cleaning items that most people purchase in the grocery store.

2. This statement is based on the classic exchange between F. Scott Fitzgerald and Ernest Hemingway. Fitzgerald observed that "The rich are different from you and me," and Hemingway replied, "Yes, they have more money."

Rejoinder to Professor DiNitto   MARK LUSK

It is clear that Professor DiNitto and I agree on most points, so one must search for the key underlying difference in our perspectives. While we both agree that poverty is largely structural, that blaming its victims solves nothing, and that most social welfare programs are paternalistic, we seem not to agree on the essence of the social contract implied in social welfare.

As Dr. DiNitto has noted, I invoke the idea of a social exchange in social welfare. But beyond the modern formal social exchange theories of Blau and Homans (Turner, 1991), I would look to the roots of such theories in the writing of John Stuart Mill and other utilitarians who noted the importance of what Rousseau called the "social contract."

Implicit in this social philosophy, which lies at the heart of the American Constitution, is the belief that the function of government in free societies is to guarantee freedom. In *exchange,* the free citizen is expected to maximize his or her own welfare and respect the rights of others. The state maintains the peace, taxes its citizens, controls crime, and to a degree, regulates the market. As these kinds of free societies have evolved, their citizens have chosen to place additional responsibilities on the state, including the protection of the poor. As I noted in my opening statement, never has such protection been "freely given." It has always been with the expectation that to the best of their abilities, recipients would seek to improve their circumstances and aspire to be self-sufficient.

As Professor DiNitto has noted, early and even recent welfare programs have demeaned recipients and provided benefit levels that are often too low to bring anyone out of poverty. I have no argument with that. Moreover, I could also note that the largest portion of so-called welfare is actually "wealthfare," given in the form of corporate and agricultural subsidies, defense contracts, tax breaks to the wealthy, and deductions for the middle class. I would not argue with that either. That the U.S. government misallocates much of its budget, that it regularly invades privacy, and that it does little to guarantee equal economic opportunity is not what this debate is about. What it *is* about is that government (which is no more than we choose it to be) has the right to expect that welfare recipients will strive to the best of their ability to become self-sufficient and productive members of our society.

The liberal agenda of the second half of this century has stressed only one part of the social contract: the responsibilities of government. This has been pressed forward with great success. Few could argue that during the past four decades the rights of minorities, women, children, the poor, and the elderly have advanced significantly. Yet this agenda has failed to address the other part of the contract—the responsibilities of individuals to themselves, their families, their communities, and their nation. Conservatives, who paradoxically have been strongly oriented toward individualism, have capitalized on these themes and done much to reverse the forward progress of this nation in guaranteeing equal opportunity.

Social workers will only place themselves out of the mainstream of liberal western democratic tradition if they argue that social benefits should not be contingent upon the expectation of client change. Taxpayers (and as Dr. DiNitto notes correctly, this category includes the poor themselves) will not easily relinquish a sizeable portion of their income without the expectation that it will be spent responsibly. Thus, social welfare benefits should be contingent on expected changes in client behavior. Such expectations are fair, constitutional, and in the mutual interests of both society and welfare recipients. It is important that we build a coherent and unified income maintenance program based on *incentives* to be self-sufficient rather than on coercion (Ozawa, 1982). This will only be possible when we make the social contract explicit.

A new liberal paradigm for social welfare is emerging which balances rights with responsibilities. This framework embraces concepts such as community, reciprocity, family, privatization, decentralization, democratization, civic responsibility, the work ethic, and public service. Programs emerging from this approach will include a National Service Corps, community enterprise zones, social service vouchers, investment in job training, and home ownership rather than public housing (see Stoesz and Karger, 1991). I count myself among those progressives who believe that in exchange for freedom, citizens have an obligation to work for their community and for their nation.

REFERENCES

Blau, P. M. (1964). *Exchange and power in social life.* New York: John Wiley & Sons, Inc.

Budget of the United States Government, fiscal year 1990. (1990). Washington, D.C.: U.S. Government Printing Office.

Donahue, J. D. (1989). *The privatization decision: Public ends, private means.* New York: Basic Books.

Goodwin, L. (1981). Can workfare work?. *Public Welfare* 39, (Fall), 19–25.

Hasenfeld, Y. (1983). *Human service organizations.* Englewood Cliffs, NJ: Prentice-Hall.

Ozawa, M. N. (1982). *Income maintenance and work incentives: Toward a synthesis.* New York: Praeger.

Reid, P. N., & Peebles-Wilkins, W. (1991). Social work and the liberal arts: An essay on renewing the commitment. *Journal of Social Work Education* 27(2), 208–219.

Stoesz, D. (1989). A new paradigm for social welfare. *Journal of Sociology and Social Welfare* 16(2), 127–150.

Stoesz, D., & Karger, H. (1991). *Reconstructing the American welfare state.* Savage, MD: Rowman and Littlefield.

Turner, J. H. (1991). *The structure of sociological theory.* Belmont, CA: Wadsworth Publishing Co.

Walz, T. H., & Askerooth, G. (1973). *The upside down welfare state.* Minneapolis: Elwood Printing.

ANNOTATED BIBLIOGRAPHY

Gilder, G. (1981). *Wealth and poverty.* New York: Bantam Books.

This is a provocative explanation of the causes of poverty and other social problems that undergirded the conservative Reagan era approaches to social welfare. Gilder blames social welfare programs for social problems.

Murray, C. (1984). *Losing ground: American social policy, 1950–1980.* New York: Basic Books.

This is another book of the times that criticizes efforts to ameliorate poverty through use of the strategies of the Great Society. Murray recommends more restrictive measures to reduce poverty.

Piven F. F., & Cloward, R. A. (1971). *Regulating the poor: The functions of public welfare.* New York: Random House.

This classic discusses how social welfare benefits have expanded and contracted to meet the demands of the labor market and how poor people have been used as pawns in this system.

Walz, T. A., & Askerooth, G. (1973). *The upside down welfare state.* Minneapolis: Elwood Printing.

The authors take a look at how welfare works in an opposite fashion to what many people think, in that the rich get the most government benefits at the least expense to them, while the poor get the least benefits at a much greater expense to them.

Can Workfare Programs Bring Large Numbers of People out of Poverty?

EDITOR'S NOTE: Workfare is a relatively recent innovation in social policy. Reintroduced in the Family Support Act of 1988, the program is designed to encourage recipients of AFDC payments to find regular employment and become financially self-sufficient. Workfare seeks to provide job training, education, job placement, and day care, all of which help poor people secure employment. The program has been widely promoted as an effective alternative to government assistance, and even as a new and dynamic solution to the poverty problem. Workfare, it is claimed, can significantly reduce the numbers of people in poverty. Skeptics are not convinced. They argue that workfare programs do not deliver the services which are needed to help the poor obtain remunerative employment. They point out that many poor people who do find work earn incomes which are below the poverty line. Opponents argue that contrary to the claim that workfare brings people out of poverty, the program actually functions to provide a cheap supply of unskilled labor and thus to maintain people in poverty.

This issue is debated by Ralph Segalman, Ph.D., who argues YES, that workfare can bring large numbers of people out of poverty. Dr. Segalman is Professor Emeritus of Sociology at California State University, Northridge. He has served as a consultant to many governmental and private organizations and has published widely in the field of social policy. His books include *Cradle to Grave: Comparative Perspectives on the State of Welfare* (1989), Macmillan (with David Marsland); *The Swiss Way of*

Welfare: Lessons for the Western World (1986), Praeger; and *Poverty in America: The Welfare Dilemma* (1981), Greenwood (with Asoke Basu).

Joel Blau, DSW, argues NO. He is an Assistant Professor at the School of Social Welfare, State University of New York at Stony Brook. He has published in various social work and social policy journals and is the author of *The Visible Poor: Homelessness in America* (1992), Oxford University Press.

YES

RALPH SEGALMAN

Workfare[1] can work, but only under a certain set of conditions. Much of the present clamor for workfare will probably lead to its being discredited because as a "stand-alone" program, it cannot work. As a part of a fully integrated welfare reform program, workfare can be one of its most important elements. Much of what is happening in the country today with "real workfare" programs is doomed to failure. Much of what is being called workfare today is not by any strict definition what workfare was originally intended to be. The New York City and Los Angeles County "workfare programs" are basically voluntary programs, serving primarily those adult persons on Aid to Families with Dependent Children who elect to enroll in education, job training, and job placement programs. By and large, the enrollees in these programs are not the target population of workfare— namely, those who are members of the residential underclass with a dependency history of many years. Many of these people are also victims of intergenerational poverty. New York and Los Angeles have the largest and second largest welfare programs in the world, and they involve the major portion of the AFDC clientele. Thus, they are valid examples of the degree to which workfare is being tried.

Necessary Components
for a Viable Workfare Program

By themselves, voluntary programs of education and job training and placement do not constitute real workfare. Workfare can only be defined in its original intent as a program designed to insure that if eligible welfare recipients do not work, they will not receive benefit payments (assistance allowances for rent, food, clothing, incidentals, etc.). This concept of workfare gained popularity because it became obvious that the present system of benefits to welfare recipients, no matter what their behavior, was creating generations of dependents rather than socially productive people. Work was seen as the most important element in bringing people to self-sufficiency. Work is one of the primary ways of getting people into a socially responsible pattern of behavior that is not violence prone.

Work has always been viewed by behavioral scientists as not only crucial to the economic improvement of people, but much more. When people adopt a pattern of working, it changes their entire life, their values, and the values of their children in a manner which welfare does not. Even if the welfare recipients show only minimal progress, the very example of their working provides their children with a picture of what an adult life should be. That is what workfare was supposed to be in theory. What is lacking in its implementation, however, is well-thought-out methods of assuring that it can be carried out.

The way workfare is implemented is crucial to any chance for its success. If it is a "stand-alone" program, whose only real goal is to coerce recipients into taking any kind of job, then it is most likely to fail. For any program to work, it must contain positive elements for its participants. It cannot be merely coercive. There are a number of elements that must be present for a successful workfare and welfare program. Some of them are not cheap, and those conservatives who view workfare as a quick way to reduce expenditures will be disappointed.

The most expensive element in a good workfare program undoubtedly has to be provisions for child day care. Some have argued that for the middle class, the total immersion of children in day care might represent a threat to family life. But, for the children of families who have lived in intergenerational poverty, good day care, while not only allowing the mother to work, represents one means of breaking the cycle of poverty and dependency by introducing these children at an early age to the values of the mainstream society.

The most obvious requirement for workfare is the availability of jobs. Previous studies have shown that make-work jobs cannot provide the core of an effective workfare program. The goal for welfare clients should be real employment. This will require a very strong effort on the part of government and industry to find these opportunities for employment.

The present de facto policy of only half-heartedly impeding the flow of illegal immigration to the United States probably lessens the number of beginning jobs available to the welfare population. Also critically important for an effective welfare reform-cum-workfare program is getting across to all clients that there is a time limit beyond which welfare cannot be extended. Welfare needs to be explained as temporary, and immediately at the point of application each of the welfare adults in a family should be asked to participate in a case plan with the goal of reemployment and self-sufficiency, either in the span of six months to a year, or by the time the children are grown in the case of unemployable heads of families. The case plan would require an understanding that additional children in the family would no longer lead to increased welfare allotments. The family would be assured of the willingness of welfare managers to be flexible and cooperative with the family, but only if the family showed it was making efforts toward self-sufficiency.

Another important element of welfare reform, including workfare, is the need for education and job training. There are a number of exemplary programs which are doing this with voluntary welfare participants. This must be expanded to all mandatory programs, and mandatory clients will need the role examples of voluntary clients.

Many workfare trainees have been afraid to move into permanent low-paying jobs for fear of losing Medicaid (welfare-related health care benefits). These benefits must continue to be available during the transitional period, until health benefits can be earned as part of the new worker's job benefits.

Another critical requirement for an effective workfare program is the reintroduction into the welfare system of the trained caseworker. The caseworker would have two major responsibilities: (1) to monitor welfare clients to insure that they comply with the requirements and goals of the workfare program, and (2) to serve as an advisor, educator, and facilitator for the people assigned to them. The caseworker should not be a product of those schools of social work which view the client as the victim and thereby ignore the possibilities and the need for individual change.

Why Workfare Hasn't Worked

One of the impediments to a clearly worked out welfare reform program has been the inability to differentiate between the different categories of welfare recipients. I argue that there are three general categories of people on welfare. The first category is those people who have had recent temporary reverses which have put their economic lives in crisis. These are people with positive life experiences in areas such as employment, education, effective child rearing, etc. Those of this group who cannot resolve their economic and support difficulties by themselves will make use of the voluntary programs of job training, education, placement, and support provided by the welfare department. Many in the group will be able to resolve their economic and support difficulties by themselves. The implementation of a coercive workfare program for most people in this group is unnecessary. All that is required is that they be clearly informed of what is available. Their own motivation will move them along toward achieving self-sufficiency. This does not, of course, include teenage unmarried mothers who would be required to complete their education and remain under the supervision of competent adults. The notion of teenage mothers as "head of household" is as logical as a self-directed nursery school.

The second group has the opposite characteristics of most of the first category. This is the residual welfare population, most of whom are second, third, and even fourth generation welfare recipients. They are the hard-core underclass. When others moved up and out of welfare, they stayed behind. This population has developed over a forty-year time period, and it will take a maximum effort and many years to reverse the situation. It may well be that the only major change that can take place is with the young children in this population. Coercion here should not necessarily be focused exclusively on adult employment. Previous results of mandatory workfare with this population have been mixed, at best. Often, there are not enough suitable jobs for people with this low level of employment skills and inappropriate work habits. Often, the sanctions of workfare have bogged down with a plethora of expensive legal challenges and appeals. For this population, the focus should be more on the young children than on their unemployable parents. This means creating extended required after-school programs and required school support programs to ensure that these children come into intensive contact with responsible and trained adults. These responsible adults will convey the kind of norms and values that the children do not get at home or on the streets. For this group, the requirements of Learnfare are appropriate. Conservatives have long had reservations regarding child care. They see it as one more force in the destruction of the American family. In this view, the mother and father no longer provide the basic infusion of what is right and wrong or how one should deal with the world. There may be some validity to this argument for the middle class and other self-sufficient populations, but in my opinion, these reservations about child care do not apply where there is no father and where the mother is ill-equipped to raise the children.

In the third category are those with characteristics between the first and second groups. These are people who are neither clearly in temporary crisis nor clearly definable as members of the residual underclass. In fact, they show some of the characteristics of both groups. Many may have become so discouraged by intermittent unemployment as to be vulnerable to membership in the residual underclass. Others of this population group may make use of programs available in both welfare and voluntary agencies, as well as participate in the general employment marketplace. For this population category, rewards and coercions would be most effective. The traditional model of workfare is appropriate for this group, especially during periods of medium and high levels of employment. One of the weaknesses of workfare planning in the past has been the fiscal abandonment of work education and job training during periods of high unemployment. This has led to the movement of people from category three to category two. During such periods, some make-work programs may be necessary, although I have serious reservations about the use of these artificial government-funded jobs on a long-term basis.

Conclusion

The cost of a real workfare program that covers all of those eligible and provides for all the necessary support services is not inconsequential. As we have noted earlier, if the original intent of workfare was to save money, then its supporters will be disappointed. Integrating the long range benefits of workfare into a comprehensive program is a necessity if we are to save generations of people living in a worsening state of permanent dependency. We need to do this not only for their sake, but for the general health of the American society.

If workfare is to be effective, it will require bold expenditures for child care, support services, training, and effective education. It will require a responsible, accountable staff with discretionary functions and controls to individualize rehabilitation. It will require jobs and general popular support. It will require effective control of illegal immigration. Real workfare will be expensive.[2] What the public needs to know is that "welfare as usual" may prove to be the most expensive, not only in dollars, but in terms of the human costs of the underclass and the related populations. It appears that America can ill afford not to put its mind and resources into welfare reform, including workfare.

NOTES

1. An earlier version of this statement was produced by Ralph Segalman and Alfred Himelson, Professor of Sociology, California State University, Northridge.

2. This entails the use of privatized commercial organizations for recruitment, education, training, placement, and program monitoring, as has in part been utilized in Los Angeles county. This strategy may prove to be less expensive than relegating such assignments to established governmental agencies that have failed in the past with this population.

Rejoinder to
Professor Segalman

Joel Blau

Yes, Professor Segalman, I have heard of the underclass. I have also heard of pauperism, the undeserving poor, and the culture of poverty. These are, in historical sequence, the terms that preceded it. One part of the population of poor people has always been written off. The only difference this time is that the social sciences have lent the act of writing them off some intellectual legitimacy.

I say "lent it" because I have no doubt that some poor people have out-of-wedlock children, engage in criminal behavior, and do not work for long periods of time. Professor Segalman expresses doubt about whether this behavior could possibly have systemic origins and suggests that I am defending "welfare as a way of life." I disagree. On the contrary, I would suggest that if anyone is defending welfare as a way of life, it is Professor Segalman, because he is defending a system which requires (as any economics textbook shows) high rates of unemployment. The fact is that under the comparatively laissez-faire version of capitalism that we have in the United States, some people—*regardless of their demographic characteristics*—must be unemployed. To pore over the demographic characteristics of the *particular* people who happen to be unemployed and then advocate a coercive workfare program as the remedy for their "deviant" behavior, is a pretty disingenuous argument.

Professor Segalman does acknowledge that by itself, "welfare reform" will not succeed unless day care, health care, and other supportive services accompany its implementation. I agree wholeheartedly with this qualification and second my opponent's warning to advocates of workfare that it will be more, rather than less, expensive. Nevertheless, I would suggest to Professor Segalman that it is hardly accidental for workfare to have been implemented in this manner. As I indicated in my opening remarks, and as the U.S. General Accounting Office has confirmed, the work in workfare is certain, but somewhere between planning and implementation, the supportive social services almost always disappear.

Like Professor Segalman, I, too, wish that welfare could be limited only to those who really need it. The difference between us is that he thinks workfare can help to whip the poverty out of the most recalcitrant poor people, and I think that people would not be poor, or engage in so much questionable behavior, if they had adequate social supports and were paid a decent wage. For Professor Segalman, demands for a decent wage evoke an image of the failed revolutionary movements in Eastern Europe. My response to this charge is that the failed revolutionary movement in Eastern Europe wanted much more than a decent wage, and if that failure is going to be used to taint the demand for such an elementary prerequisite as a decent wage, then our distinctly American version of private enterprise is in much worse shape than even I had thought.

NO

JOEL BLAU

Workfare is a failure. At a time when paid work does not bring half of the adult poor out of poverty, there is no reason to believe that workfare will do anything more than punish the poor for being poor while increasing the supply of cheap labor.

Workfare and the Family Support Act of 1988

The centerpiece of current workfare programs is the Family Support Act of 1988. The culmination of years of conservative attacks on the welfare system, the Act mandates that by 1995, 20 percent of AFDC recipients in every state must be involved in a job search, job training, or work program. In addition, although only twenty-eight states previously offered public assistance to two-parent families, all fifty states are now required to do so. The Act also legislated one year of transitional Medicaid and day care benefits, as well as more rigorous enforcement of child support payments by absent fathers. For the most part, these regulations sound good. Many people think welfare clients ought to work. Why, then, would anyone possibly object to a law that provides them with a little nudge in the right direction?

As with most conservative work programs, the problem with the Family Support Act is that it takes back with one hand what it gives with another. While the Act links assistance to work, it does clearly mandate the creation of adequate supportive services (U.S. General Accounting Office, 1991). Intimations of this tendency are already evident in the Act itself. For example, the legislation not only requires states to render just six months assistance each year to two-parent families, but demands that by 1997, 70 percent of these recipients work sixteen hours a week in exchange for their benefits. Likewise, since day care services have been in short supply even in the transitional year, there is a strong probability that after the first year, people in low wage jobs will find that both day care and health care services have vanished. Work programs do get people to work harder, but they rarely provide them with the promised services that are essential to their success and they do not get people out of poverty.

Current Research on Workfare

One reason that the Family Support Act will not get people out of poverty is that the research which shaped the legislation never showed that it could be done. Conducted by the Manpower Demonstration Research Corporation from 1982 to 1987, this research examined experimental work programs in eight different localities. Those who participated in these programs had an employment rate only about 5 percent higher than those who did not participate. In the San Diego experiment, for example, 61 percent of the participants got jobs within 15 months, but then so did 55 percent of the control group. The San Diego experiment yielded the highest total income: its participants received $5,313 in one year from both work and welfare. In Arkansas — the program where clients had the lowest average income — there was a 37 percent differential in income from work, yet that differential amounted to only $156 over one year. More to the point, income from both work and welfare combined to produce an annual total income of just $1,611 (Gueron, 1987).

These gains are exceedingly modest. Nevertheless, any attempt to replicate them nationally is likely to dilute them even further. The MDRC program studied the effects of workfare on mothers of school age children who were applying for assistance. The Family Support Act shifts the target population to recipients with children three years old (one year old or more at the states' option) who are receiving public assistance. This new population is clearly harder. By the time attempts to reach it are combined with the difficulty of implementing a small experimental program in every state, the benefits that the MDRC research identified will disappear completely.

Workfare and Ideology

If the research does not promise much, and the legislation offers still less, what is the force driving the demand for workfare programs? The answer is, plainly, the conservative political climate. Conservatives have taken the 1 percent of the federal budget that is spent on AFDC and turned it into the primary explanation of the nation's social ills. Forget the military budget, the savings and loan scandals, low wages, and our declining standard of living. If the economy is squeezing people and they feel threatened by a pervasive sense of social disorder, talking about workfare programs has the considerable virtue of directing attention to those at the bottom, rather than at the top of the income ladder. There, with some political sleight of hand, one can blame poverty on unmarried welfare mothers who would quickly ascend into the middle class if only they would work hard and/or get married instead of having babies.

From 1970 to 1991, the value of the welfare grant in Illinois, the median state, declined 42 percent. Declines in AFDC were so precipitous that by 1990, no state paid AFDC benefits equal to the federal poverty line, and Alaska, which offered the largest amount, paid a family of three $891 a month, or just 82 percent of the poverty line. At the other extreme, Mississippi, the least generous state, paid out grants that equalled only 14 percent of the poverty line, or $120 a month. Although about two-thirds of AFDC recipients are children, every state has set the rate for public assistance at levels well below the minimum required for subsistence.

Conservatives often insist that welfare mothers have babies to increase their benefits. But this argument is internally inconsistent. If economic motivation is to be attributed to people, the incentive must be there. In the case of welfare it isn't. When a mother with two children has a third child, the median differential for all 50 states and the District of Columbia is only $65 a month. No wonder that even with all the talk of a proliferating black underclass, the pregnancy rate for black teens has been declining over the last twenty years.

Perhaps the greatest myth about poor families is that their poverty is not somehow connected with the function of poverty within our economic system. Poverty, after all, serves a distinct purpose. Simply, some people — typically employers — benefit when wages are low and public assistance is even lower. As long as income for those at the bottom of the economic ladder remains meager, the people who receive this income will be poor. Unless wages and benefits are increased, any insistence that they join a work program diverts our attention from this fact.

Still, nothing in this analysis is meant to imply that welfare clients should not work. Obviously, they should. In this respect, conservatives are right: work *is* preferable to welfare. The issue, then, is not whether people should work, but rather the conditions of that work, and the extent of the social supports with which they are provided. Conservative work programs fail because they tend to use work as a punishment and add some very transitory social supports a little later. Reversing this sequence is absolutely crucial to the success of any work program. If we make the supports generous and give them *first,* people will need very little encouragement to obtain a job.

Such a program would entail far more than the simple insistence that people on welfare join a work program. It would require a higher minimum wage, equal pay for equal work, and a full range of antidiscrimination policies. Provision would also have to be made for quality day care services, as well as readily available parental leave. With adequate education, job training, and a real commitment to create jobs, few able-bodied people would remain on welfare (Rose, 1990).

Of course, this program would be more expensive. Yet, cost alone would not constitute the main difficulty. Rather, the main difficulty is political: the implementation of this program would require a fundamental revision of our economic system and of the poor people within it. Poverty is a very costly social expense, but many people who are well off benefit from its existence. By getting more people to labor for little money, conservative work programs are designed to preserve these benefits for the well off. Undoubtedly, the poor will work harder in workfare programs. Nevertheless, even after they participate in these programs, the poor will most emphatically still be poor.

Rejoinder to Professor Blau   RALPH SEGALMAN

Professor Blau has apparently not yet been informed of the discovery of the underclass. Despite the work of Auletta (1982), Bernstein (1982), Bode (1980), Dornbusch (1986), Hirsch (1983), Lewis (1968), McLanahan (1988), Mead (1988), Murray (1984), Segalman and Basu (1980), Sheehan (1976), Wrong (1986) and others, he still believes in the victim theory of unemployability. In the United States, some children learn in class (with the help and encouragement of their parents who care enough to stay together and focus on their child's future). Other children fail in class and become less employable. Many of these children eventually become heads of welfare households who are intellectually supported by liberals who claim that unemployability is an effect of the social system. I believe that this kind of jockeying for position about the residual AFDC population is of no use to society or to welfare clients. Only if a true rehabilitation (welfare reform-cum-workfare) program is undertaken can they be helped. Is it not time for the supporters of "welfare as a way of life" to realize the damage being done to the welfare clientele? Is it also not time for such supporters to join with the conservatives who want to solve the problem? Together, they might gain popular support for a true welfare reform program. Welfare is damaging to its clients; however, it can also be expected to become increasingly restrictive with diminishing benefits.

Professor Blau suggests a revision of our economic system to raise wages for the currently unemployed and the marginal poor. Simple economic theory makes it clear why low-level wages for unskilled and untrained workers will not rise in coming years. You cannot wait for a revolution which will probably never come. There was a revolution in 1918 over this same issue in East Europe. Didn't it die from unpopularity and failure? Only people who utilize their opportunities for learning and training can look forward to economic mobility in the coming decades in America. Those who want to help the welfare population should press them to do what they press their own children to do; namely, to make the most of their educational opportunities, to seek better opportunities, to work hard in class and in training, and to learn and replicate how the working world behaves. Workfare need not be a coercion. It can be what everyone really needs: a chance to make something of themselves.

REFERENCES

Auletta, K. (1982). *The underclass.* New York: Random House.

Bernstein, B. (1982). *The politics of welfare: The New York City experience.* Boston: ABT Books.

Bode, J. (1980). *Kids having kids.* New York: Watts Publishing.

Dornbusch, S., et al. (1986). A report to the National Advisory Board of the study of Stanford and the schools on the main findings of our collaborative study of family and the schools. Stanford, California, Stanford University Department of Sociology, Feb. 27.

Gueron, Judith. (1987). *Reforming work with welfare.* New York: The Ford Foundation.

Hirsch T. (1983). Crime and the family. In Wilson, J. Q. (Ed.), *Crime and public policy.* San Francisco: Institute for Contemporary Studies, 53–58.

Lewis, O. (1968). *La vida.* London: Panther Press.

McLanahan, S. (1988). Family structure and dependency: Early transitions to female household headship. *Demography* (25) February, 1–16.

Mead, L. (1988). The new welfare debate. *Commentary* (85), 3.

Murray, C. (1984). *Losing ground.* New York: Basic Books.

Rose, N. (1990). From the WPA to workfare: It's time for a truly progressive government work program. *Journal of Progressive Human Services* (1)2, 17–42.

Segalman, R., & Basu, S. (1980). *Poverty in America: The welfare dilemma.* Westport, CT: Greenwood Press.

Sheehan, S. (1976). *A welfare mother.* New York: New American Library.

U.S. General Accounting Office (1991). *Welfare to work: States begin jobs, but fiscal and other problems may impede their progress.* Washington, D.C.: U.S. General Accounting Office.

Wrong, D. (1986). The great American trouble (Review of *Crime and human nature* by James Q. Wilson and Richard J. Herrnstein and *Confronting crime: An American challenge* by Elliott Cursie.) *The New Republic,* Jan 20, 27–32.

Annotated Bibliography

Block, F., & Noakes, J. (1988). The politics of the new-style workfare. *Socialist Review* 88(3), 31–58.

This presents an excellent analysis of how the modest results of the Manpower Demonstration Research Corporation's experiments were inflated to produce the Family Support Act.

Rose, N. (1990). From the WPA to workfare: It's time for a truly progressive government work program. *Journal of Progressive Human Services* (1)2, 17–42.

This is a fine historical summary of the political and economic constraints that have prevented the establishment of an effective government work program.

Does AFDC
Foster Dependency?

EDITOR'S NOTE: Aid to Families with Dependent Children (AFDC) is designed to provide temporary assistance to low-income families in times of serious financial need. The program has helped many families cope with a loss of income caused by unemployment, illness, the death of a primary income earner, and other contingencies. Through AFDC support, many families have become self-sufficient again. Despite its importance, AFDC is one of the most heavily criticized programs of the American welfare state. Also known as "welfare," AFDC is accused of encouraging laziness, scrounging, immorality, and dependency. Critics contend that AFDC payments are an incentive to the poor to become indolent rather than earn their own living. The program, they believe, has produced a whole generation of dependent people who live off taxpayers instead of contributing to society. Supporters of AFDC argue that the official data do not support this claim. The majority of AFDC recipients do become financially self-sufficient. Many others make every effort to find work. In any case, AFDC benefits are so meager that people could not subsist on welfare. The idea that AFDC fosters dependency is, they believe, simply a political ruse intended to undermine this valuable program.

In this debate, Murray Spencer Sumner argues YES, that AFDC does foster dependency. Sumner is a pseudonym for a nationally recognized authority who has published extensively on issues of social welfare policy.

Michael Reisch, Ph.D., argues, NO, that AFDC does not foster dependency. Dr. Reisch is Professor and Director of the Department of

Social Work Education at San Francisco State University. His research interests include the political economy of social welfare, history and philosophy of social work, community organization, and social work values and ethics. He is the author of *From Charity to Enterprise: The Development of American Social Work in a Market Economy* (with Stanley Wenocur) (1989), University of Illinois Press; *The Future of Non-profit Management in the Human Services* (with Albert Hyde) (1988), San Francisco State University; *The Political Economy of Social Work in the 1980s* (with Stanley Wenocur) (1983), University of Connecticut; *New and Innovative Approaches to Community Organization Practice* (with Stanley Wenocur) (1986), University of Connecticut.

YES

MURRAY SPENCER SUMNER

Introduction

Since the Colonial era, policy makers in the United States have attempted to balance efforts to address the problem of poverty in children and families with concerns about the effects of those efforts on public morals and the health of the economic system. For over 200 years, the public welfare policies they produced with the support of a broad spectrum of the American people were based upon prevailing cultural values which sought to strengthen individual and familial responsibility and emphasized the primary role of market system mechanisms in creating and distributing material goods.

Since the 1930s, a new public ethos has emerged which has steadily eroded the value foundation of U.S. social policies toward the poor. Instead of policies based upon a social contract involving mutual responsibilities between individual and society, greater emphasis has been placed on the concept of "entitlement." This has changed the direction of U.S. social policy from one which focused on the alleviation of temporary conditions of dependency — e.g., widowhood, physical illness or injury, and unemployment — to one which has created a new form of more or less permanent dependency on government support. This shift is primarily responsible for the emergence of a new social phenomenon during the past 25 years — a permanent underclass composed largely of inner city residents who are chronically unemployed and welfare dependent, and who are disproportionately represented in social problem statistics on street crime, drug abuse, and adolescent pregnancy. They represent a subcategory of low-income people "whose actions violate the law or [do] not fit mainstream values" (Gans, 1992).

Recent statistics on criminal behavior, adolescent pregnancy, drug and alcohol abuse, and, above all, reliance on AFDC as the primary means of income support reinforce the perception that this underclass is growing and threatening to undermine the quality of life in the nation's urban centers. The AFDC program has played a major role in the development of this underclass as it has evolved from a system of temporary relief to one of permanent economic subsidy. In so doing, it has created a lifestyle by which millions of people have become dependent on government support and lost the will or capacity for self-sufficiency that is the cornerstone of the nation's socioeconomic system. Recent AFDC policy debates have finally recognized the significance of this issue and focused attention on the societal danger of the creation of a permanently dependent "underclass" by the AFDC program.

The Meaning of Dependency

Dependency can be defined as the inability of a group of people to exist or function satisfactorily without the aid or use of another. In that sense, the development of independent adults is inextricably tied to their ability to contribute constructively to the society in which they live.

For over two centuries, bolstered by the "Protestant work ethic," U.S. social policies have been shaped by moral distinctions between the "worthy poor" (the extrinsically dependent), such as widows, orphans, the elderly, and the infirm, and the "unworthy poor" (the extrinsically dependent), particularly able-bodied, employable adults. Since the 1930s, however, and particularly since the 1960s, welfare benefits, primarily AFDC, have eroded this distinction, made recipients psychologically dependent on government "handouts," and provided them with a disincentive to participate as productive individuals in the marketplace. Charles Murray's (1984) research concludes that long-term reliance on AFDC for economic support atrophies the work habits of recipients and contributes to intergenerational poverty. As a result, AFDC recipients "are even more dependent on the public sector and further removed from the American mainstream today than they were two decades ago" (Moroney, 1986, p. 18).

It is not the *receipt* of public assistance that has fostered dependency among some low-income Americans—however much their economic and social status relied upon that assistance. It is the combination of prevailing expectations of the recipient population, the nature of the assistance itself, and the often unstated and underlying goals of the act of providing assistance which have led to the emergence of a growing number of dependent individuals and families.

Policy developments in the past century have led us into this current quagmire. The severe depressions of the 1890s and 1930s undermined the ideological linkage between poverty and individual responsibility (Katz, 1986). Since the advent of New Deal reforms, government obligation to assist the dependent elderly and dependent children have been considered part of the social contract. Social security recipients and beneficiaries of child welfare-related programs are rarely stigmatized. The focus of recent anti-welfare arguments has properly been on adult caregivers who receive AFDC and on the impact on their children of being part of an AFDC family.

Moreover, these growing numbers of dependents exacerbate the fiscal crises many states are currently experiencing. In some states like California, Florida, New York, and Texas, an onslaught of welfare recipients — many from out of state or from other countries — are overwhelming the resources of taxpaying citizens. Recently, there has been as much as a 16 percent increase in the welfare rolls of some states, accompanied by a declining ratio of taxpayers to AFDC recipients (from 7:1 in 1980 to 6:1 in 1990), which is evidence that the state's high benefits draw many potential welfare recipients. Some states' economic and fiscal woes can be attributed to the growing number of immigrants and refugees from Latin America and Asia who have placed disproportionate burdens on states' budgets. As much as 12 percent of the children in the AFDC population are from outside of the state in which their families receive benefits.

AFDC Benefits and the Creation of Dependency

Although AFDC was created to provide relief for the children of widowed or abandoned families, over 30 percent of its present recipients are adults — many of them able-bodied, employable adults who have opted for the welfare lifestyle. One-third of the families headed by these adults remains on welfare for more than a year — a period usually considered to connote nontemporary participation in the program. Nearly one-sixth of all AFDC families receives benefits for more than eight years — the bulk of the intergenerational AFDC population that is at the core of the burgeoning underclass. Even welfare advocates acknowledge that 20 percent of the children on AFDC live in families which are "highly welfare dependent."

It is not surprising, therefore, that in those states like New York, California, and Massachusetts which provide higher levels of AFDC benefits, a higher percentage of AFDC families use the program as a more or less permanent form of income support than in relatively low-benefit states. In California, for example, a typical AFDC family consisting of a mother and two children receives $800/month in benefits and food stamps and is automatically eligible for Medi-Cal, the state's health insurance program for the poor, as well as a host of other state subsidies. Not including the cash value of Medi-Cal and the other state programs they may utilize, this family receives an income equivalent to the pre-tax wages of a full-time employee earning $5/hour (about 10 percent above the minimum wage), who does not receive free health benefits or any other state subsidy. Given this comparison, the attractiveness of AFDC benefits, which until recently were adjusted annually to the cost of living, becomes apparent. This is why in poll after poll, a large majority of Americans oppose increases in welfare benefits and strongly favor the imposition of work requirements on adult welfare recipients.

Conclusion: Creating Alternatives to Dependency

The linkage between AFDC and dependency rests on a conceptual foundation that makes explicit the relationship between social policies, social problems, the society's socioeconomic system, and the cultural values which underlie them. The value foundations of social welfare systems in modern capitalist societies have emphasized marketplace values and individualism, because those are the values which enable the system to function. The recent collapse of socialist governments in Central and Eastern Europe underscores the comparative success of capitalist societies in producing and distributing wealth while maintaining civil liberties and democratic political processes. Social policies which undermine the values upon which this system is based ultimately erode its effectiveness as an engine to produce wealth for its citizens.

In a market economy which now contradictorily rewards AFDC families with incomes higher than those earned through entry-level service and manufacturing jobs, it is not surprising that a large proportion of children in the lower socioeconomic classes are at some time in their lives supported by AFDC. Public assistance has enabled many female heads of households to choose a lifestyle which abjures work, the mutuality of responsibility between individual and society, and widely held moral tenets. In so doing, a growing number of children are being raised in an environment which nurtures values that ill prepare them for the demands of the educational system or the marketplace. A vicious cycle is therefore created in which children continue to have children as a means to establish economic and social independence. In the process, the children they bear grow up with fewer and fewer models of behavior that will enable them to escape the dependency trap and move into the economic and social mainstream.

A final distinction between AFDC recipients and other groups who receive government subsidies is based on the absence of any reciprocity in the relationship between AFDC recipients and the society which assists them. Pinker suggests that in relationships of a dependent nature, the extent to which receivers of benefits or services are able to reciprocate defines their status in our society (Cited in Moroney, 1986, p. 25). As Bertha Reynolds pointed out in her classic, *Social Work and Social Living* (1951), the absence of mutuality in the exchange between the provider and the receiver of aid renders the recipient an unequal partner in the relationship. When applied to society, this "unilateral exchange" produces a "profound sense of stigma" and fosters ongoing dependency, because in order to receive assistance, the recipient must undergo a process (a means test) in which s/he is made to feel inferior.

The way to establish this reciprocity is not through the continuation of a program that engenders such dependency. Rather, it is to recognize that our nation's prosperity is based on a foundation of human capital investment. If we were truly committed to ending welfare dependency and promoting greater self-sufficiency, we would invest in job training, education, child care, health care, and housing programs that would create viable alternatives to the "welfare lifestyle." Without such a commitment, the maintenance of social policies that provide no incentives for individuals to become contributing participants in our society will inevitably lead more people to opt for the surety of welfare over the challenge of the marketplace. This will not only foster growing dependency among children and their families, but it will also contribute to the deterioration of our longstanding cultural values of self-reliance and competition. At a time of increasing global economic competition, we can hardly afford to take this risk by maintaining social programs like AFDC which promote attitudes and behaviors in the next generation that are antithetical to those that made our nation's economic and political systems the model for the rest of the world.

Rejoinder to Murray Spencer Sumner

MICHAEL REISCH

Sumner's argument reflects two of the basic characteristics of conservative critics of the welfare state and their historical antecedents, which upon closer examination reveal both the fundamental flaws in their position and their underlying biases. First, conservative critics decontextualize the problem they are analyzing—i.e, they remove it not only from the economic, political, social, and cultural environment in which it has emerged, but also from the historical context which produced it. Incredibly, for example,

Sumner divorces his discussion of the growth of the so-called "underclass" from the dramatic shifts which have occurred in the United States and world economies — shifts which have all but eliminated the kind of entry-level jobs that provided previous generations with an escape from poverty and from the temporary humiliation of the relief rolls. He ignores the impact that two decades of fiscal cutbacks and programmatic stagnation have had on the economic well-being of low-income families and on the prospects of their children, who have grown up in an era of shrinking employment opportunities, declining spending for public education and housing, and increasing antipathy for poor people and their communities. He makes no mention of the effects of a resurgent institutional racism and sexism, manifest not only in political rhetoric and popular culture, but also in the rollback of antidiscrimination legislation and the attack on the principles of affirmative action. Finally, Sumner fails to note the remarkable confluence of interest between the political and ideological forces which condemn AFDC policy, and those which promote governmental fiscal, monetary, and spending policies that have widened the gap between rich and poor to the greatest distance since such statistics were kept.

Second, Sumner's position transforms what is essentially a social and institutional problem into one of individual behavior and values. This is an often repeated tactic of opponents of public assistance, who for centuries have justified society's lack of compassion for those who have suffered from its fundamental propensities toward inequality (what Richard Titmuss termed its "diswelfares") by condemning welfare recipients for their immorality or their lack of "basic family values." This approach has several critical flaws.

As William Ryan aptly noted in his classic, *Blaming the Victim,* it attributes to the *differences* between people the cause of the inferior position or prevalence of particular problems within one group or class. It implies that the problems of those under analysis are the result of individual decisions (and that the successes of their social "betters" are similarly the consequences of superior judgment and not the result of conscious political choices). This position ignores the role which the socioeconomic and political system has played in creating the current distribution of wealth and power in our society, and the role that our cultural system has played in justifying, defending, and rationalizing this distributional pattern. Lastly, this approach promotes "solutions" to the problems under scrutiny that would leave the environment which produced them virtually untouched under the assumption that only individual, and not structural changes, are needed.

Sumner's arguments — so frequently seen these days in state proposals to reduce AFDC benefits or to take other punitive actions against AFDC recipients — represent a misguided and mean-spirited attempt to solve longstanding social and economic crises by attacking those who have suffered most from them. Based on a faulty set of assumptions, it panders to the worst instincts and prejudices of the electorate and substitutes a vindictive panacea for proactive and preventive social policies. Finally, by repeating tired and often refuted distortions about AFDC recipients, it diverts our attention from constructive policy making and narrows the range of alternatives to the short-sighted and failed options of the past.

NO

MICHAEL REISCH

Since the early 1980s, the fragile fifty-year consensus on U.S. social policy has been shattered by attacks on the role of government in addressing individual and social problems and by persistent challenges to the efficacy of social welfare programs in combatting poverty. The most recent example of the latter is the attempt of the Bush Administration to blame the April 1992 civil disturbances in Los Angeles on the "failed social policies of the 1960s." In the 1990s, the impact of widespread recession and extensive government fiscal crises has intensified the debate over the purposes and functions of societal efforts to assist low-income families. Many states have attempted to solve their budget crises by striking at the most vulnerable segments of the population: families who receive AFDC.

One aspect of this current "war on the poor" (Katz, 1989) has been the reemergence of new forms of the historic argument that AFDC — widely termed "welfare" — has the insidious effect of fostering "dependency" on the populations who receive it. Even sympathetic social democratic scholars like William Julius Wilson (1987) and Harrell Rodgers (1990) have partially accepted these premises. This argument, eagerly seized upon by opportunistic politicians, perpetuates persistent myths and stereotypes about low-income individuals and families who receive AFDC and contains more than a dash of racism, sexism, and class bias.

The position that AFDC fosters dependency is flawed for several reasons. For one, it ignores the history of public welfare policies, the ideologies which support them, and the connection of these policies to economic and social transformation. Second, it is based upon persistent myths about who receives AFDC, the size and economic value of AFDC benefits, and the economic behavior of the poor. Finally, it is founded on the faulty assumption that participation in the AFDC program inevitably leads to long-term reliance on public assistance for the overwhelming majority of recipients.

Persistent Myths about the AFDC Population

Conservatives have attempted to support their view of the linkage between AFDC and dependency by fostering the impression that a growing tide of "irresponsible" welfare recipients threatens to overwhelm the resources of the nation's hardworking citizens. Some, like California Governor Pete Wilson, have gone further and, in the face of contradictory data, attributed their states' economic and fiscal woes to swelling numbers of immigrants and refugees from Latin America and Asia. All proponents of the "AFDC fosters dependency" thesis base their assertions upon a characterization of adult recipients as individuals who must be compelled to work and who prefer the "easy life" of the dole. The similarities between these arguments and those of their historical predecessors are striking.

The facts, however, paint a very different picture. According to nonpartisan analyses, data do not lend support to the theory that eligible families move to take advantage of higher grant levels. Even in "welfare generous" states like California, the state's welfare population grew more slowly in the mid and late 1980s than its overall population, belying one of the more common myths about AFDC.

Another popular impression about AFDC that is fueling the current concern over dependency involves the composition of the AFDC population. Contrary to the myth of the "welfare queen" or the "welfare drone," 70 percent of the national AFDC population is composed of *children*; the remainder are their adult caretakers. Contrary to the myth of large welfare families in which women continue to bear children in order to increase their grants, the average family that receives AFDC consists of a mother and two children. Fewer than 10 percent of all AFDC families have more than two children—smaller than the proportion of all U.S. families (U.S. Bureau of the Census, 1991). Although the media have created the image of thousands of teenage parents having babies to go on the public dole, fewer than 2 percent of AFDC mothers are under 18 years old; over 90 percent are 21 or older.

Finally, the core of the dependency hypothesis—that receipt of AFDC promotes long-term, intergenerational reliance upon public welfare—is strongly refuted by a wealth of available data. Most families who receive AFDC use its benefits for a short period to soften the impact of structural economic or social forces beyond their control, such as layoffs, worker displacement, illness, family breakup, or environmental disaster (Friedman, 1989). The median time for the first period of aid is nine months, and the majority of recipients are on aid for fewer than two years (Levitan, 1985). Two-thirds of two parent families on AFDC are off assistance within a year (California State Legislature, 1989). Although the notion of intergenerational welfare dependency is at the heart of recent efforts to cut public assistance benefits nationally, only 20 percent of children whose families received one quarter or more of their income from AFDC became "highly welfare dependent" as adults. Statistics from state governments as diverse as California, New York, and Maryland demonstrate that only 10 to 15 percent of all AFDC recipients receive benefits for more than eight years (i.e., are "long-term recipients").

Finally, again contradicting widely held stereotypes, more than half of all able-bodied adult AFDC recipients have been employed for some time during the past two years (Levitan & Shapiro, 1987). Studies of welfare reform programs in California, Massachusetts, Wisconsin, New Jersey, and Maryland consistently reflect the preference of most adult AFDC recipients for work over welfare. Yet, governments at the state and national level have never provided AFDC recipients with basic needs such as child care, health care, and job training to help them meet the societal expectation that they work. In fact, changes in AFDC policy during the 1980s have actually created a disincentive for recipients to obtain part-time employment or to try to reenter the labor market on a full-time basis (Edelman, 1987). Consequently, many AFDC recipients who are eager to work are on growing waiting lists, even in those states whose "workfare" programs are less attractive.

The Myth of Economic Irrationality

This leads to the last argument against the proposition that AFDC fosters dependency: an examination of the economic rationality behind the behavior of AFDC recipients. Proponents of the dependency hypothesis attempt to have the argument both ways. On the one hand, they favor either a revived "less eligibility" standard which would compel adult AFDC recipients to reenter the labor market by reducing AFDC payments to a level well below the minimum wage and eliminating all corollary benefits such as Medicaid and subsidized housing, or a system of economic incentives (such as temporary continuation of child care and health care benefits) which encourage AFDC recipients to enter a "workfare" or job training program as a step toward leaving the welfare system. On the other hand, however, some proponents of the dependency hypothesis favor approaches to the alleged problem of welfare dependency which rely heavily on coercive measures to compel workforce participation by recipients. Initiatives to reduce benefits if families remain on public assistance more than six months, or if they have another child while receiving benefits, are examples of this approach.

Recently, many state programs have combined both carrot and stick elements in programs which assume that low-income people, under state compulsion, behave rationally in their personal economic decision making. That is, when confronted with unavoidable choices that have clear and different economic consequences, they will select the choice that is "best" for them from a strictly economic standpoint. Such programs further assume that participating in a low-wage job, without fringe benefits, with little opportunity for advancement, and with no employment security would be preferred over AFDC by "rational" adults. In fact, strictly from the point of view of economic rationality, there is considerable evidence that although most adult AFDC recipients prefer employment to welfare, they behave quite rationally in occasionally choosing AFDC over the marketplace for a limited period of time. A comparison of the hypothetical family incomes of an AFDC family of three and a one-wage-earner family of comparable size is instructive in this regard.

In those few states with "liberal" AFDC benefits such as California, New York, and Massachusetts, the family of three will receive benefits which equal slightly over 70 percent of the federal poverty line. Even if the family receives an average food stamp grant — and many eligible families do not — its income will rise to only 86 percent of the poverty line. It is only when all other possible benefits are factored in — subsidized child care, energy assistance, housing subsidies, subsidized school meals, WIC benefits, surplus food giveaways, mass transit passes, and, above all, medical assistance — that the family's "income" rises above the poverty line. By contrast, while a family in which the sole wage-earner works full-time at minimum wage work would produce an income above that of AFDC benefits, this family would probably be ineligible for the supplemental benefits the AFDC family could potentially receive.

It is important, however, to point out several additional factors often overlooked in such comparisons. First, few families on AFDC receive this optimal "benefits package." In fact, it would require an enormous investment of time and energy and a high degree of sophistication in dealing with bureaucracies to receive this hypothetical optimum. Second, as a result of federal and state cutbacks during the past decade, far fewer families receive benefits even from *some* of these programs. Federal spending on public housing alone has decreased 81 percent since 1981. Third, in most states the level of AFDC benefits and the availability of other supportive social services are well below those provided by the states cited above. Fourth, the cost of living in states with higher AFDC benefits erodes the seemingly higher value of these benefits. For example, 60 percent of California's AFDC families live in the state's ten metropolitan areas. In these areas, the "fair market rent" for a two-bedroom apartment — described by HUD guidelines as "decent, safe and sanitary . . . of a modest (nonluxury) nature" — is *higher than the total AFDC grant*. The same is true in 48 other states and the District of Columbia. In California, this problem is compounded by the fact that only 11 percent of these families live in publicly owned or subsidized housing—the lowest rate in the nation and considerably below the dismal national average of 28.3 percent. Fifth, the purchasing power of AFDC benefits has declined 25 percent since 1981 and the median state benefit has dropped 38 percent in the past two decades. While safety net programs pulled 20 percent of all low-income families out of poverty in 1979, they now provide that assistance to only 10 percent of such families. Finally, a strictly economic model of decision making assumes that AFDC families do not (or, perhaps, should not) care about other noneconomic factors in making life choices, such as the safety of their neighborhoods, the quality of their children's schools and child care settings, recreational and cultural opportunities for their families, and the ability to develop high quality relationships with their children.

It is difficult, therefore, to argue against the rationality of AFDC families. Like all low-income families in history, they attempt to find the surest path to economic survival and family integrity. At times, these goals are best served by entry into the market economy. In fact, the behavior of most AFDC recipients indicates that work is the preferred option when opportunities exist. At other times, however, it is rational from both economic and noneconomic standpoints for such families to apply for public assistance rather than trust their fates to the vicissitudes of the market.

Conclusion

Until we restructure our economic system to guarantee the basic necessities of life for those who participate in it and for those who cannot, we must continue to provide adequate income supports for our nation's children and their caretakers who are unable—for whatever reason—to support themselves. Public opinion polls demonstrate that despite the persistence of negative stereotypes about AFDC recipients, nearly two-thirds of those queried recognize that the children and families who receive AFDC are really poor and desperately need the assistance; and two-thirds of those polled believe the country is not spending enough money on poor children and families. Our social policies should reflect this compassionate tendency in our society (Schorr, 1986; Schorr & Schorr, 1988) as well as the abundance of socioeconomic data which justify the liberalization of AFDC programs (Danziger & Weinberg, 1986; Schorr & Schorr, 1988). To take this step, however, we must rid ourselves of false assumptions about AFDC recipients based upon lingering prejudices. First among these is the myth that AFDC fosters dependency.

Rejoinder to Michael Reisch MURRAY SPENCER SUMNER

Dr. Reisch's essay essentially repeats the classic defense of the welfare state without examining its underlying assumptions. Of even greater significance, he does not take into account the dramatic differences in the socioeconomic environment which has emerged since modern AFDC policies were first introduced — differences which have been shaped, to a considerable degree, by these policies themselves. In so doing, Reisch precludes the possibility of a realistic debate on the efficacy of current AFDC policies and the development of more effective, long-term alternatives. Instead, the solutions he proposes would perpetuate the current cycle of dependency and dependency-related behaviors, which have produced a dramatic increase in the nation's negative social indicators in adolescent pregnancy, drug abuse, and violent crime, among others.

A clearer picture of the AFDC problem can be obtained by simply standing on its head the broad array of statistics Dr. Reisch parades in defense of his position. According to the data he cites, 30 percent of the AFDC population is composed of adult recipients; one-fifth of the children in the program *do* become "highly welfare dependent" as adults; and about one-seventh of all AFDC families are intergenerationally dependent. No efforts to minimize the relative degree of the problem can diminish the severity of its economic and social consequences. No amount of rhetoric which strives to gild the lily can refute the observations of an overwhelming number of public welfare officials, community leaders, social workers, and AFDC recipients themselves: the AFDC system is not working because it fosters a pattern of behaviors and attitudes which contradict those well-intentioned programs striving to create greater self-sufficiency in recipients.

If the size of AFDC families has remained constant (or even decreased as Dr. Reisch implies) in recent years, this means that the proportion of adult AFDC recipients to children has grown. It is the implications of this growth which are so disturbing to the so-called conservative critics of the nation's welfare system, and which lie behind the current drive to reform its abuses and failures. Children do not choose to go on AFDC, adults do. Children do not voluntarily become dependent on the AFDC program, adults do. It is the behavior of adults, therefore, that must be altered if the system is to function as it was originally designed in the 1930s: as a *temporary relief* from unforeseen and unavoidable loss of family income caused by the death, disability, or abandonment of a primary wage-earner and not, as it has often become, a more or less permanent source of economic support that fosters an alternative family lifestyle. This socially irresponsible and economically unproductive behavior can only be changed if the fundamental tenets of AFDC policy which encourage such dependency are reexamined in our current political and economic context.

If Dr. Reisch is correct that adult AFDC recipients act rationally in choosing the certainty of AFDC over the uncertainty of the marketplace, in so many words he acknowledges that the AFDC program promotes conduct in which individuals rely on non-marketplace solutions to meet basic economic needs. In addition to its negative impact on the nation's potential workforce and overall economic productivity, such behavior is clearly undesirable because of its impact on the children in these families, many of whom grow up without adult role models who have made the life choices more likely to lead to mainstream economic success.

It is ironic that defenders of AFDC, like Dr. Reisch, are among those children's advocates who bemoan the absence of role models for children in the nation's ghettoes. Proponents of his position simply cannot have the argument both ways. In order to obtain support for the programs they advocate to benefit children, they must recognize that childrens' problems are the results of adults' behavior, most notably dependency on the welfare system. Unless the policies which foster this behavior are overhauled, the repetitive cycle of generations being born without hope, without prospects, and without even a conception of an alternative lifestyle will never end.

REFERENCES

California State Legislature (1989). Senate Committee on Appropriations and Joint Oversight Committee on GAIN Implementation. Sacramento: CA.

Danziger, S. H., & Weinberg, D. H. (Eds.) (1986). *Fighting poverty: What works and what doesn't.* Cambridge, MA: Harvard University Press.

Edelman, M. W. (1987). *Families in peril: An agenda for social change.* Cambridge, MA: Harvard University Press.

Friedman, B. M. (1989). *Day of reckoning: The consequences of American economic policy.* New York: Vintage Books.

Gans, H. (1992). Point of view. *The Chronicle of Higher Education* (January 8), p. 56.

Katz, M. B. (1989). *The undeserving poor: From the War on Poverty to the war on welfare.* New York: Pantheon Books.

Katz, M. B. (1986). *In the shadow of the poorhouse: A social history of welfare in America.* New York: Basic Books.

Levitan, S. A. (1985). *Programs in aid of the poor,* 5th edition. Baltimore: The Johns Hopkins University Press.

Levitan, S. A., & Shapiro, I. (1987). *Working but poor: America's construction.* Baltimore: The Johns Hopkins University Press, 1987.

Murray, C. (1984). *Losing ground: American social policy, 1950–1980.* New York: Basic Books.

Moroney, R. M. (1986). *Shared responsibility: Families and social policy.* New York: Aldine Publishing Co.

Reynolds, B. C. (1951). *Social work and social living.* NewYork: Citadel Press.

Rodgers, H. R., Jr. (1990). *Poor women, poor families: The economic plight of America's female-headed households.* Armonk, NY: M. E. Sharpe, Inc.

Schorr, A. L. (1986). *Common decency: Domestic policies after Reagan.* New Haven, CT: Yale University Press.

Schorr, L. B., with D. Schorr (1988). *Within our reach: Breaking the cycle of disadvantage.* New York: Doubleday.

U.S. Bureau of the Census (1991). *Poverty in the United States: 1991.* Current Population Reports, series P-60, No. 163. Washington, D.C.: U.S. Government Printing Office.

Wilson, W. J. (1987). *The truly disadvantaged.* Chicago: The University of Chicago Press.

ANNOTATED BIBLIOGRAPHY

Gilder, G. (1981). *Wealth and poverty.* New York: Basic Books.

This influential book written by George Gilder, one of Reagan's chief domestic policy architects, had a major impact on the social thinking of conservatives throughout much of the 1980s.

Katz, M. B. (1986). *In the shadow of the poorhouse: A social history of welfare in America.* New York: Basic Books.

Written from a left perspective, Katz's book is an excellent study of the historical forces that shaped the American welfare state.

Mead, M. (1986). *Beyond entitlement: The social obligations of citizenship.* New York: Free Press.

Mead, a well-respected conservative thinker, captures the intellectual crux of the social and political arguments of the New Right against the American welfare state.

Piven, F. F., & Cloward, R. (1971). *Regulating the poor: The functions of public welfare.* New York: Pantheon Books.

Although this classic book is somewhat dated by not covering the recent events in the Reagan and Bush administrations, it still provides one of the most coherent historical critiques on the relationship between the welfare state and social control posed by the American left.

Is There an Underclass?

EDITOR'S NOTE: The idea that poor people form a distinct class, separate from the rest of society, with their own culture, attitudes, and behaviors, is not a new one. In the nineteenth century, the wealthy used the term the "dangerous and perishing classes" to describe the inhabitants of the tenement slums of the cities, and during the middle decades of this century, the notion of the culture of poverty was popularized. In recent times, the term "underclass" has gained currency. The idea of the underclass is today also associated with poor inner city communities and particularly with those communities in which crime, drug use, unemployment, and illegitimacy are conspicuous. Despite the popularity of the underclass concept, some experts question its usefulness. They point out that only a small proportion of poor people can realistically be categorized as belonging to the underclass, and that this has limited relevance to the task of formulating policies that respond effectively to the poverty problem. Of even greater concern is the political connotation of the term. By denigrating poor people as deviant and criminal, they are segregated from society and can be conveniently forgotten.

W. Joseph Heffernan, Ph.D., argues YES, the underclass does exist. Dr. Heffernan is Professor of Social Work at the School of Social Work, University of Texas at Austin. He has undertaken extensive research into social welfare policy and the history of social welfare programs. He has published *Social Welfare Policy: A Research and Action Strategy* (1992), Longman; and *Social Work and Social Welfare: An Introduction* (1992), West.

Kathleen Heffernan Vickland takes the opposite view, arguing that there is no underclass. She is program manager at SRI International, with a primary research interest in international economic development. She is co-author of *Reforming Financial Systems: Policy Change and Privatization* (1992), Greenwood; and the author of several articles on scholarly journals.

YES

W. JOSEPH HEFFERNAN

Research and policy debates about an underclass are hampered by the absence of a clear operational definition of the term. While I would like to begin with an operational definition that is consistent with the consensus use of the term in the popular and social science press, such a definition is impossible because the term is most often used in nonfocused and essentially political ways. As Herbert Gans has observed, "One of the ways that America and its policy makers avoid dealing with poverty is to label some of the poor as morally deficient and, therefore, not worthy of help" (1992, p. A-56). Michael Harrington's *The Other America* (1962) popularized and politicized the notion that the very poor were somehow different from the rest of society. Harrington used as a metaphor an exchange between F. Scott Fitzgerald and Ernest Hemingway. In this exchange, Fitzgerald reportedly observed that "The rich are different from you and me," to which Hemingway replied, "Yes, they have more money."

Culture of poverty theorists sided with Fitzgerald and argued that the poor not only have less money, but they are also a distinct social class with their own special mores and norms. Harrington and the 1960s liberals further argued that these norms must be considered in the design of social policy. Structural poverty theorists sided with Hemingway and saw the lack of money as the only significant difference between the poor and others. Now most observers view both structural and cultural aspects as contributing to poverty, particularly multigenerational poverty. In more recent years a new concept has entered the technical and popular debate. The concept is of an underclass, a subcategory of the poor who are not only decidedly different in their mores and norms of adjustment, but who also face structural and institutional discrimination. These patterns of adjustment render some social programs counterproductive for members of the underclass.

Conservatives use the concept to argue for the reduction of social programs, while liberals use the concept to justify the redesign of social programs. The latter argue that the poor are not a single class, but a set of classes, and programs that will help some poor may in fact be harmful to other poor people. It is clear that once a subpopulation is defined for social policy planning purposes, it is also primed for political exploitation. The truth is that if we specify the distinctions of a social underclass, the David Dukes of the world will distort these distinctions for their own selfish ends.

Defining the Underclass

The central problem faced here is the absence of a clear operational definition of the term "underclass." Presently, it is being used to note the coincidence of a number of social ills, including, but not limited to, welfare dependency, fatherless families, and the operation of an irregular economy. Various experts have defined the characteristics of an underclass in terms of the duration of poverty, the geographic concentration of the very poor in inner cities, and specialized (and socially destructive) patterns of behavior. However, there is no "correct" definition of this or any other term used in the social sciences. Definitions are dependent on the way a problem is conceptualized. Thus, conceptualization is intended as a symbol of the phenomenon under investigation. In the formulation of various propositions, social scientists deal only with the concepts and not their underlying realities. A common error of scientific reasoning is to substitute the concept for the phenomenon its symbolizes. This error is called the "fallacy of reification." The danger of reification is always real, and stretching any definition beyond its conceptual framework inevitably leads to problems. Defining a disease like AIDS, establishing a poverty line, or specifying child abuse in terms of specific behavior are political problems as well as intellectual puzzles.

No one can banish the concept of the underclass from its proper and improper use in policy debates; nor can anyone magically prevent street-level social workers from allowing this concept to distort the daily reality they must face. The question becomes: "Does the planning utility of the concept outweigh the disutility of the stereotypical thinking it will almost certainly engender?"

Abstract concepts are not irrelevant to social policy; often, they are critical. There can be no doubt that the concept of an underclass has a particularly nasty label. At worst, it reminds one of Adolf Hitler's use of the Germanic expression "untersubmenchen." At best, it is reminiscent of Oscar Lewis's (1969) development of the concept of the "culture of poverty." Lewis argued that the poorest in our society develop a protective culture, which is passed from one generation to the next. This view was expanded to include the idea that the protective features of this culture worked so well that some of the poor do not even try to escape their poverty. As suggested above, liberals used this thesis to suggest that remedial cultural programs would need to accompany service, training, and income support programs in the War on Poverty. A conservative variation of the same concept was articulated by Edward Banfield (1963) in *The Unheavenly City*. Banfield argued that a disproportionate number of inner city blacks entered into what the middle class would label as a dysfunctional lifestyle. This occurred not only because society offered ghetto residents meager rewards for enlisting into the lifestyle of the middle class, but also because the welfare system actually offered rewards for a deviant lifestyle. Alteration of the real opportunity structure and the welfare system would be required to stem the growth of the underclass. It was Banfield who set the terms of the 1980s debate about the welfare system generating its own dependency. This is hardly a new idea in the history of welfare policy debates. What is new is the effort to specify a specific subpopulation of the poor to whom this generalization applies.

The "underclass literature" is diverse. Moreover, the same term is used to define different phenomena, and different terms are used to identify identical phenomena. This is the way science seeks to break away from old paradigms such as structural versus cultural explanations for persistent poverty. Gunnar Myrdal (1961) used the word "underclass" in 1961 to describe an economic class that was being made permanently underemployed and unemployed by structural shifts in the economy. Myrdal's was the first widely recognized use of the term, but at that time it did not have much significance in the policy debates. The widespread belief that the economy was strong enough to lift all people out of poverty left little room for Myrdal's insight. This was the first time the concept was ignored, to our collective loss.

At a descriptive level, the journalist Ken Auletta (1982), described the underclass as: (1) long term welfare recipients, (2) impoverished street criminals, (3) the released but untreated mentally ill, and (4) a diverse collection of the urban poor who didn't conveniently fit into some more recognizable category. After a short silence, William Julius Wilson revived the term. For Wilson (1987), the underclass was a sociological concept that was a referent for spatially disadvantaged persons living in Census tracks with abnormally high rates of "dysfunctional family and employment conditions." Those who were left behind in the ghetto were outside of the economic opportunity structure. Thus, "structural" poverty generated "cultural" poverty. Finally, Errol Ricketts and Isabel Sawhill (1988) offered their definition of the concept as a subpopulation characterized by behaviors that are not only at variance with mainstream American values, but are highly likely to impose social costs on the rest of society. These groups are geographically concentrated in the "center" of Northeastern industrial cities.

The common element in these definitions is their untested empirical assumption that these groups actually exist, and that this grouping serves

FIGURE 20.1 IS THERE AN UNDERCLASS?

Operating System

Objective Reality	The Underclass Exists	The Underclass Does Not Exist
The Underclass Exists	No error	Type I error
The Underclass Does Not Exist	Type II error	No error

some theoretically relevant social science and/or social planning purpose. Definitions without purpose are theoretically barren, and definitions without empirical referents are incapable of generating verifiable propositions.

For the purpose of this debate let us pretend that we do not know whether an underclass exists. The underclass then becomes the hypothetical underclass, and our question becomes akin to one of a Type I or Type II error of hypothesis testing (see Figure 20.1).

Conclusion

I argue that a Type I error is the more dangerous one. Even given a substantial latitude in any definition of an underclass, I think that a walk down the mean streets of urban America will confirm this population exists. Moreover, an examination of the case records of multigenerational welfare families will confirm their self-defeating behaviors. I would add that the "urban underclass" is also found in small town and rural America. The objective reality is that sound welfare policies which help the vast majority of families in trouble are destructive for a minority of those families. Put simply, I believe it is clear that more generous welfare payments do cause some illegitimacy; that interstate differentials in welfare payments do cause some welfare recipients to migrate; and that publicly funded abortions cause some recipients to use abortion as a means of birth control. This list could go on endlessly. Although the numbers may be very small — perhaps even tiny — the time has come for liberals to accept the fact that all welfare programs are harmful to some people. On the other hand, conservatives must accept the fact that none of the welfare programs are harmful to all of the people. If we ever hope to target welfare programs more effectively, we must begin to accept the fact that there is a social underclass. In short, I would like to banish the term but not the concept.

Rejoinder to Professor Heffernan

KATHLEEN HEFFERNAN VICKLAND

I have just two observations on Dr. Heffernan's essay. His own argument opens the door to my first point by noting that, "the poor are not a single class, but a set of classes." The subcategory "underclass," which we have already seen is small, is itself composed of a multitude of diverse subgroups, some as different from one another as the underclass is from the rest of the poor. For example, some individuals exhibit destructive behavior only briefly; others are in a seemingly unending cycle of rebellion against the laws and mores of society. Surely this distinction is of extreme concern to the policy community. Similarly, the underclass could be divided into further segments (urban/rural, young/old, etc.) until the policy community is faced not with meaningfully sized populations but a series of individual case studies that do not facilitate research and policy design. By accepting the concept of an underclass, which is unspecific, hard to quantify, and only refers to a small portion of the welfare population, we open a Pandora's box of meaningless segmentation.

Secondly, the negative side effects of assuming that the underclass exists when it does not (a Type II error) are perhaps underestimated. One could argue that the political backlash to the underclass concept is so great as to overpower the negative implications of the Type I error referred to by my opponent. Moreover, the political backlash is not theoretical but real and palpable. We see it now in the form of budget cuts at the national, state, and local levels, reductions in individual donations to charity, and heightened, perhaps even potentially explosive, interclass tension. In addition, the political backlash (Type II error) harms the entire welfare population, while the mistargeting (Type I error) harms only one-thirteenth of the welfare population. For these reasons, I urge that we abolish both the term and the concept of an "underclass."

NO

KATHLEEN HEFFERNAN VICKLAND

In any debate, one must first define the terms. We have all been in the disappointing situation in which we have debated with someone only to find that we agree after all. The problem was that we hadn't agreed on definitions at the start of the debate. We wouldn't want that to happen here. In any case, we have agreed to build our discussion on Errol R. Ricketts and

Isabel V. Sawhill's (1988) definition of the underclass as "A subgroup of the American population that engages in behaviors at variance with those of mainstream populations . . . [and which are] likely to inhibit social mobility . . . [and] impose costs on the rest of society" (p. 318–319).

In some ways, the concept of an underclass is not new, but is a throwback to the "culture of poverty" developed by Oscar Lewis. This school of thought argued that poverty is a result of the adoption of lifestyles, beliefs, and values which do not result in full participation in the social and economic mainstream. In attempting to come to grips with the question of an underclass, we must ask: (1) Does this underclass exist? (2) Is this term helpful in reducing the incidence and/or severity of poverty in America?

Defining the Underclass

First, does this underclass exist? According to Ricketts and Sawhill, who are considered to have done some of the best empirical research on the subject, the definition of underclass only applies to one percent of the American population, roughly one-thirteenth of all people living under the poverty line. Common sense supports this empirical finding. As Peterson (1991) points out, "many poor people are clearly not members of any underclass. The elderly poor, widows, orphans, the severely sick and disabled, and the simply unlucky can find themselves suddenly plunged into poverty without warning" (p. 622). Surely, a label that applies to only one-thirteenth of the poor population is not going to be of great assistance in solving the nagging problem of poverty. What about the other twelve-thirteenths? Even moving the entire underclass off the welfare rolls would only slightly diminish the overall poverty rate.

While the nature/nurture debate is far from resolved, most people agree that incentives matter. People respond to changed economic circumstances and new opportunities. Enterprise or duty-free zones around the world, from Southern China to Northern Mexico, have graphically demonstrated the rapid, positive response people can make to increased job opportunities. Under the right circumstances, the behaviors ascribed to the underclass diminish or are even eliminated.

Other empirical measures of the underclass indicate that the term may apply to anywhere from 0.2 to 5 percent of the population of the New York SMSA (Hughes 1989). This vast range illustrates an additional problem with the underclass concept: the sensitivity of the empirical estimate to the definition and measurement technique. Indeed, Hughes concludes that the concept is "too volatile an organizing principle to be accepted lightly." In addition, my previous point remains valid: even at the high end of the range, the concept only applies to a minority of the total poor population. The underclass therefore does not exist in sufficient numbers to validate the common usage of the term or to spend disproportionately large amounts of policy analysis time and dollars to its study. However, the term could still have some validity, especially if it can be proven to be helpful in other ways.

A term is useful to the social policy community if it: (1) divides the world into meaningfully sized categories worthy of study (which the term "underclass" does not); (2) illuminates characteristics about groups of people that will facilitate poverty reduction in that group; or (3) conveys to voters and decision makers information and a sense of the worthiness of a cause, or, at the very least, does not create antipathy toward measures designed to reduce poverty.

Dangers of the Term "Underclass"

Although the term "underclass" illuminates characteristics about its members, it is not the characteristics that will help treat the problem. One can forcefully argue that deviant behaviors result from, rather than cause, poverty. Poor people are not innately less moral or more lazy than the middle class or (certainly) the rich. Applying the concept of an underclass will be an unfortunate case of treating the symptom rather than the underlying reason for the disease. Thus, the term is not helpful in this respect. Nor is the concept useful in enhancing or even maintaining political support for poverty reduction measures. Terms such as "single mothers," "the disabled," or "the working poor" all evoke sympathy, empathy, or at the very least neutrality in voters and members of Congress. The word "underclass" is not only unhelpful, it is extremely harmful.

The concept of the underclass ranks one group of people as unequal to the other. This occurrence is much more than an unfortunate word choice; it is indication of an unacceptable segmentation of American society into high and low social classes. America was founded partially in rebellion to the classist immobility of old Europe; we must not allow those tendencies to seep into mainstream thinking by being party to the common usage of a misguided term. The use of the term inflicts even more damage. By consigning people to the underclass, we rob them of any possible hope for improvement in their situation. In short, the term "underclass" adds fuel to the ever-louder "us" versus "them" debate presently marking social welfare policy. By labelling "them" deficient, we indicate that they do not merit our assistance, and we distance ourselves from all responsibility for their plight or their future.

In more compassionate times, perhaps the political implications of the term would be softened. Unfortunately, most people would probably agree that mainstream America in the 1990s has less sympathy for the plight of the poor and the homeless, less confidence in the ability of our social programs to solve their problems, and less enthusiasm for allocating dollars for their care and feeding than in the past. The we/they division implicit in the term underclass is potentially explosive politically, especially as we now struggle with a lengthy recession, higher unemployment rates, and worsening race relations. In short, the term should be discarded because it lacks validity and specificity, and because it is potentially damaging to American society.

Rejoinder to
Ms. Heffernan Vickland

W. JOSEPH HEFFERNAN

I begin my rebuttal with the observation that "poor is the scholar whose student does not exceed him." With that in mind, Ms. Vickland has still not destroyed my argument.

Ms. Vickland suggests that the underclass make up only a tiny proportion of the poor, and that the concept of the underclass is politically dangerous. I agree, but the point remains that current welfare policy can be, and perhaps is, harmful to the one-thirteenth for whom the concept applies. If we had an advance in oncology which could cure twelve but might kill the thirteenth cancer patient, surely we would spend scarce research dollars to better identify and prescribe treatment.

We do not yet know enough to dismiss, or worse ignore, the underclass. This one-thirteenth consumes an unspecified, but certainly large proportion of the welfare budget over time. Their persistent presence on welfare rolls is always fodder in the political game of cutting benefits and/or introducing harsh policies for all recipients. I will admit that the concept of an underclass carries the implicit danger of misdirecting policy and/or policy analysis priorities. However, ignoring the concept carries the greater danger of continuing policies which are harmful to a significant subpopulation of those in need. If the concept of an underclass is useful in times of high interclass compassion, it is all the more necessary in times of interclass antipathy.

REFERENCES

Auletta, K. (1982). *The underclass.* New York: Vintage.
Banfield, E. (1963). *The unheavenly city.* Boston: Little Brown.

Gans, H. (1992). Point of view. *The Chronicle of Higher Education* (Jan. 8), 56.

Harrington, M. (1962). *The other America.* New York: Penguin.

Hughes, M. (1989). Concentrated deviance and the 'underclass' hypothesis. *Journal of Policy Analysis and Management* 8(2), 274–282.

Lewis, O. (1969). The culture of poverty. In Moynihan, D. P. (Ed.), *On understanding poverty.* New York: Basic Books, p. 187–200.

Myrdal, G. (1961). *A challenge to affluence.* New York: Pantheon.

Peterson, P. (1991). The urban underclass and the poverty paradox. *Political Science Quarterly* 106(4), 617–656.

Ricketts, E., & Sawhill, I. (1988). Defining and measuring the underclass. *Journal of Policy Analysis and Management* 7(2), 316–325.

Wilson, W. J. (1987). *The truly disadvantaged.* Chicago: University of Chicago Press.

Annotated Bibliography

Katz, M. B. (1989). *The undeserving poor.* New York: Pantheon Books.

The author presents a broadly conceived review of the shift in central assumptions implicit in the anti-poverty policies from Johnson to Reagan. Katz argues for a new review of the cultural perspective by examining the distribution of power and wealth.

Kaus, M. (1992). *The end of equality.* New York: Basic Books.

Kaus, a senior editor for *The New Republic,* presents an argument for a reconsideration of work, family, and welfare policy that would substitute civic liberalism for the redistributive policies. In his view, these policies have done a disservice to the underclass and have exacerbated racial and class tensions.

Mead, L. M. (1992). *The new politics of poverty.* New York: Basic Books.

Mead examines what he sees as the cause and consequences for a significant portion of the adult population who appear unwilling or unable to enter the labor force.

Wilson, W. J. (1987). *The truly disadvantaged.* Chicago: University of Chicago Press.

In this examination of the rise of social pathologies in the urban ghetto, Wilson presents a broad social democratic agenda that goes well beyond the race-specific agenda found in liberal and conservative orthodoxies.

Can an Asset-Based Welfare Policy Really Help the Poor?

EDITOR'S NOTE: Governmental programs for the alleviation of poverty have traditionally provided resources for consumption. While it is obviously necessary to meet the consumption needs of the poor, proponents of asset-based social policies believe that the poverty problem can be more effectively addressed by helping the poor accumulate both the economic and human capital which will lift them out of their condition. Programs which encourage the poor to save by matching their deposits with government resources are far more useful than income support programs which merely maintain the poor at basic consumption levels. Critics of this approach are not so sure. While they agree that an asset development program is worthwhile, they are doubtful that it offers a ready solution to the problem of poverty. Poverty, they contend, is so widespread, serious, and intractable that large-scale government intervention rather than individualized programs is needed. Solving the problem of poverty requires economic planning, the creation of new jobs, enhanced education and training, massive social investments, and other similar measures rather than the subsidization of individual savings.

These arguments are examined by Michael Sherraden, Ph.D., who argues YES, that an asset-based welfare policy can really help the poor. Dr. Sherraden is Professor of Social Work at the George Warren Brown School of Social Work at Washington University, St. Louis, Missouri. He the co-author of *The Moral Equivalent of War: A Study of Non-Military Service in Nine Nations* (1990), Greenwood; and *Assets and the Poor: A New American Welfare Policy* (1991), M.E. Sharpe.

James Midgley, Ph.D., argues NO. He is Professor of Social Work and Associate Vice Chancellor for Research at Louisiana State University. He has published widely on issues of international social policy with particular reference to the developing countries. His major books include *Professional Imperialism: Social Work in the Third World* (1981), Heinemann; *Social Security, Inequality and the Third World* (1984), John Wiley; *Community Participation, Social Development and the State* (1986), Methuen; *Comparative Social Policy and the Third World* (1987), St. Martin's Press (with Stewart MacPherson); *The Radical Right and the Welfare State: An International Assessment* (1991), Barnes and Noble, (editor with Howard Glennester); and *Profiles in International Social Work* (1992), NASW Press (editor with Terry Hokenstad and Shanti Khinduka).

YES

Michael Sherraden

My great-grandparents were immigrants who homesteaded in Kansas in the 1870s. They were given 160 acres of land by the federal government. They worked hard, raised twelve children, held barn dances on Saturday nights, and left the community and the country a little better off. The Homestead Act, a massive asset give-away program, was one of the most successful domestic policies in American history. It was based on the Jeffersonian idea that people become better citizens in a democracy when they have a stake, assets, and ownership. Although the United States is no longer a nation of small farmers, the concept of stakeholding is just as relevant today as it was at the beginning of the republic.

Despite the prominence of asset ownership in American values and American history, social policy in the modern welfare state — and especially means-tested policy for the poor — has been focused almost exclusively on the distribution of income for consumption. Indeed, means-tested policy usually prohibits savings and the accumulation of assets.

Of course, income and consumption are essential — many Americans do not have enough to eat, many are without basic shelter, and many do not have medical insurance of any kind — but income-based policy, by itself, does not help poor households develop economically. Income-based policy traps families in a cycle of spending that goes from check to check. Yet, the simple reality is that not many families manage to spend their way out of poverty. After more than fifty years of income-maintenance policy, we have confirmed that it is correctly named — it provides only maintenance, not development.

Assets: A Different Perspective

We should consider a different approach. Social policy, including welfare policy, should promote asset accumulation. In addition to the income and consumption policy of the current welfare state, asset-based policy would focus on savings and investment.

The rationale for this new direction can be stated in two parts. First, for the vast majority of households, the pathway out of poverty is through savings and accumulation. The attainment of important economic development goals almost always requires the prior accumulation of assets. Assets are needed to move to a better neighborhood, to send a child to college, to purchase a home, to start a small business, or to achieve other economic goals. Second, when people begin to accumulate assets, their thinking and behavior changes as well. One way to say this is that while incomes feed people's stomachs, assets change their heads. Accumulating assets leads to important psychological and social effects that are not achieved in the same degree by receiving and spending an equivalent amount of regular income. In contrast to mainstream economic thinking, I am suggesting that assets do more than provide a storehouse for future consumption, and these psychological and social effects of asset accumulation are very important for household "welfare" or well-being. Why do assets matter?

- Assets lead to greater household stability.
- Assets create long-term thinking and planning.
- Assets lead to development of knowledge and skills (creation of human capital).
- Assets provide a foundation for risk taking.
- Assets increase personal efficacy and self-esteem.
- Assets increase social status and influence.
- Assets increase political involvement and community participation.

Altogether, these effects of assets can contribute substantially to the well-being and development of poor households.[1]

The Distribution of Assets

Assets are much more unevenly distributed than income. Looking at income, the top 5 percent of the population receives about as much annual income as the bottom 40 percent. But looking at assets, the top one percent holds about as much assets as the bottom 90 percent.[2]

Asset statistics also tell us a great deal about racial inequality. African Americans have virtually never – and still not today – had the same access to asset accumulation as have European Americans. For example, at the time my great-grandparents were receiving free land from the government, the promise of "forty acres and a mule" for freed slaves was not kept (Oubre, 1978). Today, the continuing discriminatory record of banks and savings and loan associations in making real estate loans to African Americans is a national disgrace. Statistics show that even when they have the same income, blacks are much less likely to be granted a loan than are whites.[3] What is the result? African-American households have only about one-eleventh the assets of white households (U.S. Bureau of the Census, 1990).

Assets and Domestic Policy

The importance of asset accumulation has been virtually ignored in the antipoverty policies of the welfare state. However, through the tax system, we do support asset accumulation for the nonpoor, primarily in two categories, tax expenditures for home equity and tax expenditures for retirement pension accounts. In these two categories, the federal government spends well over $100 billion each year and the total is rising rapidly.[4] These two categories make up the bulk of asset accumulation in most American households, heavily subsidized by federal government. Almost everyone would agree that these policies of asset accumulation have been highly successful and good for the country. Thus, we have asset-based policy for the nonpoor, and we spend quite a lot of money on it. But we do not have asset-based policy for the poor.

Poor people, by and large, do not benefit from asset accumulation tax policies because they have marginal tax rates that are zero or too low to receive substantial tax benefits. Perhaps worse, welfare transfer recipients, under current law, are restricted from accumulating ordinary savings and even business assets. Welfare policy, as currently structured, is antisavings policy.

This policy does not make sense. As a nation, we should not be telling welfare recipients that they cannot save for a business, a home, or their children's education. An asset-based policy would, in contrast, structure, encourage, and provide incentives for asset accumulation.

Individual Development Accounts

One way to achieve this goal is to create a system of Individual Development Accounts (IDAs). IDAs would be a relatively simple and universal system of accounts similar to Individual Retirement Accounts (IRAs). IDAs would be optional, earnings-bearing, tax-benefitted accounts in the name of each individual, initiated as early as birth, and restricted to designated purposes. Regardless of the category of social policy (housing, education, self-employment, retirement, or other) assets would be accumulated in these long-term restricted accounts. The federal government would match deposits for the poor, and there would be potential for creative financing through the private sector.

In developing a single IDA policy structure, the government would limit complexity and better integrate various asset-based initiatives into an overall national strategy. Also, the policy would be essentially direct-to-the-beneficiary, with very limited intervention by a welfare bureaucracy. The following general guidelines should be considered for IDAs:

- IDAs should complement income-based policy.
- The policy should be simple both conceptually and administratively.
- The accounts should be voluntary.
- The accounts should receive favorable tax treatment.
- Federal and state governments should provide deposit matches for the poor.
- Creative participation by the corporate and nonprofit sectors should be actively encouraged.

Once the structure of Individual Development Accounts is in place, even with minimal direct funding from the federal government, there would be opportunities for a wide variety of creative funding projects from the private and nonprofit sectors. To build IDA accounts, one can imagine corporations "adopting" a school or a neighborhood, church fund raisers, contributions from civic organizations, bake sales, car washes, carnivals, student-run businesses, and so forth. The key is to establish a policy structure that could leverage private money with tax benefits, spark creative ideas and partnerships, attract diverse funding, and gradually expand as the policy demonstrates its worth.

Policy Development

At this writing, discussion of asset-based policy is increasing. An Individual Development Account Demonstration bill has been introduced in the U.S. House (HR 2258, Section B) by Tony Hall (D-OH) and Bill Emerson (R-MO); it has 135 cosponsors from both parties. A similar bill has been introduced in the Senate (S 2086) by Bill Bradley (D-NJ). The states of Oregon and Iowa are in the process of planning statewide IDA applications. Local IDA experiments have sprung up in Tupelo, Mississippi, and Bozeman, Montana.

A New Direction: Social Policy as Investment

Social policy should invest in the American people — and encourage them to invest in themselves — so they become stakeholders and active citizens. The key is to combine social policy with economic development through a program of asset building and stakeholding.

As a closing thought, Individual Development Accounts, or some other form of asset-based domestic policy, could become for the twenty-first century what the Homestead Act was for the nineteenth — an investment-oriented policy to develop individual capacity, strengthen families and communities, promote active citizenship, and contribute to economic growth.

NOTES

1. These suggested effects of asset accumulation are discussed in *Assets and the Poor* (Sherraden, 1991). They are offered as propositions that have considerable intuitive appeal and certain theoretical and empirical support, although specific tests with poverty populations will be desirable.

2. Asset distribution data are from the Federal Reserve's Survey of Consumer Finances for 1989. Asset distribution in the United States grew considerably more unequal during the 1980s.

3. Evidence of discrimination by race in home purchase and mortgage lending is overwhelming and pervasive. Studies consistently report steering of clients by real estate agents, redlining of neighborhoods, and systematic loan denials by race. The Community Reinvestment Act of 1977 requires the Federal Reserve Board to keep statistics on mortgage lending, and these statistics indicate strong racial bias, particularly against African Americans.

4. A good source for estimates of tax expenditures is U.S. Congress, Joint Committee on Taxation (1989), *Estimates of federal tax expenditures for fiscal years 1990–1994*. Washington, D.C.: U.S. Government Printing Office.

Rejoinder to Professor Sherraden
JAMES MIDGLEY

Michael Sherraden's work represents one of those rare instances in social science endeavors when a scholar formulates a truly original idea which makes a major contribution to social policy research. Despite its importance, a major drawback of Professor Sherraden's asset-based approach is its resolute individualism. While I respect Professor Sherraden's personal preferences, it should now be clear that individualist solutions to our pressing social problems do not work. Fifteen years of rampant individualism in economic and social policy have generated even more poverty, inequality, deprivation, and despair than before. As I argue in my statement, approaches that have dealt with the poverty problem with some degree of success involve concerted, planned intervention by the state. Professor Sherraden's asset-based approach advocates the introduction of individualistic measures like IDAs, when large-scale collective action is needed.

Professor Sherraden's book (1991) does make passing references to the value of collectively held assets. He describes the city of Benito Juarez in Mexico, where assets are developed and held collectively by the community, and he supports the notion of state investment in education as a way of enhancing collectively owned human capital. While Professor Sherraden obviously approves of these measures, he does not pursue the notion of collective asset development but instead uses these references to support his case for IDAs and the perpetuation of ineffectual individualist policy options.

A particularly troubling aspect of the individualistic asset approach is its potential to be used in the campaign against collective involvement in welfare. IDAs are attractive to the political right not only because they assign primary responsibility to individuals, but because their selective approach targets public resources on small, deprived sections of the population, and in this way, reduces government social expenditures. This results in lower taxes and higher business profits. Ultimately, selective individualized programs legitimize the abolition of successful forms of collective welfare such as social security.

The advocacy of the asset approach poses a real danger to social security. Like IRAs, IDAs could replace social security and it is likely that their institutionalization will result in even more frequent attacks on social security in the future. Social security is already being criticized as a sinecure for the prosperous which, critics contend, should be replaced by social provisions that 'target' resources on the poorest groups. The political right supports public supplements to IDAs because they contribute to a wider campaign to abolish social security and other forms of collective provision.

If collective measures are abolished, the success of selective asset-based programs for the poor depends on the future willingness of government to fund these provisions. This is a promissory note that should be carefully scrutinized. When the middle class withdraws from collective programs such as public education, social security, and national health care, tax resistance increases and budgetary allocations for remaining selective programs inevitably decline. Asset-based programs are at risk of facilitating a reduction in popular support for social programs and reducing their ability to help the poor. If this seems an implausibly conspiratorial scenario, it is important to remember that one of the first asset-based programs in American history, the land grant program for freed slaves (which Professor Sherraden refers to), failed largely because it focused on an impoverished minority instead of encompassing the population as a whole.

NO

JAMES MIDGLEY

Of various alternatives to conventional policies for the alleviation of poverty, the asset approach is the most original and radical. As formulated by Sherraden (1991), this approach re-orients existing anti-poverty policies by encouraging the accumulation of wealth rather than the payment of benefits for consumption. By helping the poor to save, the asset approach purports to really help the poor.

The Asset-Based Approach

The asset-based approach is critical of conventional anti-poverty programs. Many existing programs such as AFDC, Food Stamps, and Medicaid promote the consumption of goods and services. They fail, however, to encourage savings and engender behaviors that make the poor responsible, independent, and self-reliant. While it is obvious that basic needs can only be met through consumption, critics contend that the continual provision of consumption goods to the poor simply maintains them at minimal levels of living. If the goal of social policy is the eradication of poverty, the poor must be offered an opportunity to escape poverty. Proponents argue that the asset approach helps poor people accumulate resources to lift themselves out of poverty, and it allows them to become self-reliant and self-respecting citizens.

At the core of the asset approach is the Individual Development Account (IDA) which, like the Individual Retirement Account (IRA), encourages savings. These accounts would be established for all individuals, and would be tax benefitted to foster asset accumulation. Depending on the financial circumstances of the depositor, individual savings would be matched by state contributions at varying rates. For example, a person in severe financial need would have a match as high as 90 percent, while someone who is working and enjoying a relatively good income would receive no match at all. The matching system would be highly flexible and would permit the government to supplement savings as the economic circumstances of individuals change. The accounts would be managed by individuals themselves so that they would become familiar with investment options and learn to use their money wisely. However, the account would be restricted so that withdrawals could only be made for approved purposes such as the purchase of a home, education, retirement, or the establishment of a business. Accumulated IDA assets could be transferred to children at death or prior to death if desired.

Although the asset approach would not replace AFDC or other programs that assist the poor in meeting their basic needs, it would encourage AFDC recipients to deposit a part of their benefits into IDAs and generously match their contributions. In this way, poor people would derive concrete financial benefits, and their predilection to be dependent on the state would be reduced. Asset accumulation through IDAs would be a long-term process, but would foster thrift and responsibility among the poor who have little propensity to save.

Consonant with the tenets of Jeffersonian liberalism, the political philosophy underlying the asset approach is essentially individualist in character and firmly rooted in the American experience. Indeed, this approach was first used in the United States in the form of the Homestead Act of 1862, which delivered about 200 million acres of land to settlers. However, similar approaches have been adopted in other countries. Of interest are the provident funds established in many former British colonial territories to provide an alternative to social security (Midgley, 1984). An asset approach was also introduced by General Pinochet's regime in Chile to replace the country's longstanding social security system (Borzutsky, 1992).

Can Assets Really Help the Poor?

The mobilization of capital through personal savings is regarded by most economists as highly desirable. Whether operated on command, corporatist, or free-market principles, modern economies require investment to renew infrastructure and establish productive enterprises. By encouraging ordinary citizens to save, the economy benefits and those who save benefit as well. Through savings, they accumulate the resources needed to purchase goods and services and in this way, they contribute to aggregate demand, generating more production and employment.

While the advocacy of asset accumulation is noncontentious, the role of assets in solving the problem of poverty is more problematic. Few would disagree with the idea that the poor should be encouraged and even helped to save, but it is unlikely that the implementation of an assets approach through the creation of IDAs will, of itself, really help the poor.

It is obvious that the poorest sections of the population, such as AFDC recipients, do not have the financial resources to save at appreciable levels. Even if supplemented by government, it is difficult to believe that their meager savings can help them to escape poverty within a reasonable period of time. AFDC benefit levels are appallingly low, and despite propagandistic claims that recipients enjoy a comfortable level of living at taxpayers expense, they endure a daily struggle to survive. The poorest sections of the population subsist on incomes which are below minimal physical survival levels, and below the minimum standards of decency which a civilized society should tolerate. It is unlikely that these people can somehow find the resources to contribute to IDAs, and that their meager savings, even if supplemented by the state, will eventually propel them out of poverty. The prospects of saving to escape poverty are even more remote for those who have lost their homes and who live on the streets surviving through begging, scavenging, or scrounging.

The asset approach is designed to encourage responsibility and self-sufficiency among the poor. Indeed, its potential as a means for inculcating puritan attitudes is far greater than that of generating the material resources needed to escape poverty. But while it has become fashionable to indict the moral behavior of the poor, it is doubtful whether poverty can be solved through the cultivation of middle-class values. Those who work with welfare mothers know that they manage their meager budgets with the hard nosed acumen of small town bankers. Their need for material resources, realistic employment opportunities, day care for children, and adequate housing is far greater than their need for lessons on the virtues of thrift, sobriety, and self-reliance.

In addition to the problem of inadequate resources, the asset approach presents difficult economic, organizational, and political challenges. The costs of subsidizing IDAs would be considerable, especially if the government supplements them to a significant degree. Also, there are formidable organizational issues to be resolved if the IDA program is to be implemented on the national level and if it is to be sufficiently flexible to adjust quickly to people's changing economic circumstances. However, proponents of IDAs have no doubt that these problems can be overcome, and they believe that political obstacles can be surmounted. Although the asset approach has secured bipartisan political support, it is not certain whether this support will endure when the political ramifications of the program's funding requirements are fully understood. To finance IDAs for the poor, it is proposed to abolish a variety of tax benefits which the nonpoor currently enjoy. Given the realities of the political process, it is by no means certain that political support for these proposals will be sustained as well-organized constituents react negatively to plans for reducing the benefits they currently enjoy.

More fundamentally, the asset approach, like most other attempts to deal with poverty on an individual level, fails to address the basic causes of poverty and deprivation in society. Poverty is rooted in economic and social structural factors, and not in the declining propensity of individuals to save. Economic decline associated with de-industrialization and global economic changes, reduced employment opportunities in traditional blue-collar occupations, falling wages for those in regular employment, deteriorated urban areas, declining educational standards, cutbacks in the human services, and entrenched inequalities are far more relevant in understanding the nature of poverty today. If the problem of poverty is to be effectively addressed, these realities must be addressed at the national level through comprehensive economic and social policies. Like other programs that attribute poverty to individual misfortune and assign primary responsibility for escaping poverty to the individual, attempts to encourage the poor to save, however worthwhile, cannot eradicate poverty.

Programs for the alleviation of poverty that have had the greatest degree of success in the past have implemented macro-economic and social policies and mobilized the resources of the state on a large scale. Despite its many shortcomings, the Johnson administration's attempts to address the poverty problem resulted in a significant decline in the incidence of poverty (Marmor, Mashaw, & Harvey, 1990). The experiences of Western Europe and the newly industrializing East Asian nations, which have highly interventionist governments, offer further evidence of the effectiveness of collectivist solutions which combine economic and social policies through the powerful agency of the centralized, interventionist state (Esping-Anderson, 1985; Midgley, 1986).

Of course, such strategies are unlikely to garner much political support in America's highly individualistic enterprise culture, where the power of the central government is used to promote the accumulation of wealth among those who are already wealthy, rather than deal with pressing social ills. In this political climate, the asset approach may make a contribution. However, despite its advantages, it is unlikely that the asset-based approach can *really* help the poor.

Rejoinder to Professor Midgley   MICHAEL SHERRADEN

Jim Midgley is a very thoughtful observer of social development and welfare state policies. He is well informed both historically and internationally, and he is among the few scholars who successfully incorporate social theory with applied policy issues. Under any circumstance, it would be a pleasure to exchange views with him, and I am particularly pleased to have this opportunity to discuss asset-based welfare.

On this occasion, however, Professor Midgley's comments are a little off the mark. His "no" statement relies on a number of general assumptions and questionable characterizations that largely miss the point of my proposal for asset-based welfare policy.

Midgley suggests that the creation of Individual Development Accounts, by itself, would not help the poor because the poor have no financial resources to save. Allow me to clarify that asset-based policy would not be put into effect by itself. I have not proposed reducing income transfers. The proposal is to balance income-based and asset-based policy by providing large incentives (in the form of matching deposit subsidies) for the poor to save. For the very poorest, the match would be as high as nine to one.

At this time, we do not know how many poor people or welfare recipients would find a way to take advantage of this. Judging from discussions with AFDC recipients, my guess is that the number would be substantial. But if only a small percentage of AFDC recipients were able to start saving for their children's college education, would the program be a failure? Surely it would not.

Professor Midgley would apparently prefer no incentives or subsidies for the poor to accumulate assets (although he is no doubt aware that the nonpoor in the United States receive considerable asset accumulation subsidies through the tax system). This position is unfair to the poor, and it is paternalistic. Who is to say who can and who cannot save? How are we to explain underground savings groups that have sprung up among AFDC mothers in some housing projects? How are we to explain the thousands of development projects around the world, which Midgley knows well, that promote small savings among populations that are miserably poor? In the end, who is able to save and under what circumstances is an empirical question that cannot be prejudged. The public policy issue is: Do we provide incentives for the poor to save? Currently in the United States, we do not.

The "no" statement says that the potential for "inculcating puritan values" in asset-based welfare is greater than that for helping the poor to escape poverty. Permit me to restate that the proposal is for asset accumulation, not behavioral training. I do suggest that certain positive social and psychological effects are likely to result from asset accumulation, such as looking ahead, feeling better about oneself, attaining higher social status, and increasing participation in the community. I would not use the word "puritan" to describe these effects, but no matter what they are called, most people would think they are desirable.

Professor Midgley writes that the proposal for asset-based welfare policy fails to address the "wider causes of poverty and deprivation in society." Poverty, he says, "is rooted in economic and social structural factors." These are broad and vague statements. He seems to suggest that a single policy must fix everything from deindustrialization to racism. Are we to take no positive steps if we cannot solve every social and economic ill at once?

But let us look more closely at the word "structure." This word is often tossed around without specification. What does it mean? In a fundamental sense, assets (wealth and capital) are structure. Indeed, according to Marx, capital is the very definition of social class. In this light, proposals to increase the assets of the poor are fundamentally structural—certainly more structural than income maintenance policies.

This brings us to the word "individualistic." This characterization is a half-truth. I have not, as Midgley claims, "attributed poverty to individual misfortune," nor have I "assigned primary responsibility for escaping poverty to the individual." It is a misrepresentation to suggest that the proposal for asset-based welfare is purely individualistic when in fact the proposal is for social policy, operating through the state, to address the accumulation of wealth in society, and particularly for the poorest.

There is a larger conceptual problem here. It is a false dichotomy to assume, as Midgley seems to, that state social policy promotes communalism through income redistribution, and that the only alternative is radical individualism. On the one hand, we have to question how much communalism has in fact been created by income-based policies. To take the most prominent case, how much has AFDC really brought us together? On the other hand, we have to question whether radical individualism is the only alternative. Does the state have other policy options in addition to income redistribution?

Professor Midgley knows that it does. He has recently written a very perceptive article on Asian states suggesting that the simplistic dichotomy of welfare state income redistribution versus pure capitalism may not be useful (Midgley, 1992). It is indeed possible to have a strong state very much involved in social policy, and at the same time promote a strong ideology of individual effort and asset accumulation. I happen to be writing this response while studying social policy in Singapore, where the state is among the strongest and most interventionist in the world, but the social policy system is organized primarily around individual asset accumulation. There are pros and cons to this system—a discussion that will have to wait for another day—but the point here is that strong states and individualism need not be contradictory. The real issue is not whether the state plays a strong role in social policy—it is in fact a safe prediction that social policy will remain the primary business of all economically advanced states (even the concerted radical right movements of the 1980s did not reduce overall social expenditures in the United States, the United Kingdom, and elsewhere; see

Glennerster and Midgley, 1991). In short, the real issue is not whether there *will* be social policy, but what *kind* of social policy.

Professor Midgley raises the specter of the political use of asset-based proposals to reduce expenditures in current welfare state programs. This is a possibility with any new proposal, and I appreciate the words of caution. However, we should not overlook the very real political horrors that have been unleashed by the income-based programs that we already have. AFDC is under attack in almost every state and is regularly used as a powerful political wedge to attack social spending in general.

To round out the "no" statement, Midgley tosses in an administrative issue. He suggests that the organizational issues would be complex. But they need not be. IDAs would be an expansion of the IRA concept, and IRAs operate with almost no bureaucracy.

In the end, all of these issues are speculative until we have empirical tests. Surely there is enough positive potential of asset-based welfare to warrant experiments with different populations. If we are able to put these experiments into motion, then we will have answers to the questions raised above.

REFERENCES

Borzutsky, S. (1992). The Chicago boys, social security and welfare in Chile. In Glennerster, H., & Midgley, J. (Eds.), *The radical right and the welfare state: An international assessment.* Savage, MD: Barnes and Noble, pp. 79–99.

Esping-Anderson, G. (1985). *Politics against markets: The social democratic road to power.* Cambridge, MA: Harvard University Press.

Glennerster, H., & Midgley, J. (Eds.) (1991). *The radical right and the welfare state.* Hertfordshire: Harvester Wheatsheaf, and Savage, MD: Barnes and Noble.

Marmor, T. R., Mashaw, J. L., & Harvey, P. L. (1990). *America's misunderstood welfare state: Persistent myths, enduring realities.* New York: Basic Books.

Midgley, J. (1992). Development theory, the state, and social development in Asia. *Social Development Issues* 14(1), pp. 22–36.

Midgley, J. (1986). Welfare and industrialization: The case of the four little tigers. *Social Policy and Administration* (20)3, 225–238.

Midgley, J. (1984). *Social security, inequality and the Third World.* New York: John Wiley and Sons.

Oubre, C. F. (1978). *Forty acres and a mule: The Freedman's Bureau and black land ownership.* Baton Rouge: Louisiana State University Press.

Sherraden, M. (1991). *Assets and the poor: A new American welfare policy.* Armonk, NY: M. E. Sharpe.

U.S. Bureau of the Census (1990). *Household wealth and asset ownership: 1988*. Washington, D.C.: U.S. Government Printing Office.

ANNOTATED BIBLIOGRAPHY

Oubre, C. F. (1978). *Forty acres and a mule: The Freedman's Bureau and black landownership*. Baton Rouge: Louisiana State University Press.

Oubre's is one of the best accounts of African Americans and property in the post–Civil War period. Knowledge of this period is essential for understanding racial inequality in asset holding.

Sherraden, M. (1991). *Assets and the poor: A new American welfare policy*. Armonk, NY: M.E. Sharpe.

The author attempts to identify the effects of asset accumulation, and he proposes an asset-based policy built on Individual Development Accounts.

U.S. Bureau of the Census (1990). *Household wealth and asset ownership: 1988*. Washington, D.C.: U.S. Government Printing Office.

This is a very useful data source, published every few years, on the distribution of various types of assets by income, race, family type, and so forth. The report is based on data from the Survey of Income and Program Participation.